KV-577-782

Martial Rose
Tel: 0196

CONTINUING PROFESSIONAL DEVELOPMENT

CONTINUING PROFESSIONAL DEVELOPMENT

Issues in Design and Delivery

Edited by

Ian Woodward

CASSELL

Cassell
Wellington House
125 Strand
London WC2R 0BB

127 West 24th Street
New York
NY 10011

British Library Cataloguing-in-Publication Data
A catalogue record for this book is available from the British Library.

ISBN 0-304-33781-1

Typeset by Action Typesetting Limited, Gloucester
Printed and bound in Great Britain by Biddles Ltd, Guildford and King's Lynn

Contents

Contents

Preface

In the mid-1980s I took part in a project to develop and deliver a distance learning programme designed to ease the path of industrial managers through the maze of selecting and implementing CADCAM systems. After two years, and at a cost approaching some £300,000, the materials were launched in the industrial market. However, there was very little take-up by industry, and when I wrote up the project as a case study,[1] I concluded, somewhat lamely, that more sales and marketing effort was required. A perhaps wiser head – that of Professor Gordon Wray, FRS – asked whether it was not 'industry's fault'.

Now, some ten years later and in very different economic and employment conditions there does seem to be rising interest in continuing professional development (CPD), not only among engineers, but across the spectrum of managerial and professional occupations. The advent of knowledge-based industries (of which changes such as the CADCAM revolution were a part), and a consequent upward spiral in the numbers of managerial and professional jobs, has been matched by encouragement for CPD from government and professional institutions. According to the present minister responsible for higher education, CPD is one of the fastest growth areas in university activities.

If, as I believe, the generation and application of new knowledge is essential both for our economic well-being and to enhance our quality of life, then a concerted effort to improve the quantity and quality of lifelong learning opportunities must be a central concern. The chapters which follow present a spectrum of thought and experience of managing these opportunities. In the spirit of current thinking about lifelong learning, they will hopefully provide a stimulus for reflection, dialogue, and action.

Ian Woodward
University of Leicester

[1] I. Woodward (1987) Continuing education in computer-aided engineering. *International Journal of Applied Engineering Education*, **3**(3), 255–62.

List of Contributors

Ian Woodward, Director of Professional Development, University of Leicester

Judith Bowen, Head of Access and Independent Study, Leeds Metropolitan University

Andrew Eaglen, Project Manager for Higher Level Skills Development and Access Project (1992–94), Leeds Metropolitan University

Richard Taylor, Professor of Continuing Education, University of Leeds

Valerie A. Mitchell, Associate Dean of the School of International Studies and Law, Coventry University

Edward Thomas, Professor of Continuing Education, University of Bristol

Hazel Knox, Depute Director of Department of Continuing Education, University of Paisley

Denise Hevey, Director of the Vocational Qualifications Centre, The Open University

Julia Carter, Lecturer in Continuing Education, City University

Mike Scannell, Lecturer and Researcher, Putteridge Bury Management Centre, University of Luton

Geoff Chivers, Professor of Continuing Education, University of Sheffield

John Cusworth, Head of Development and Project Planning Centre, University of Bradford

Tom Franks, Director of Professional Development and Training Programme, Development and Project Planning Centre, University of Bradford

Roger Aspland, Lecturer in Education and Professional Development, University of East Anglia

Roseanne Benn, Senior Lecturer in Adult Education, University of Exeter

Clive Nicholas, Continuing Education and Training Officer, University of Exeter

David Guile, Research Officer, Institute of Education, University of London

Michael Young, Head of the Post-16 Education Centre, Institute of Education, University of London

Malcolm Maguire, Principal Research Fellow, Institute for Employment Research, University of Warwick

Alison Fuller, Vocational Education and Training Research Associates

Peter Simpson, Head of School of Organisational Behaviour, Bristol Business School

Tony Lyddon, Employee Development Manager, GKN Chep Ltd

Boris Boulstridge, Human Resources Manager, Advanced Materials Division, Courtaulds Aerospace

Neville Cooper, Senior Lecturer, North Warwickshire and Hinckley College

Clare Rapkins (*née* Madden), formerly CPD Manager, The Chartered Institute of Public Finance and Accountancy.

Jennifer Tann, Professor of Innovation Studies, University of Birmingham

Alison Blenkinsopp, Director of Education and Research, Department of Medicines Management, University of Keele

Introduction: A Note on UK Systems and Structures for CPD

Much of this volume deals with ideas which are applicable across international cultures and systems. As one important example of this, the main theme running throughout many of the chapters is the interface between the world of work and the delivery of CPD by the higher education sector. This is a relevant issue in many economies, whether developing, transitional or developed. Three chapters have a specific international focus: 'Policies and Structures for University Continuing Professional Development', 'Comparability of Qualifications across Europe', and in the sphere of developing and transitional economies 'Managing Impact at a Distance'. However, throughout the book a substantial amount of the research and case study material is drawn from UK sources and there are numerous references to UK structures and systems. Therefore it may be helpful to the reader who is not acquainted with the UK to have available a brief description of the national framework of CPD. This introduction serves that purpose.

The framework is presented from three perspectives:

- the supplier/consumer relationship
- the role of government and public funding
- the role of employers and professional bodies

THE SUPPLIER/CONSUMER RELATIONSHIP

This is virtually a free-market relationship. Suppliers, be they consultants, partnerships, private companies, in-house training and development functions, charitable or voluntary organizations or higher education institutions (HEIs), are free to develop CPD services and offer these to their chosen market. The market, whether individual or corporate, is similarly at liberty to choose a preferred supplier. Even within the boundaries of both private and public-sector organizations, managers are not necessarily required to use the services of their own in-house training and development function. It is not uncommon to find a situation in which the Human Resource Development (HRD) department has to sell its wares to employees and line managers from its own organization.

Some regulation of the supply side of the market does occur. Where professional bodies have adopted CPD policies, requiring or encouraging their membership to participate in a minimum amount of CPD each year, they may establish a list of approved courses, seminars, etc. More importantly perhaps, where CPD leads to a recognized qualification such as (enhanced) membership of a professional body, or a university or institute award, quality assurance procedures are applied to regulate supply. In the UK this regulation is *not* a state function. As an example, the authority to confer degrees is vested in universities as autonomous institutions. There is no direct state control of aims, content, process or assessment criteria. Through its committee structures the individual university willl approve degree regulations, which generally include specific provision for internal and external quality assurance procedures. Where these degree programmes form part of the requirements for (enhanced) membership of professional institutions, quality assurance may also be carried out by the relevant professional body (which is similarly free of state control). However, regulation by professional bodies is the exception rather than the rule and, where applied, tends to govern structured career progression in disciplines such as medicine. The vast majority of professionals and employers who wish to invest in CPD are at liberty to choose their preferred supplier and preferred programme of learning.

The virtual lack of market regulation has a number of advantages. It provides for dynamism: new products and services can be rapidly generated (though both the professional and higher education institutions take their responsibility for quality assurance seriously, and this can at times lead to a time lag between market demand and the availability of programmes leading to a recognized qualification). Secondly, it generates variety: consumers can choose from a range of CPD products since the lack of regulation creates a climate favourable to diversity. Finally, it can contribute to innovation, quality improvement and sensitivity to costs: the rules of the market apply and suppliers need to achieve competitive advantage.

The disadvantage is that the consumer, faced with a diversity of products, costs and methodologies, is required to make sophisticated choices. Most UK consumers, both individual and corporate, have been schooled (quite literally) in a publicly funded education system which prescribed for them many of the variables – aims, content, location, process, assessment and costs – with which they are confronted when making choices about CPD.

THE ROLE OF GOVERNMENT AND PUBLIC FUNDING

In a number of chapters there are references to various UK government programmes and structures. The articulated policy of the present government is one of intervention in CPD activities only where there is evidence of market failure, and at policy level there is commitment (by all major political parties) to the concept of lifelong learning. Since there is a perception that in comparative terms the UK workforce is less well educated than that of other developed national economies, a major thrust of government intervention in recent years has been to encourage improved access to, and take-up of, opportunities leading to qualifications.

This intervention is accomplished through what may seem to be, and in fact is, a bewildering array of organizations. In broad terms these are of two types, the first being directly controlled government bodies (such as ministries). Organizations in the second category are also publicly funded, but are not under direct political control, though the conditions attached by government to their receipt of public funding does to an extent determine the scope of their activities and (arguably) limits their independence. In a peculiarly British piece of jargon, this second category has the generic label 'quasi-autonomous non-governmental organizations' (quangos).

Government ministries

Until 1995, responsibilities were split between a number of ministries (known in the UK as Departments). Where specific government departments face onto particular professional groups they may involve themselves with CPD. An example of this, quoted in the final chapter, is the financing by the Department of Health of a centre for pharmacy postgraduate education.

A broader remit has been held by three ministries: the Department of Trade and Industry (DTI), the Employment Department (ED) and the Department for Education (DFE). As Denise Hevey points out (in Chapter 5) the DTI has been responsible for the international validity of professional qualifications and also has responsibility for science policy as part of its remit for competitiveness. These areas obviously impinge on CPD.

Within a broad portfolio concerned with the labour market, the Employment Department has been concerned with a wide range of interventions in vocational training and development, financing both relevant research and innovations in the design and delivery of CPD programmes.

The Department for Education has been the primary source of policy and finance for the public education system, making available funds which can be applied to the development and provision of vocationally relevant degree and other qualification programmes, and to short-course development and provision.

The separation of spheres of policy, and allocation of responsibility to different ministries, has produced overlaps and at times a lack of coordination. Two measures have been taken to resolve these problems – the establishment of multi-departmental government offices at regional level and the merging of the Departments of Education and Employment into a new single ministry, the Department for Education and Employment (DFEE).

Quangos

In broad terms, quangos serve to translate government policy into strategy and operational detail. There are three main quangos which affect CPD – the National Council for Vocational Qualifications (NCVQ), Training and Enterprise Councils (TECs) and the Higher Education Funding Councils.

The NCVQ was set up to develop a unified framework for vocational qualifications in the UK, since it was felt that there was a proliferation of awards which were confusing to the consumer. It was also felt that existing programmes of vocational training and development lacked relevance to the needs of the world of work, and therefore the new ladder of National Vocational Qualifications (NVQs) should be specified in terms of actual work competences rather than predetermining the knowledge and skills requirements, learning process and duration of study. The NCVQ has drawn up broad guidelines at five levels for these new vocational qualifications. The levels form a progression, from Level 1 to Level 5, in terms of both job complexity and responsibilities. Industry lead bodies interpret these guidelines into specific sets of competences for discrete work tasks, which then form the basis for a particular NVQ. There is no prescription of learning process or duration – these are decided by the learners and/or providers.

TECs were established to reflect the diverse needs of local economies. They replaced the national Training Agency (which in its turn had replaced the Manpower Services Commission). Each TEC is required to develop a strategy for, among other things, training and development in its local area. TECs are private companies, directed by boards drawn from representatives of local industry and commerce, and to a lesser extent from representatives of the public sector. In addition to administration of public funds following nationally predetermined rules and procedures, TECs have discretionary cash available for local initiatives. Much of the TECs' funding comes from the Department for Education and Employment, channelled through the regional government offices, and this allows government to influence the activities of TECs. The 'Investors in People' (IiP) initiative is one example of this. IiP is a standard to which employers may (voluntarily) commit themselves. In very simple terms, it requires that a development plan be generated for all employees and carried out in practice. Employers who meet the standard are awarded 'Investors in People' status. TECs are rewarded financially according to the number of employers in their area who commit to and achieve this status. Therefore there is a financial incentive for TECs to promote IiP and provide assistance for employers to achieve the status.

The Higher Education Funding Councils are responsible for much of the finance of the UK's university system. Formulae are applied to different categories of students to determine how much financial support an individual university will receive. By adjusting the weightings within these formulae, the funding councils can make it financially more attractive for universities to recruit, say, science students rather than arts students, or to recruit full-time as opposed to part-time students. Secondly, the funding councils can stimulate supply of higher education through financial mechanisms, or (as at present) restrain growth. Proponents of CPD would argue that funding councils' policies could make it financially more attractive to provide vocationally relevant and flexibly delivered programmes, particularly at postgraduate level, and that this would do much to stimulate lifelong learning. The funding councils do provide pump-priming funds for new initiatives in continuing vocational education (CVE), though this is a fairly small amount of cash in comparison with their support for 'standard' teaching and research activities.

The universities themselves may be seen as quangos, since they are autonomous organizations which administer public funds (though this categorization might not be recognized by academics). Of importance to the CPD framework are changes in institutional status which have occurred within the UK's higher education sector. An expansion of higher education in the 1960s saw the creation of polytechnics, under local authority control, as well as growth in student numbers within universities. The higher education sector was therefore split between universities on the one hand and polytechnics and colleges of higher education on the other. This situation has now ended, and (with very few exceptions) there is one unified sector in which almost all higher education institutions are now universities. This change is having its impact: for example, the credit accumulation and transfer schemes (CATS) described by Hazel Knox (Chapter 4) were a feature of the polytechnics and are now spreading throughout the higher education system. Nevertheless, important differences remain between institutions from the two former sectors, and there is still a tendency to differentiate between 'old' and 'new' universities.

A note on national variations

Though a unified state, the United Kingdom is a mix of different national entities; this affects the framework for CPD. Not all London-based ministries or quangos necessarily have direct roles in the Scottish, Welsh or Northern Irish framework.

The differences in structures are quite substantial and beyond the scope of a brief introduction to describe in detail. Three of the more pertinent examples which are referred to in this volume are:

- TECs have been established within England and Wales, whereas in Scotland Local Enterprise Companies have a much broader remit for economic development, and in Northern Ireland the function is carried out by an arm of central government;

- in Scotland, Scottish Vocational Qualifications (SVQs) are preferred to NVQs;

- different Higher Education Funding Councils operate in each constituent country, and can develop and apply different policies.

THE ROLE OF EMPLOYERS AND PROFESSIONAL BODIES

The Confederation of British Industry (CBI) is perhaps the most important umbrella association for employers. The CBI was instrumental in establishing National Education and Training Targets (NETTs) for the UK workforce, expressed in terms of National Vocational Qualifications. These targets have been accepted by government, and at local level TECs are encouraged to play an important role in their achievement. The higher education system has been rapidly expanded to help with this drive towards a better qualified workforce; however, the targets for lifelong learning are not nearly so explicit as targets for (what is seen as) initial vocational education. Interestingly, the expansion of higher education has also seen growth in the numbers of mature students now acquiring first and postgraduate degrees (see, for example, Chapters 4, 6 and 8), and many of these students might well be labelled post-experience rather than initial learners.

A number of (mainly large) employers have adopted their own schemes to encourage lifelong learning. The Ford Employee Development and Assistance Programme is perhaps the best known of these and is described in Chapter 13.

There are a large number of professional bodies in the UK, which fall into two types. For some professions, such as medicine, registration with the appropriate professional body is essential if an individual is to practise the profession. These bodies have a regulatory role, and many now choose to insist on quantified amounts of CPD for members to maintain their right to practise. Where there is no regulatory function, membership is, of course, entirely voluntary, and CPD tends to be encouraged rather than required. Chapters 7, 16 and 17 address issues surrounding lifelong learning in specific professions and in the context of the policies of professional bodies.

THE FUTURE FOR UK SYSTEMS AND STRUCTURES FOR CPD

The development of the framework for CPD is a matter of national (economic) concern, and there are signs that continuing education in general is now assuming greater importance in national policy. Demand for workers with high-level skills is rising, and there are qualitative changes in the labour market such as greater participation by women, increases in part-time working and fewer opportunities for career-track employment as opposed to short-term assignments. These changes in the market for CPD are not, in my view, as yet adequately reflected in the structures and systems of the UK. The future may hold a shift of emphasis from initial to post-experience education, new arrangements for financing CPD, greater incentives for employers to invest in training and development, and even the emergence of a dedicated and more unified system better able to provide flexible and multi-disciplinary opportunities.

CPD is a rapidly developing and expanding feature of the modern labour market, and of the educational systems which contribute to the fund of competences among the workforce. Systems and structures are constantly evolving, and for those with professional involvement in this development there is really only one safe prediction for the future – continuing change, growth and the challenge of being part of a dynamic industry.

Chapter 1

Dimensions of Continuing Professional Development

Ian Woodward

The term ['continuing professional development' (CPD) describes learning activities that are undertaken throughout working life and are intended to enhance individual and organizational performance] in professional and managerial spheres.

[The importance attached to CPD is growing, largely due to the accelerating pace of economic, social and technological change: there is no longer any serious argument that initial professional education alone is adequate to equip individuals with the knowledge and skills needed for their lifetimes' employment.] Attention is now focusing on the best means of delivering effective CPD to ensure that the goal of enhancing individual and organizational performance is attained. There are three main dimensions to consider:

- an improvement dimension, concerned with the translation of theories of learning into effective means of delivering CPD;

- a market dimension, concerned with analysing demand and seeking to develop the market in line with knowledge about the effectiveness of different approaches to delivery;

- the development and contribution of the infrastructure for CPD.

Underpinning and informing these three areas is a base dimension: the economic rationale. This base dimension provides a justification for investment in CPD, and is therefore the logical starting-point to set the parameters for discussion of methodologies, markets and their development, and the infrastructure necessary to facilitate effective lifelong learning.

THE ECONOMIC RATIONALE FOR CPD

Accepted wisdom is that nation-states, and larger groupings such as the European Union, require economic growth to ensure the well-being of their populations. Competitive success in the global market-place is held to be the key to economic growth. In this context Porter's (1990) study of the competitiveness of nations has been influential in shaping economic policy. He argues that competitive advantage requires the adoption of continual change, and is dependent on, among other factors, the specialized knowledge and skills possessed by the workforce:

> firms gain and sustain competitive advantage in international competition through improvement, innovation, and upgrading. Innovation ... includes both technology and methods, encompassing new products, new production methods, new ways of marketing, identification of new customer groups, and the like.
>
> (p. 70)

> The human resources most decisive in modern international competition ... possess high levels of specialized skills in particular fields.
>
> (p. 9)

The wealth-creation sector, with which Porter is principally concerned, is underpinned by a 'factor pool of infrastructure', including, for example, the education system, health service and commercial processes such as capital formation. It would follow from Porter's arguments that the 'factor pool of infrastructure' should also display a commitment to improvement and innovation in order to increase its impact on wealth-creation sectors.

In essence, stressing the importance of innovation is an argument which prioritizes knowledge. It is the generation of new knowledge and its subsequent dissemination and application within organizations which lead to new products and processes (Boisot, 1987). The kernel of the problem is not *whether* the generation and application of knowledge in the workplace is of importance, but *how best* to effect that process. It is also argued that this is a particularly critical need for the UK economy. Coates (1994) notes that the UK share of all manufactured goods traded globally has declined from 25.9 per cent in 1950 to 8.5 per cent in 1994, and compares a static rate since 1973 of UK manufacturing output with a 119 per cent growth over the same period by Japanese industry. In part at least, this haemorrhage of an important wealth-creation sector is a consequence of failed competitiveness due to a lack of change and innovation.

THE IMPROVEMENT DIMENSION: TRANSLATION OF THEORIES OF LEARNING INTO EFFECTIVE MEANS OF DELIVERING CPD

That there is a relationship between lifelong learning and competitive advantage is not a new concept. Revans (1982) concluded that for organizations to remain competitive, the rate of learning has to be at least equal to, or greater than, the rate of external change. Traditionally, at least in the popular mind, 'learning' is associated with formal, structured activities which, in a vocational sense, are intended to lead to improved job performance. The transfer of knowledge and skills from the artificial learning environment to working practice, needless to say, does not always occur in practice.

The MUTs phenomenon

As part of professional CPD requirements a partner in a small accountancy practice attended a one-day course in auditing. The course was well constructed and the need for change in auditing practice was accepted by the participants on the day. A major feature of the change was to move away from being 'mechanical unthinking tickers' (MUTs) as auditors to providing a more professional consultancy service to clients. Despite a conviction that this was the right way to proceed, the accountant subsequently made no changes to his own professional practice. Client expectations, his partners' expectations, and the firm's financial ability to provide a more thorough service prevented change.

The lack of positive outcome is a familiar problem to most CPD practitioners, and is not necessarily related to the relevance or otherwise of the topic to delegate needs, nor the excellence of the instructional design and delivery. Annett and Sparrow (1985) suggest that where (off-line) training and development is a recurrent function of the work situation, transfer of new knowledge into working practice may be more readily effected. In these situations, it may be that the volume of activity renders it part of the accepted norm of working practice, rather than a diversion from the usual working routine. Hence the acquisition of knowledge and its transfer to working practice is the rule rather than the exception. However, on a pragmatic level, for organizations where the volume of training and development is below the level needed to effect successful transfer, 'invest in more training' is doubtless advice which individuals and employers would find difficult to accept.

Vygotsky (1978) provides a further insight into conditions for effective learning. When individuals undergo a new experience, this is either accepted and their stock of knowledge is enhanced, or it is rejected. The conditions for acceptance or rejection depend on the proximity of the new experience to their existing stock of knowledge. A new experience which is remote from or otherwise at variance with what is already known will be

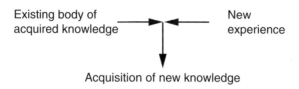

Figure 1.1 Vygotsky's theory of proximal learning

rejected. Where there is consonance between the new experience and what is already known, the stock of knowledge will be augmented and enhanced (see Figure 1.1).

There are two implications inherent in the theory. The first is that new learning should be incremental, building on existing stocks of knowledge and experience. The second is more fundamental: individuals whose knowledge and experience are limited will be less disposed to new learning, and hence to change and innovation, than those with a more diverse knowledge base. This phenomenon may occur at organizational as well as at individual levels.

The design and production divide

The company in question operated on two sites some thirty miles apart. Research and development (R&D) was carried out at one location, and manufacturing at the other. The two sets of professional engineers – design and production – seldom if ever met, other than at senior management level. They faced an acute business problem: a significant percentage of their (high technology) products were failing acceptance testing. The attitude of the R&D staff was 'If we can make one, why can't they make a thousand?' The contrary view from production was 'Why can't they come up with designs we can make?' At one site, the experience and training of staff was restricted to R&D, and at the other to production. In addition, there was a culture of mutual animosity between the two groups. The (obvious) solution to the problem – learn more about each others' discipline, possibly by forming multi-disciplinary teams – was rejected by both engineers and management.

The (collective) experience of the company was one of functional specialism: we do our jobs and they should do theirs. The notion that an investment in learning about others' functional specialisms could be beneficial was so far remote from this collective experience that it was rejected out-of-hand. Notably, the rejection was not of a learning experience, but of the *opportunity* for a learning experience. Theories of adult learning have long recognized that adults set their own objectives and direct their own learning, if with advice and counselling (see, for example, Brookfield, 1986), and therefore will decide whether or not to pursue a particular learning opportunity.

Kolb (1984) makes a major contribution to our understanding of self-direction and the learning techniques adopted by adults. Although most attention has focused on his notion of a cycle of learning, Kolb's thesis rests on two more fundamental ideas:

that learning is a naturally occurring phenomenon;
that the ability to learn is a pro-active skill which allows us to influence and shape our (working) environment.

The importance of these two points should not be understated. People learn constantly and are highly sophisticated at the skills of acquiring knowledge and applying this knowledge. In other words, people will learn whether or not there is a structured intervention. As a consequence, experiential learning has primacy over artificial, constructed interventions, and therefore to be effective CPD interventions must take into account (combinations of) three variables:

- The stock of prior knowledge, attitudes and values held by participants. This is essential to ensure that the new experience will be complementary rather than remote or contradictory, and hence will be accepted rather than rejected.

- Other learning experiences gained during the time span of the intervention. Taking these into account suggests control of the situation either by isolating participants from the workplace, or by planned integration of (any) off-line intervention with established or new working practices.

- Future experiences to ensure that those skills and insights which have been acquired continue to develop. Future variables are, of course, hard to control, though carefully considered career or succession planning will assist with this process.

The difficulties of exerting control over the work situation are self-evident. Organizations are themselves a complex of variables – personnel, systems, culture, are diverse and subject to change. In consequence two distinct trends are now emerging. The first is the movement towards the *learning organization* (Pedler *et al.*, 1991; Senge, 1993), seeking to develop organizational systems and cultures which constantly review, refresh and augment their stock of knowledge, and hence establish competitive advantage. This approach has its roots in the economic analysis of Porter (1990), who concludes that it is only at organizational level, rather than at individual or national levels, that the chain reaction from innovation to economic growth can be secured and maintained.

The second movement is towards *individual commitment* (Maguire *et al.*, 1993; Metcalfe *et al.*, 1994). This trend imposes individual responsibility – rather than the employer's or the state's duty – to plan for and finance lifetime learning. The economic justification derives from calculation of the 'private rate of return' (Blaug, 1969): the relationship between levels of educational attainment and lifetime earnings achieved by individuals. The better an individual's qualifications, the more he or she is likely to earn. Second, the nature of work itself and of the labour market is changing to become more competitive. Individuals can no longer expect a job for life, and hence will have to take charge of their own destiny through personal investment in CPD in order to maintain employability.

I have argued above that experiential learning, gained in the working environment has primacy over off-line activities. Individual commitment to CPD cannot therefore hope to equal the potential impact of organization commitment. Measures of lifetime earnings which may justify the movement towards individual commitment do not necessarily equate with measures of value added, which can only be achieved in the final analysis through improved organizational performance. Hence, though individual commitment is certainly not without value (least of all to the individual), investment in learning organizations, with both systems and cultures which offer employees continuous, incremental and diverse learning opportunities, must – from the perspective of learning theory – have greater impact.

THE MARKET FOR CPD

Since CPD is directly concerned with professional and managerial work performance, the study of the labour market – along both quantitative and qualitative axes – is of pivotal importance. Handy (1995) describes the employment market of the future in the formula 'half by two by three': half as many people will be paid twice as well, and deliver three times the added value. This (apocryphal) view is shared by Rifkin (1995) – those with high-level skills, 'symbolic analysts', will have the chance to find relatively stable employment in, for example, technical, professional, educational and possibly voluntary spheres, whereas blue-collar workers have little prospect of stable employment. This employment trend may already be reflected in the increase in numbers of entrants to higher education. The decision to expand

UK higher education in the late 1980s certainly met with no consumer resistance: the targets set by government were met with relative ease, both from an increase in recruitment among the 18-year-old age cohort and from mature students. Not surprisingly, given this expansion, graduate participation in the workforce is increasing. Many graduates, however, are not entering traditional, career-track graduate employment, but are working at lower levels in the labour market. It is a moot point whether this trend represents a 'drawing down' of graduates into low-level occupations and hence under-utilization of their skills, or an upgrading of job requirements in recognition of the need for high-level skills to be apportioned vertically throughout organizations. Whatever the consequence of increased graduate participation, it seems likely that the growth in demand from adult post-experience learners for higher education will be sustained. In turn, the very fact that they possess a stock of knowledge and experience which is not found among standard 18-year-old entrants must generate new forms of teaching and learning. In particular, higher education will need, as a minimum, to recognize as valid their stock of experiential learning, and to adopt teaching and learning methodologies which complement and utilize this stock. Progress is being made with recognition of validity, with development of techniques for accreditation of prior learning (APL). However, it is questionable whether, with the exception of specialist continuing education units, teaching and learning methodologies are rapidly changing to meet the requirements of post-experience learners.

In addition to an increase in professional, managerial and associate professional employment, and a corresponding decrease in manual jobs, the UK Employment Department (1994a) notes four further trends which can be expected to influence provision and take-up of CPD:

- a higher age profile for the workforce, reflecting both the demographic dip in the 16–34 age range, and the tendency among young people towards longer 'stay-on' rates in education;

- increased participation by women in the labour market;

- an increase in part-time and self-employment;

- employment growth in the small firms sector.

The first of these provides an additional volume indicator since a decrease in young, recently educated entrants to the labour market will require older cohorts to update and upgrade their skills. The final three trends provide qualitative indicators: there will need to be consideration of aims, content and delivery mechanisms to meet the requirements of increased female participation, the needs of the self-employed and part-time staff; and the time and resource constraints which inhibit employees of smaller organizations from participating in traditional 'off-line' CPD. Certainly, a greater degree of flexibility in delivery will be required. Well-established techniques such as distance learning and part-time provision will need to expand, and there will need to be further development of the use of the workplace as a learning resource, and of the new interactive and multi-media technologies to offer greater flexibility in the timing and location of provision.

Aims and content must certainly continue to include technocratic subjects. However, the implication of Handy's formula (half by two by three) is that discipline-specific competence will no longer be adequate in a slimmed-down, professional labour force. Technocratic competences will need to be matched with managerial skills, and with the capability to convey to others an understanding of one's own discipline. Moreover, if it is accepted that a prime purpose for CPD is to promote innovation, then its remit must extend beyond the acquisition of defined interdisciplinary skills and knowledge, to promote the capability to analyse and question the accepted tenets of practice. Schon (1987) identifies this capability as the process of 'reflective practice', the constant review of experience against the specialized knowledge base which professionals possess and utilize. Argyris (1993) analyses similar processes in team settings, where in order to realize effective organizational development, team members must display openness rather than conceal their real agenda for action. These are sophisticated skills which cannot be adequately developed through brief training episodes, and which require the integration of CPD interventions with practice (Bines, 1992).

While survey research shows that much employer-sponsored training and development occurs at managerial and professional levels, it is of short duration and designed to meet the immediate requirements of the organization (Wickens, 1991; Abbot, 1993; Employment Department, 1994a). If employer demand remains narrowly defined and restricted to immediate needs, then it is difficult to see how the fundamental competences necessary to establish a culture of improvement, change and innovation can be developed. While these competences may be engendered through individual commitment to self-development, their enaction into practice in any meaningful way requires a much more extensive commitment to the adoption of the learning organization. This point is further elaborated below in discussion of infrastructure for CPD; at this juncture suffice it to say that a critical market problem would seem to be the development of a greater understanding among employers of the breadth and value of CPD, and of their role in fostering conditions for effective implementation.

Before turning to discussion of organizations and structures, in the context of the market it remains to define the intended audience for CPD: in effect to analyse what is understood by 'professional'. The term 'profession' no longer refers to an exclusive and homogeneous group of occupations with shared characteristics. Indeed, the homogeneity of traditional professions, such as the law, medicine or religion, perhaps owed as much to the social class of their practitioners as to any notion of professionalism. More recently the spread of occupations which might be grouped under the generic heading of professions has grown and diversified. Many of these groups have adopted characteristics of the traditional professions, establishing associations which set standards for membership, requiring a combination of formal entry level qualifications and a period of assessed internship. Whether the processes of formal study and internship run in parallel or are sequential, the combination of study and practice is a common requirement for entry to professional associations (Eraut, 1994). A second common feature is the relationship between professional status, and the (legal) ability to carry out certain tasks. The clearest examples of this relationship are still to be found in the traditionally organized professions, where, for example, it is unlawful to engage in aspects of medical practice without formal registration with the professional body. In other professions, there may be elements of *de facto* regulation where access to professional indemnity insurance may depend on membership of an appropriate association. Finally, consumers may prefer that certain tasks are carried out by recognized professionals – veterinary science provides an example of consumerism protecting professional standards.

While the concept of the 'professional manager' has gained ground, management as a profession is still largely exempt from either *de jure* or *de facto* regulation which governs other professional occupations. As an example, it is not necessary to obtain membership of the Institute of Directors to take on the legal and strategic responsibilities which attach to the title of Company Director. Similarly, individuals can be responsible for personnel, marketing, production and other functional management roles without any requirement for membership of the relevant professional institution.

Defining 'profession' by either membership of recognized professional associations or by a management job function is clearly inadequate. There are simply too many areas which might be considered as professions but which fall outside this definition: academics, journalists, higher grade civil servants, etc. If it is difficult to define 'profession', the idea of 'professionalism' may be more productive. Barnett's (1994) analysis of 'skill' provides a helpful insight:

There are four criteria for the application of the term 'skill':

1 A situation of some complexity.
2 A performance that addresses the situation, is deliberate and is

not just a matter of chance.

3   An assessment that the performance has met the demands of the situation.

4   A sense that the performance was commendable.

(p. 56)

Taken together, the four criteria describe events which require a significant knowledge base and its considered application, a review procedure and a sense of excellence in the execution of the process. At the risk of self-indulgence in exemplifying this analysis, CPD practitioners may find much here that strikes a responsive chord. A complex knowledge base is required to analyse situations and to design and execute learning solutions, which are then reviewed and assessed by stakeholders (hopefully) to applaud their value. However, a panoply of other skills are also required by CPD practitioners: who among us does not regularly find themselves moving furniture, filling in expense claims or word-processing course notes? In other words, jobs may have some components which are professional in nature, and also other elements which can be skilled or purely manual, and do not meet all of Barnett's four criteria. Using this as a basis for defining 'professionalism', it follows that some activities undertaken by, for example, technicians which involve solving complex problems are professional in nature, though the technician may not be regarded as a 'professional'.

As knowledge continues to grow and situations become more complex, it is inevitable that 'professionalism' will be a component of a much wider range of jobs. Any market definition of CPD which targets only members of recognized professional associations, or those in management roles, will be inadequate to meet this challenge.

THE INFRASTRUCTURE FOR CPD

CPD involves four groups of stakeholders:

- governments, parastatal and professional bodies, and supranational bodies such as the UN, European Union and international trade and professional associations;

- employers;

- individuals;

- providers of CPD services.

The basis for UK government policy is to secure 'a sustained increase in the quantity and quality of the skills in Britain's workforce, as the key to business success and personal opportunity. This requires a partnership spanning business, education and training, within a common framework and towards common goals set by the Government' (Department of Trade and Industry and Employment Department, 1992). Tansley (1994) elaborates the goals of policy as: 'to ensure that there is a suitable institutional framework for training; and to intervene in areas where there is market failure.' The translation of this policy into operational terms is concisely described in *Training in Britain* (Employment Department, 1994b). This includes:

- Support for the development and achievement of National Education and Training Targets (NETTs), including targets for high-level, professional qualifications.

- The development, through the National Council for Vocational Qualifications, of a framework of National Vocational Qualifications (NVQs) extending from Level One for occupations which are relatively low-skilled, to Level Five for professional and managerial occupations carrying significant responsibility. The rubric defining the two higher levels reads:

  Level 5 competence which involves the application of a significant range of fundamental principles and complex techniques across a wide and often unpredictable variety of contexts. Very substantial personal autonomy and often significant responsibility for the work of others and for the allocation of substantial resources feature strongly, as do personal accountabilities for analysis and diagnosis, design, planning, execution and evaluation.

  Level Four competence in a broad range of technical or professional work activities performed in a wide variety of contexts and with a substantial degree of personal responsibility and autonomy. Responsibility for the work of others and the allocation of resources is often present.

- A campaign to encourage employers to invest more systematically in human resource development – 'Investors in People' (IiP).

- The establishment, at local level, of a network of Training and Enterprise Councils (TECs), and in Scotland Local Enterprise Companies (LECs). These are limited companies, with the majority of their directors drawn from local business and industry, to reflect local needs. The TECs are largely funded by central government through the Department for Education and

Employment, and are performance-measured against targets such as attainment of NVQs and the number of employers subscribing to the Investors in People initiative.

- Provision of tax relief for study leading to NVQs, and the availability of career development loans to stimulate individual commitment to CPD.

- The financing of development projects in higher education to enhance the quality and quantity of CPD provision.

Perhaps the most fundamental critique of government initiatives as they affect CPD is that of Porter (1990). In his view there should be no state intervention beyond provision of the general education service; rather, it is the task of employers to develop the capabilities of human resources. This view contrasts with the actuality of the situation, certainly in much of Western Europe. Pump-priming funds to initiate new developments, levies on employers to finance systems of continuing education and training, guaranteed paid leave for CPD, general subsidies to providers and tax relief for individuals all figure in the financial intervention of European Union states (Hughes, 1994). Porter simply does not take into account the political dimension. A failure to develop human resources will impact on economic performance, and hence governments feel obliged to intervene, particularly in democracies where poor economic performance can have adverse electoral consequences. There is therefore no real question of whether governments should intervene, since they will do so anyway. The more pertinent question is whether their interventions are well considered and beneficial.

In the UK the establishment of infrastructure includes targets for vocational qualifications. Perfectly adequate capabilities can, of course, be possessed without the validation of a formal qualification or membership of professional associations. However, comparative figures show the UK workforce to be poorly qualified in comparison with competitor nations. Market forces, in the shape of employers recruiting or investing in the development of highly qualified labour, were not redressing the deficiency; therefore intervention in the shape of National Education and Training Targets is justified. However, the development of NVQs, which are a central feature of the targets, was based on consultation with representatives of employer organizations, and largely excluded consultation with other stakeholder groups. The specification for NVQs, the basis for which are sets of vocational competences assessed in workplace environments, has been the subject of criticism (Smithers, 1993). By defining competences only in terms of observed behaviours, the NVQ philosophy was open to charges of omitting from specifications the knowledge base which is essential for the achievement of complex tasks, and the improvement processes associated with reflective practice. This deficiency may be redressed with the development of higher level NVQs with which professional associations are now involved. Second, the consultation process to derive specifications has not involved employers at organization level to any significant degree, nor providers or individuals. The assessment procedures which were evolved include compilation of portfolios of achievement. This is proving to be a complex and lengthy process, and it remains questionable whether either employers or individuals will invest time in this process. Finally, there is the omission of any mention of change, improvement or innovation in the rubrics for NVQs at Levels Four and Five. These could be inferred from 'analysis and diagnosis, design, planning, execution and evaluation', but it surely would have been appropriate to make explicit a commitment to innovation.

The infrastructure also includes Training and Enterprise Councils and Local Enterprise Companies: effectively the implementation arm of national policies. The establishment of TECs was intended 'to give leadership of the training system to employers, where it belongs' (Employment Department, 1988). Two-thirds of TEC board members are drawn from the senior management of private sector business and industry within a given locality, reflecting an emphasis on wealth creation and on local solutions to local problems. They have a remit to manage publicly funded programmes to the best advantage of their local area, and are measured and rewarded against agreed quantified targets. League tables of TECs' performance against these targets have been published, but quantification of this kind is far from being a thorough evaluation of their performance. Ashton (1994) questions employers' ability to 'identify the skills they are seeking ... they have difficulty in explaining their requirements in terms that are meaningful and practical for those whose function it is to deliver the skills'. This need not necessarily be a difficulty when there is a dialogue between employer and provider. Taking as an example the concept of 'leadership', a skilled provider will elicit from employers the necessary detail through reference to different styles of leadership – autocratic, participative, etc. However, if employers are given responsibility for interpretation and direction at local level of national policy, then they clearly should be able to explain their requirements in meaningful terms. Second and more fundamental is the problem of employers' tendency to adopt a short-term approach by prioritizing the solution of immediate skills needs through brief training episodes. Replication of this tendency at a local strategic level is clearly a danger inherent in placing responsibility in the hands of TEC boards. The role given to TECs is a significant one, and their performance would bear a more thorough evaluation. The evidence available suggests that dependence on TECs for management of CPD policy could be a high-risk strategy.

Finally, there are the three initiatives of Investors in People, career development loans and tax relief to consider. Both tax relief on fees and career development loans will promote individual commitment to CPD. Investors in People on the other hand seeks to promote organization commitment, identified earlier as the weak link in the cycle of learning necessary for effective CPD. Investors in People is clearly a step in the right direction towards the development of learning organizations. Employers adopt and are audited on the IiP standards which require periodic review, planning and implementation of programmes for employee development at all levels in organizations. There is, however, some distance between the IiP standard and the practical approach to building a learning organization, advocated by Garvin (1993):

> A learning organization is an organization skilled at creating, acquiring, and transferring knowledge, and at modifying its behaviour to reflect new knowledge and insights.
>
> (p. 80)

> The first step is to foster an environment that is conducive to learning. There must be time for reflection and analysis, to think about strategic plans, dissect customer needs, assess current work systems, and invent new products. Only if top management expressly frees up employees' time for the purpose does learning occur with any frequency.
>
> (p. 91)

This contrasts with the colourful appraisal of industry performance provided by Caulkin (1995). He describes an epidemic of anorexia as a passion for cost-cutting reduced company head count in both the UK and the USA. This process may have been justified by reference to delayering in pursuit of laudable objectives such as 'Business Process Re-engineering' (Hammer and Champy, 1993) which, with its advocacy of flattened structures and multi-disciplinary teams, is closely allied to the concept of the learning organization. However, the net effect in Caulkin's view has been extremely detrimental: 'Unfortunately, cost-cutting is not enough to ensure survival. Only growth and innovation can do that. Now that they are trying to kick the slimming habit, however, companies are discovering the destructive side effects' (Caulkin, 1995, p. 28). Not only are there inadequate numbers of professional and managerial employees to contribute to the generation of innovative products and processes, but those who remain have had their motivation and loyalty severely damaged by successive waves of redundancies.

If the infrastructure for CPD is to reflect the interests of the four groups of stakeholders, then both strengths and weaknesses are apparent in the UK framework. The lead now being taken by professional bodies in the development of competency-based approaches to CPD is positive and provides for integration between groups of stakeholders: providers such as higher education institutions, employers providing workplace learning and the development of broadly based competences by individuals. The Engineering Council's development of new CPD pathways culminating in Chartered Engineer status provides one example of a carefully considered approach which requires educational achievement; work-based learning and attested performance in work situations; multi-disciplinarity; individual commitment including 'Learned Society Activity' and the maintenance of competences through an action plan, and offers flexible pathways to achieve these outcomes (Engineering Council, 1995). Notably, the Council makes explicit their goal of assisting *individuals* to achieve professional registration. The prime concern of professional bodies is maintenance of standards through development of individual members, not of employing organizations. The definition of CPD adopted by the CPD in Construction Group also makes this explicit: 'the systematic maintenance, improvement and broadening of skills, and the development of personal qualities necessary for the execution of professional and technical duties throughout *the practitioner's* working life' (quoted in Johnston, 1993, p. 64; emphasis added).

The essential coalition between individuals and employers to ensure effective CPD may be better achieved through the requirements imposed by professional associations, but while there is much in the direction of a national policy and creation of an infrastructure which is sound, the questionable area remains employer commitment. There are, of course, examples of good practice among employers (including case studies outlined in this volume). However, good practice examples do not mean consistent performance on a national basis. I have elsewhere argued (Woodward, 1995, p. 4) that employers,

> though perhaps appreciating the need for professional development, harbour doubts about the award of qualifications, since these may lead to expectations of promotion or other employment benefits. Individuals, on the other hand, value qualifications because they can enhance job security and prospects. In the current national context, this creates a three way tension.

Within this 'eternal triangle' (see Figure 1.2) the axis linking individual commitment to national policy appears sound: the infrastructure to create opportunities for CPD is developing through the activities of professional bodies and higher education institutions, and is underpinned by the availability of loans and tax relief. The two axes linking national policy to employers, and individual commitment to employers, appear less well established, and it is these two areas of connectivity which may require further intervention.

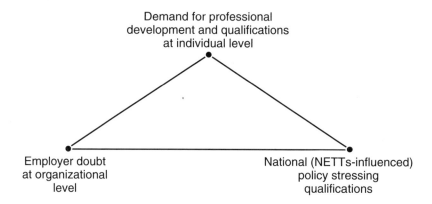

Figure 1.2 The eternal triangle: economics, organizations and the individual

DIMENSIONS OF CPD

In the chapters that follow, the themes of infrastructure, individual commitment, flexibility in CPD provision, the learning organization and the development of reflective and innovative practice are expanded. I have argued that CPD is an economic imperative, and that the essential task is to meet this challenge through effective learning opportunities which provide not only technocratic knowledge but also those skills necessary for pro-actively generating new knowledge and directing continuous innovation. Doubtless individual demand for CPD will grow, as will the range of occupations which exhibit 'professionalism'. The potential to enhance individual and organizational performance is therefore significant, since knowledge and its dissemination lies at the root of innovation, but this potential can only be realized through the commitment of *both* individuals and employers.

REFERENCES

Abbot, B. (1993) Training strategies in small service sector firms. *Human Resource Management Journal*, **4** (2), 70–87.

Annett, J. and Sparrow, J. (1985) Transfer of training: a review of research and practical implications. *Programmed Learning and Educational Technology*, **22** (2), 116–24.

Argyris, C. (1993) *Knowledge for Action: A Guide to Overcoming Barriers to Organizational Change*. San Francisco: Jossey-Bass.

Ashton, D. (1994) Labour market demand for high level skills. In I. Woodward (ed.), *Managing High Level Skills Training*. Leicester: University of Leicester.

Barnett, R. (1994) *The Limits of Competence: Knowledge, Higher Education and Society.* Buckingham: SRHE and Open University Press.

Bines, H. (1992) Issues in course design. In H. Bines and D. Watson, with J. Astley *et al.*, *Developing Professional Education.* Buckingham: SRHE and Open University Press.

Blaug, M. (1969) *The Economics of Education.* Harmondsworth: Penguin.

Boisot, M. (1987) *Information and Organisations: The Manager as Anthropologist.* London: Fontana.

Brookfield, S. D. (1986) *Understanding and Facilitating Adult Learning.* Milton Keynes: Open University Press.

Caulkin, S. (1995) Take your partners. *Management Today*, February, pp. 26–30.

Coates, D. (1994) *The View at Half Time: Politics and UK Economic Under-performance.* Professorial Inaugural Lecture, University of Leeds, 12 December.

Department of Trade and Industry and Employment Department (1992) *The Strategy for Skills and Enterprise: Guidance from the Secretary of State for Employment and the President of the Board of Trade.* London: DTI and ED.

Engineering Council (1995) Pathways. In *Competence and Assessment.* Sheffield: The Employment Department, Issue no. 29, June, pp. 42–9.

Eraut, M. (1994) *Developing Professional Knowledge and Competence.* London: Falmer.

Employment Department (1988) *Employment for the 1990s.* Cmd 540. London: Employment Department.

Employment Department (1994a) *Labour Market Skills and Trends.* Sheffield: Employment Department.

Employment Department (1994b) *Training in Britain.* Sheffield: Employment Department.

Garvin, D. A. (1993) Building a learning organization. *Harvard Business Review*, **71** (4), 78–91.

Hammer, M. and Champy, J. (1993) *Re-engineering the Corporation.* London: Nicholas Brealey.

Handy, C. (1995) Life inside and outside the organisation. *Common Purpose Magazine*, Spring, pp. 10–13.

Hughes, A. K. (1994) *Developing European Professions: Delivering Continuing Professional Development in Europe.* Bristol: University of Bristol Department for Continuing Education.

Johnston, R. (1993) The role of distance learning in continuing education and professional development. *International Journal of University Adult Education*, **23**(1), 61–76.

Kolb, D. A. (1984) *Experiential Learning: Experience as the Source of Learning and Development.* Englewood Cliffs: Prentice-Hall.

Maguire, M., Maguire, S. and Felstead, A. (1993) *Factors Influencing Individual Commitment to Lifetime Learning: A Literature Review.* Research Series No. 20. Sheffield: Employment Department.

Metcalf, H., Walling, A. and Fogarty, M. (1994) *Individual Commitment to Learning: Employers' Attitudes.* Research Series No. 40. Sheffield: Employment Department.

Pedler, M., Burgoyne, J. and Boydell, T. (1991) *The Learning Company: A Strategy for Sustainable Development.* New York and Maidenhead: McGraw-Hill.

Porter, M. E. (1990) *The Competitive Advantage of Nations.* London: Macmillan.

Revans, R. W. (1982) *The Origins and Growth of Action Learning.* Bromley: Chartwell Bratt.

Rifkin, J. (1995) *The End of Work: The Decline of the Global Labour Force and the Dawn of the Post-market Era.* New York: G.P. Putnam Sons.

Schon, D. (1987) *Educating the Reflective Practitioner.* San Francisco: Jossey-Bass.

17

Senge, P. M. (1993) *The Fifth Discipline: The Art and Practice of the Learning Organisation*. London: Random House.

Smithers, A. (1993) *All Our Futures – Britain's Education Revolution,* a *Dispatches* Report on Education. London: Channel Four Television.

Tansley, D. (1994) Government policy and the training of unemployed adults: the priorities and the practice. In I. Woodward (ed.), *Managing High Level Skills Training*. Leicester: University of Leicester.

Vygotsky, L. S. (1978) Interaction between learning and development. In M. Cole *et al.* (eds), *Mind in Society*. London: Harvard University Press.

Wickens, P. D. (1991) Innovation in training creates a competitive edge. In J. Stevens and R. MacKay (eds), *Training and Competitiveness*. London: Kogan Page.

Woodward, I. (1995) The eternal triangle: economics, organisations, and the individual. *Network News: HE Projects Newsletter*, **1**, 2–5.

Chapter 2

The Two Cultures Debate Revisited
Higher Level Skills Development and the Attitudes of the World of Work and the World of Higher Education

Judith Bowen, Andrew Eaglen and Richard Taylor

Since (at least) the 1960s there has been a debate about the relationship between the world of higher education and the world of work. This debate has focused on the tension between the perceived university culture which is held to value the pursuit of knowledge for its own sake, and the culture considered to dominate the world of employment which places emphasis on the utilitarian application of specific job-related skills. The debate then is not new, but in the context of moves towards mass participation in higher education, and the importance now being attached to lifelong learning, there is a need to reconsider the relationship between the higher education and employment sectors.

The origin for our reconsideration of the debate was survey research to identify, within the Leeds area in the north of England, employers' needs for continuing vocational education, and the extent to which provision by two local universities met those needs. The main findings and conclusions drawn from this research are presented at the end of the chapter, following our broader national analysis of the similarities and tensions between university and employment cultures.

THE HIGHER EDUCATION SECTOR

Universities are not socially autonomous institutions. Organizationally and financially they have become increasingly integrated into the British state during the twentieth century. This has been particularly so, of course, over the last twenty to thirty years as the higher education system has expanded. This obvious truth can be traced, at one level, through the bureaucratic history of the national management of universities – from the gentleman's club atmosphere of the original mechanism for financing universities through to the current formula-driven, government controlled Funding Councils (Gosden, 1983).

This close involvement with the state has been characteristic of universities' place within the established institutional hierarchy of British society. In pre-industrial society, the ancient universities provided the classical education and the high culture atmosphere which played an important role in the social reproduction of the ruling order. As the needs of the changing social order changed, so the roles of universities have altered radically. But their fundamental functions, both to provide what are perceived to be the appropriate skills and knowledge for the élite and to act as one of the key agents of hegemony, have remained constant.

These functions derive from a second truism: that, within a remarkably hierarchical society obsessed with status, universities have been seen traditionally as at the pinnacle of the educational pyramid. Indeed, right up until the 1980s universities were still highly élite institutions in the literal sense of being accessible to only a tiny proportion of the population (Anderson, 1992). This contrasted markedly with virtually all comparable societies.

They have also been, of course, highly élitist in terms of their student and (academic) staff composition. This is so well known as to need little emphasis here, but it is still nevertheless of critical importance to note the overwhelmingly middle-, upper-class and white dominance in universities. Until the 1970s, there was extreme gender imbalance too, and even though the composition of the student body has since become far more equal in this respect, staff imbalances, especially at senior levels, remain (Taylor et al., 1985).

The direct results of this long-standing exclusivity have been to perpetuate élitist social reproduction, to preserve predominantly conservative institutional structures and attitudes and, not least, to constrain curricular development within eurocentric and indeed often 'nineteenth-century' parameters.

Much has changed in the last decade. However, before moving on to discuss these developments, which form the main context for our discussion of higher level skills, some qualifications must be made to this image of generalized conservatism. As sociological analysis has shown time and again modern social institutions are never monolithic. This has applied with particular force to universities, and indeed to education generally. There have always been tensions between the needs of the state and the conservatism that this entails, and the inherently liberal inclinations of the educational profession. The 'conservatism' is easily explained, as indicated earlier, by universities' place within the élitist hierarchy: but why has liberalism also been so prominent? In part, this results from the fractured ideological structure of the wider society in the nineteenth and twentieth centuries, and arguably in earlier centuries too (Anderson, 1965). There has been a long tradition of liberal individualism, associated with private property rights, and philosophical and political arguments centring on the importance of individualism. In the context of universities, this individualism was naturally to the fore, as was, more importantly, the free-thinking, critical questioning inherent in the liberal framework.

Educators have been concerned to a significant extent with fostering habits of independent thinking and original intellectual development. Obviously, this has been even more prominent at university than at school level. Most important of all, there has been an inherent tendency to criticize the *status quo*. This questioning attitude is fundamental to the western intellectual tradition and is of course related to the tradition of 'blue skies' research.

Structurally, this has been a dangerous development for the established order in the twentieth century. The greater the sophistication of the economy, the greater the need for graduates equipped with appropriate skills. But the more universities have expanded to meet these needs, the more difficult it has become to maintain the élitist and conformist ethos. There is thus a contradiction between the economic imperative for university expansion and the social consequence of greater numbers of critical, questioning graduates. Moreover, given the fundamental long-term problems of the British economy, the potential for a disgruntled if not alienated, déclassé group of graduates has become considerable. In the last twenty years or so, a subculture of graduate professionals has developed who are distanced from the predominant late capitalist environment not only through their educational experiences but because of their subsequent employment in public sector and/or welfare oriented professions.

In these ways, then, university culture is heterogeneous – hence the ongoing tensions between the state and universities over the years, although there have also been disputes over straightforward resourcing issues in more recent years. However, there is no doubt that the dominant ethos has been conservative. A good representation of what might be termed the 'old Tory' view is given by Kenneth Minogue:

> Academic inquiry is a manner of seeking to understand anything at all, a manner distinguished no doubt by its motives and preoccupations, but distinguished above all by a quite different logic from that of practice. This means that there is a consistent difference in the kind of meaning that is found in academic discourse, by contrast with that found in the world at large. To ignore this difference, and to treat universities simply as institutions which provide educational services for society is like treating a Ming vase as a cut-glass flower bowl: plausible, but crass.
>
> (Minogue, 1973, p.76)

Implicit in this position is unbridled élitism. Sometimes this is linked to explicitly authoritarian models of wider social and political organization but more often it holds to an *a priori* assumed need for any society to have an intellectual élite whose role is to pursue knowledge untrammelled by the sordid concerns of the everyday world.

In sharp contrast to this and, needless to say, commanding more support these days from the established order, is the crudely utilitarian view of universities' functions. This view can be characterized, or perhaps caricatured, as the demand for ever greater numbers of graduates at increasingly cheaper unit cost, and concentrated upon somewhat narrowly conceived vocationalism. The validity or otherwise of research endeavours should be judged, it is argued, by the same yardstick.

These two conservative cultures in universities coexist rather uneasily with the liberal perspectives outlined earlier. Certainly, most universities, for most of the time, adhere to liberal principles of critical enquiry and the disinterested pursuit of truth; and they regard these principles as justifiable, indeed essential, not only for quality assurance and consequent funding reasons, but as *a priori* values.

Finally, in this catalogue of cultures, there are those who espouse a more progressive, 'social purpose' view of universities and whose influence is felt particularly in continuing education and associated parts of the system. The relationships between this historically socialist and egalitarian tradition and the contemporary movements for accessibility are contentious. On the one hand, it can be argued that at last mass higher education and accessibility give tangible, practical form to what has always previously remained socialist, and often romantic, rhetoric; on the other hand, these contemporary movements can be seen as incorporating, within the mainstream, essentially capitalist structures, a previously independent and alternative tradition, thereby neutralizing it.

Schematically, then, there are *four* cultures of the university in the mid- to late twentieth century, which replicate the original 'two cultures' argument between F. R. Leavis and C. P. Snow. These university cultures provide a good analytical framework for discussion of the development of the last decade and the place of higher level skills. There can be no doubt of the determination of the state (in this case, principally in the form of government and civil service) in the latter years of the twentieth century to continue 'the drive towards efficiency and utilitarianism', and of the determination of ministers of education to encourage a shift of emphasis in universities towards the scientific and technological subjects.

Such views are by no means confined to governmental and related circles. Voices in both industry and in universities themselves have called for a reorientation of university priorities and activities along similar lines. Two educationalists have argued, for example, that from the nineteenth century on Britain has persistently clung to an outmoded, pre-industrial set of educational priorities, dominated by Oxford and Cambridge and their attachment to the classical education model (Roderick and Stephens, 1982). Despite the rhetorical support given to technological education in the 1960s (by the then Prime Minister, Harold Wilson, among others), Britain remained one of the lowest per capita investors in higher education in the industrialized world, and in the late 1960s, the proportion of students in 'arts plus social studies ... [at] 42.4% was just about the same as it ever had been since before the war' (Sanderson, 1975).

Other critics have been somewhat harsher in their condemnation of what is seen as the obscurantism of the universities' attitudes. David Weir, for example, argues that:

> it is the arts based culture which dominates. ... Since the late
> 19th century other advanced industrial societies ... have devel-
> oped educational systems which attach more priority to science
> than to the arts ... and these technologies are even further
> down in the power structure of British society.
>
> (in Roderick and Stephens, 1982, p.92)

Furthermore, such critics would argue, their analyses of the innate educational conservatism of the university sector were confirmed by the packages of financial cuts imposed on the universities in 1981, and the subsequent continuing restrictions imposed on universities.

Thus, despite its increasing control over the university sector, the government was not able to reshape the universities to the degree it would have liked, towards vocationally and technologically oriented programmes of study. Undoubtedly, this was a major factor in the creation of the binary system from 1965, bringing into being thirty polytechnics, and thus attempting to bypass, to some extent, the problem of the universities' intransigent traditionalism.

Since the decision of the government, in the late 1980s, to move to an explicit policy of mass higher education, the context of post-compulsory education has changed fundamentally. Despite the present hiccough, there is no doubt that we are well on the way to a mass higher education system. One in three 18-year-olds are now in higher education – and it must not be forgotten that more than half of university students are now over 21 years old. Equally important, the ending of the binary line has led to a similarly fundamental shift of practice, if not yet of culture, in virtually all universities. Modularization, the expansion of continuing education and continuing vocational education, and of part-time degree provision, have all been combined with a far greater emphasis upon access and curriculum development to achieve generic and transferable skills and greater links to industry and, generally, vocational training.

There is considerable diversity across the unified university sector. Some of the changes noted above have hardly affected Oxford and Cambridge, for example. And the ancient universities, and some of the other élite research institutions, really have little in common with many of the new universities. Indeed, there is obviously far more common ground – in terms of mission, curriculum, student body and overall ethos – between many new universities and some of the larger further education colleges, many of which have significant elements of higher education within their provision.

Nevertheless, for the bulk of the university sector, these irreversible developments will lead to fundamental cultural changes. Within this changed environment, continuing vocational education can and should have a central role to play. Our analysis of this role is derived from a project to evaluate the extent to which university provision of continuing vocational education meets the needs of employers. The project was carried out by staff of two neighbouring universities – the University of Leeds and Leeds Metropolitan University – with very different traditions and missions which, nevertheless, are both now fully committed to higher level skills development within the context of an expanded continuing education and vocational education role.

There are inevitably difficulties, however. The university system has been under great pressure in terms of student numbers, declining units of resource and ever-increasing research demands. In this context of rapid and often seemingly incoherent change, higher level skills and similar developmental programmes often appear as 'yet one more damned thing' to cope with. Hard-pressed heads of departments need to be convinced of the cost effectiveness and long-term relevance of higher level skills – and other developmental initiatives – before they are prepared to become fully involved.

The survey of university provision and local employers' needs thus took place at an opportune time in many ways: rapid institutional change, including expansion, modularization and an emphasis upon accessibility, were in full flow and higher level skills integrated into this programme of change. But it has also been a time of 'innovation overload'. Whether higher level skills development, and the related work-based learning and continuing vocational education initiatives, manage to embed themselves permanently in what is still in many of its essentials a conservative culture, is an open question.

THE EMPLOYMENT SECTOR

We now turn to discuss relationships between the employment sector, the universities and the state. One question which the project described below attempts to address is: to what extent can the higher education sector satisfy some or all of the training and education needs of the workforce in the second half of the 1990s and beyond? This superficially straightforward question makes assumptions about the employment sector and the non-problematic nature of the interaction between employers, the universities and the state.

The employment sector is not homogeneous. In fact the distinction between public and private sector, although in theory breaking down because of government policies and legislation over the past twelve years, remains important. Large organizations, for example, in the health sector, include key members of staff who identify more readily with the higher education sector. However, the hierarchical organizations of the health service professions means that for some groups, such as doctors, this identification will be with the older universities: the professions allied to medicine may have closer links historically with the new universities but may seek what they see as more prestigious alliances. A commitment to the concept of continuous professional development may be more important for groups who have had more limited access to diplomas and degrees. Given these different alliances nevertheless, a public sector organization such as health is more likely to seek training and education opportunities in the higher education sector.

Similarly, some private sector business, irrespective of size, will have developed links with local colleges of further and higher education in order to provide full-time and part-time day release courses for employees who are expected to gain professionally recognized qualifications. It can be argued that it is 'semi-professionals' (Etzioni, 1964) who have benefited from the wide range of diploma and degree courses which are academically respectable and quality assured and which offer, in effect, dual qualifications to employees and potential employees.

The former polytechnic sector has relied heavily over the past twenty years on extending the range of professionally acceptable qualifications; the sector has gone further than this and has promoted provision in contrast to the 'ivory tower' model and has sought to reassure its target market of the relevance of its courses. It is not that relationships of this kind are free from tension; rather, that in finance and law, for example, as well as in health, full-time vocational education was becoming the norm for recruitment of first-time entrants. Although the impact of market-based models has had its effects, the culture in a range of organizations, irrespective of size and public/private designation, is still influenced by credentialism.

During the 1980s, however, the utilitarian focus for education and training became much more important, with consequences for training budgets and formal systems of delivering staff development and upgrading skills. Arguments put forward by governments and others were that there is a strong link between education and training systems in place and a country's level of industrial productivity and competitiveness. A survey carried out in the European Community countries in 1987–88 (European Round Table of Industrialists, 1989) reported that the most serious educational problem facing Europe was not initial professional training, but the need to upgrade the skills and knowledge of the existing workforce. This had arisen, it was argued, partly because of the lack of attention in the past to 'lifelong learning' but also because of the need to compete in a very different global market environment. Flexibility and the acquisition of constantly changing skills are of paramount importance. 'Countries whose populations have the best possibilities to learn and develop their competence are going to be the nations of wealth' (Otala, 1993, p.3). This emphasis on technology-based skills but also on the ability to learn and learn continuously has added a new dimension to the 'two cultures' debate. It presents the employment sector with difficult choices in terms of priorities for training and education and creates competition for scarce resources among young people and those already within the workforce.

The workforce of the future, it is argued, will need employees willing and able to take on new roles and the new competences associated with these roles. If this is true, then an emphasis on operational training is no longer sufficient; a wider range of employees will need strategic capabilities which will help them to think ahead, to innovate and to be ready to accept change. This model places a premium on continuous professional development and targets employees at higher levels in the organization.

Lena Otala argues that, although companies had recognized the need for a more flexible approach, this had often been accompanied by a 'down-sizing' of centralized training departments. Flexibility and responsiveness mean that training 'close to the business' is preferred, and this has its own dangers:

> There is a danger of losing cumulative company know-how of
> human resource development when the responsibility for train-
> ing is too operational. At the same time the development of
> personnel training practices is no one's responsibility.
>
> (Otala, 1993, p.8)

The European Round Table survey showed that, by the late 1980s, the employment sector in Europe was experiencing severe tensions between the need to provide high quality training and education for an existing and ageing work-force and focusing on operational competences, at a time when jobs were being cut back and institutional training responsibilities devolved. It can be argued that these tensions are greater in the UK because of the relatively low levels of highly qualified people in the existing workforce. The élitist nature of higher education in the UK (and in fact post-16 education overall) has had con-sequences for the 'learning capability' of organizations. In 1988, 10 per cent of the workforce had degrees, 7 per cent higher level diplomas and 20 per cent lower technician or craft qualifications. In Germany in the same period, 11 per cent had degrees, 7 per cent diplomas and 56 per cent lower technician or craft qualifications. In the Netherlands where 8 per cent had degrees, 19 per cent had higher diplomas and 38 per cent lower technician or craft level qualifica-tions (National Advisory Council for Education and Training Targets, 1994). The evidence suggests that the UK has neglected its technician level qualifica-tions and has concentrated higher education effort on degrees. Moreover, it has only belatedly begun to increase age participation rates into higher educa-tion to levels approaching that of its European partners in the Union (30 per cent by 1993). As a result, the culture of many organizations in the sector is likely to be resistant to higher education and unlikely to turn to the universi-ties to serve their immediate problems; it is also likely to be hypercritical of the 'products' of the sector.

The government's assessment of this situation during the early 1980s led to the setting up of the National Council for Vocational Qualifications (NCVQ) and to the adoption of the CBI National Education and Training Targets, with a National Advisory Council to monitor progress on achievement.

It is not the purpose of this chapter to describe the National Vocational Qualifications (NVQ) system in any detail. However, the underlying philosophy is important in recognizing their avowed purpose in changing the culture of the employment sector. Standards are first developed, consultatively, by lead bodies from the different employment sectors. The standards are competence-based and can be assessed in the workplace. The qualification, however, is awarded by a national awarding body, specifically accredited, which organizes the moderation process and the quality assurance of the whole system.

Government ideology has also linked funding for NVQ development to individual employees rather than through taxes on employers. (The compar-ison with France is interesting; the country has had a tax on employers related to their employee budget since 1971 and an entitlement to employ-ees for paid educational leave since the same date.) It could be argued that, in spite of strenuous publicity and promotion of NVQs, there has been little incentive for employers to think strategically about education and training. It was against this background that a further initiative – the 'Investors in

People' programme – was established to promote a more strategic orientation by employers.

In reality, the adoption of NVQs has been slow (Smithers, 1994) and mainly at the lower levels (1–3). Employers have found it difficult to introduce higher levels (4 and 5) without the commitment of the higher education sector. More recently, government energy has been devoted to introducing General National Vocational Qualifications into schools as a way of providing an alternative to A-level awards. This has diverted attention away from the employment-based philosophy of NVQs which were intended originally to change the culture in the employment sector and to stimulate education and training.

The argument so far has been that it is not possible to point to a single culture which can be defined as the culture of the employment sector. Different sectors have different traditions and have responded to market pressures and government policies in different ways, depending on factors such as size, tradition, professional orientation and existing alliances. There is, however, a striking neglect of other social factors which affect the skill levels of the sector; education and training, it can be argued, has too often been divorced from changes in people's domestic responsibilities and lifestyles (Harman, 1993).

It is acknowledged that women now outnumber men in the workforce and that over the past twelve years new jobs have largely been part-time. Many of these are low skilled and training, if offered at all, will be very short-term and highly specific.

There are equal opportunities issues around employment status and the entitlement of people to education and training which will improve the quality of life and the level of skills and knowledge. It is not clear to what extent a shift in culture towards a more egalitarian sharing of work and domestic responsibilities is influencing workplace policies and practices. Most studies demonstrate that higher education replicates and reproduces gender divisions in the workforce and that self-employment and working in small organizations are particularly disadvantageous for women (Bowen, 1990).

What is clear is that the existing models do not readily match the needs of the UK workforce in the 1990s. Day release, intensive degree-level awards, reliance on individual contributions and highly specific skills training do not necessarily respond to the needs of people whose work and domestic lifestyles may actually be moving nearer together.

To summarize, it is suggested that the culture of the employment sector is changing and that tensions, similar to those in the university sector, can be identified. This is not surprising since neither sector exists in a social vacuum.

Changes in the employment sector are most easily interpreted as coming from the perceived demands of the capitalist economy. To survive in the market-place, it is argued, businesses must constantly renew their products in the light of shifts in global predominance. None the less, the influence of different stakeholders in this market economy can be discerned.

For historical reasons, the private sector in the UK has been slow to recognize the value of university education. The past thirty years has seen a move towards recognizing the importance of degree level qualifications. The move towards credentialism has been strongest among professional and semi-professional groups and the former polytechnic sector has been a significant player in this scenario. Professional groups are now reluctant to give up the status conferred by diplomas and degrees, hence the lack of progress in acceptance of NVQs at higher levels. The professions have, in some cases, recognized belatedly the need for continuing professional development and the importance of lifelong learning. Credentialism, however, remains important for them.

In organizations, especially small and medium-sized enterprises where the professional culture is weak, the economic imperative is seen to drive change. This is sometimes expressed as an impatience with formal qualifications and their associated bureaucracy; sometimes as a demand for customized courses and an emphasis on operational skills. Recognition that the market demands more knowledge-based skills is beginning to influence the kind of skills that are seen as important. Adaptability, flexibility and information technology awareness are increasingly valued.

In all enterprises, it is argued, the perceptions of people in the workforce are changing. The increase in part-time work and the significant contribution which women now make to the economy coexist alongside a culture which still places a high value on company loyalty, commitment to a corporate career and traditional forms of recognizing status. The needs of part-time workers, workers in a multinational and multicultural environment have, however, all been recognized by legislation.

It is at this point that university culture and employment culture intersect. The expansion of the university system is irreversible. Greater participation in education up to and beyond the secondary stage, together with improved standards of living for most sections of the population, mean that people are more likely to wish to exercise choice in the work situation. For both sectors the move towards a mass higher education system has brought tensions and contradictions. For the universities this is most starkly expressed as the contradiction between exclusivity and greater student participation. For businesses and the public sector this is a tension between perceived market-led demand for skills and the desire of people to control their own lifestyle.

The 1960s debate about the two cultures was over-simplified. It is no longer a question of 'more scientists and fewer arts graduates'. That debate was itself grounded in an élitist model of education. The challenge for both sectors is to find ways of responding to the demands posed by mass participation and by a possible move towards a universal higher education system. This will not be achieved by either sector becoming more 'utilitarian' in the sense of simply serving the economy. The higher level skills debate poses more serious questions for post-industrial society. It raises questions about which skills are to be valued, not because they equip people for a particular job but because they allow people to access learning which enables them to exercise a greater control over their lives.

Some would say that this is to redefine the social purpose model of higher education by introducing the concept of skills as a key component of access. For both sectors, the issues around change will need to be worked out, if not in formal partnerships, at least in a closer dialogue than has been possible in the past.

THE HIGHER LEVEL SKILLS ACCESS AND DEVELOPMENT PROJECT

This two-year project was funded and carried out collaboratively by the Leeds Training and Enterprise Council, the Leeds Metropolitan University and the University of Leeds. The broad aims were to evaluate the extent to which the current provision in the two universities meets the needs of local employers. The project team carried out surveys of employers across the main employment sectors and worked on pilot projects within both institutions to propose models for marketing and accessing education and training which would be more responsive to the different stakeholders.

The survey findings are described in a report to the Leeds Training and Enterprise Council (Eaglen, 1994). Drawing on these findings, we now outline the evidence which points to a need to reorientate both university and employment sector priorities, if the partners are to contribute to the trained and flexible workforce which, it is argued, an expanding economy requires in the competitive world of the late 1990s.

First of all the surveys showed that, not surprisingly, the employment sector does not have a uniform view on education and training. Size of organization was a significant factor in their willingness to invest in formal policies and practices. Large organizations were more likely to recruit graduates and to have identified specific skills and knowledge gaps among their workforce. They were also more likely to recognize and value formal degree and diploma qualifications.

Size alone was not sufficient to account for the diversity of responses. Some medium-sized firms, especially in the financial and legal sectors, recognized the value of formal qualifications. This was clearly as a result of their fairly long-standing associations with the higher education sector and the influence of a professional ethos within the organization. An emphasis on institute membership, graduate status for managers and mandatory continuing professional development characterized organizations in the public sector and in the private sector where a tradition of association existed. The personal development experience of senior managers was also a factor; many who had succeeded without a university education themselves felt that graduates needed management and interpersonal skills which were not always in evidence.

There were some marked differences between sectors. Traditional routes to qualifications in the printing industry, for example, were through the further education sector. This contrasts with the situation described above, where the profession, rather than the company, sets the criteria for career development.

Smaller organizations, overall, were more likely to be preoccupied with short-term operational needs. While aware of other needs, they invested in technical upgrading rather than in management skills. They gave a low profile to general qualifications and to degrees and diplomas and they saw the universities as primarily offering three-year degree programmes and attracting school leavers. Although all sectors emphasized 'value for money' as being more important than price, this was particularly true for small organizations which were also more likely to be critical of higher education's ability to deliver.

The survey findings suggested that, overall, the impact of the National Vocational Qualifications has been low. In the health sector, for example, there has been considerable investment in lower level (1–3) NVQs as a response to the changing structure and the reorganization of work practices in the new trusts, but this does not seem to have progressed to levels 4 and 5.

One way in which government policies over the past twelve years do seem to have influenced employers' attitudes to training and education is in the contribution expected of employees in the training and education process. 'Employers perceived employees to be significant influences or initiators in the process and required them to demonstrate a level of motivation to warrant what for some organisations was perceived as a sizeable investment' (Eaglen, 1994, p.13).

Another way in which expectations are changing is the great emphasis placed by all employers on flexible delivery of provision by the higher education sector. This flexibility takes many forms but includes a greater emphasis on short courses, a preference for evening or weekend timing, the use of the summer semester and opportunities for distance and open learning and the accreditation of work-based learning. Travel time to study is a significant factor for employers and employees. Currently, employers in the sample were using regional resources but also going beyond the region for part-time provision. Teeside, Nottingham and even London were mentioned. Whether this was because of traditional links or more flexible provision was not always clear.

An area in which practically all respondents were in agreement was the need for improvements in the way in which the higher education sector communicates with potential students. This covers all aspects from marketing through to pre-entry guidance, admission practices, induction and support while studying.

CONCLUSIONS

This brief summary does not do justice to the findings of the report. It does, however, demonstrate that the culture of the employment sector is changing, albeit slowly. It has been possible to identify at least four influences, some of which conflict and can sometimes be seen within the same sector.

The more conservative model, which emphasizes conventional apprenticeships and clearly delineated routes based on technical qualifications with access to higher diplomas but not degrees, seems to be weakening.

Among smaller firms in particular, a pragmatic approach to training is identified, although the emphasis here is also on core management and information technology skills. Although 'short-termist' in most respects, it recognizes the imperatives of the market economy; the potential contribution of the higher education sector is not yet recognized.

The influence of professionalism and the value of higher awards is stronger among sectors where there has been contact between universities and the established and emerging graduate professions. The conflict between the professional ethos, the recognition of the need for continuous professional development and the demands of market forces, even in former public sector organizations, is most marked in these sectors.

Finally, employers across the spectrum recognize the changing nature of the workforce and the demands that this makes on them to sponsor more flexible provision. The tension here is the extent to which this is reflected in equal opportunities policies and appraisal systems which recognize the right to training and education of all workers, whether full- or part-time.

The extent to which the university sector can or wishes to respond to this shifting culture is likely to be a significant feature of their development over the next five or so years of 'consolidation'. The project has highlighted the recognition, by both universities involved, that a move to mass higher education cannot be ignored, not least because government policy has already brought this about. The changing issues for the two organizations may differ in some respects. In the older university the tensions between the pursuit of knowledge for its own sake and the demands of the market economy may be greater than in the new university; advocates of the social purpose model may find it harder to stake a claim for a change towards admitting students from under-represented groups. The vocational and professional focus of provision in the new universities however, makes them more vulnerable to changes in the market-place and in danger currently of being less attractive to people studying for personal development objectives.

If, as the survey findings suggest, the culture of the (capitalist) employment sector is changing, higher education will not be able to stand still. Competition from further education and business and commercial organizations to provide training and education will challenge the purposes of universities. If universities are concerned with learning, then definitions of the skills required for learning will have to go beyond the demands imposed by the market-place.

The project demonstrates that universities are responding, in difficult circumstances, to the rapid transformation to a mass higher education system that is now underway. The government is intent upon accomplishing this quickly and at minimal cost, while of course retaining quality. A key element in this process is the development of closer liaison and partnership with the 'world of work'. Depending upon their cultures, market positions and histories, universities are responding to this in diverse ways. This may well result in a much more diversified sector which can then respond to the varying needs of the employment sector.

REFERENCES

Anderson, P. (1965) Origins of the present crisis. In P. Anderson and R. Blackburn (eds), *Towards Socialism*. London: Fontana.

Anderson, R. D. (1992) *Universities and Élites in Britain since 1800*. Basingstoke: Macmillan.

Bowen, J. (1990) *Opportunities and Choice for Women Graduates and Self-employment in the 1990s*. Small Firms Policy and Research Conference, Harrogate, September.

Eaglen, A. (1994) *The Higher Level Skills Development and Access Project. Report to the Leeds Training and Enterprise Council*. Leeds: Leeds Metropolitan University and the University of Leeds.

Etzioni, A. (1964) *Modern Organisations*. London: Prentice-Hall.

European Round Table of Industrialists (1989) *Education and European Competence*. Brussels: European Round Table of Industrialists.

Gosden, P. H. J. H. (1983) *The Education System since 1944*. Oxford: Martin Robertson.

Harman, H. (1993) *The Century Gap*. London: Vermilion.

Minogue, K. (1973) *The Concept of a University*. London: Weidenfeld & Nicolson.

National Advisory Council for Education and Training Targets (1994) *Review of the National Targets for Education and Training. Proposals for Consultation*. London: NACETT.

Otala, L. (1993) *Trends in Lifelong Learning in Europe*. TEXT Conference. Dublin, 1–3 April.

Roderick, G. and Stephens, M. (1982) The British education system 1870–1970. In G. Roderick and M. Stephens (eds), *The British Malaise: Industrial Performance, Education and Training in Britain Today*. Lewes: Falmer.

Sanderson, M. (1975) *The Universities in the Nineteenth Century*. London: Routledge & Kegan Paul.

Smithers, A. (1994) *Raising Educational Attainment and Enhancing Skills*. FEDOR National Conference, London, March.

Taylor, R., Rockhill, K. and Fieldhouse, R. (1985) *University Adult Education in England and the USA: A Reappraisal of the Liberal Tradition*. London: Croom Helm.

Chapter 3

Policies and Structures for University Continuing Professional Development

Valerie A. Mitchell and Edward J. Thomas

Universities in Europe are currently experiencing a period of major change. This has been considered and encouraged in recent studies from, among others, the European Union (Commission of the European Community, 1991, 1993) and the Committee of European Rectors (Seidel, 1994). These changes relate to categories of activity (teaching, research and continuing education), to the size and range of higher education (students, subjects, course structures and teaching networks), to their social and economic roles (for example, links with industry and regional development), to their wider context (closer collaboration with Western and, increasingly, Eastern European universities and other international links), and often to changing funding arrangements. European higher education will almost certainly remain a diverse system, both nationally and institutionally, with different universities pursuing different roles. A period of change can be one of opportunity or of decline. At such a time it is particularly important (and, in the case of United Kingdom universities, a requirement if central funding is to be received from the Higher Education Funding Councils) that each university should adopt a specific policy.

Continuing education has become an increasingly important activity for many European universities. Encouraged by, among others, the European Commission (1991), by the Committee of European Rectors and by the European Universities Continuing Education Network (1992), some are introducing continuing education and others are expanding it significantly. This will result increasingly in a changing balance in universities' work between initial and continuing education, a development encouraged by the European Commission. Particular attention is currently attached to expanding the provision of continuing vocational education, including continuing professional development, to assist Europe to retain and increase its international competitiveness by exploiting new technology and meeting skills shortages. There is a move to ensure good health, education, financial and other professional services (Otala, 1992). There is also encouragement to grant credits for higher education (including open and distance learning) and so to develop flexible routes to university qualifications (CEC, 1992). In some European countries university continuing education is expanding rapidly; in others the higher education structures are not conducive to continuing education (for example, some are over-centralized; others are inflexible). In other countries a clear structure has yet to be established. Given the many current pressures on universities, any institution undertaking continuing education which does not have a clear and well-understood policy will almost certainly be at a disadvantage to those which do.

This continuing education policy should be consistent with and implement the university's policy. This is not only good practice in planning but it increases the power and effectiveness of continuing education within the university and the unit(s) which provide it. The more closely a department or other unit of a university is seen to be fulfilling the policy of the university as a whole, the stronger that unit will be. Such a sequential link between the overall university policy and that of each academic and service unit of the university not only confers authority on the unit's activity but helps to ensure consistency and compatibility between the activities of the different sectors. It further provides a means of identifying and responding to inconsistencies which develop.

Against this background we:

- explore the process of creating a policy framework;

- identify the possible contents of such a policy;

- consider the implementation of a university continuing education policy by the selection of appropriate structures to achieve it;

- illustrate all these matters by case studies; and

- summarize the practical benefits to be gained from an effective university continuing education policy.

THE POLICY FRAMEWORK

In creating a policy, the aim should be to articulate institutional goals in order to give clear guidance in decision-making for both day-to-day provision and future development. To achieve an effective policy one needs not only to be able to choose appropriate objectives but also to express these in a clear and unambiguous way. Neither of these are simple tasks and a two-stage approach is preferable. The first stage is to generate a single or small number of broad *aims*, sometimes referred to as the 'mission statement'. More precise *objectives* can then be developed.

An effective policy statement is unlikely to be generated by just one person. Ownership is a key concept and widespread discussion across all staff levels and functions is desirable. Extensive consultation is valuable since:

- a wider range of ideas can be considered for inclusion within the policy;

- any ambiguities within the objectives can be located and removed;

- the policy can be formulated to meet the working needs of most (if not all) of the people using it;

- by taking part in the discussions, the users will become well-informed on the content of the policy; and

- having contributed to it, they are more likely to implement the policy with enthusiasm.

Produced in this way, the final policy should meet the needs of the organization. In particular, in the case of continuing education, it should allow a student/client-centred approach which builds on the students' knowledge, flexibility of course content (format, level, credits, time and place), a fast response to clients' needs, and facilitate continuing innovation. It should also help to ensure that the continuing education is appropriately resourced (particularly in terms of accommodation, student support, academic and support staff, administrative systems, finance and quality assurance) to meet the needs of post-experience learners which differ significantly from those of young full-time undergraduates.

As in many other activities, the law of diminishing returns operates in the case of producing continuing education policies; it is not productive to overemphasize the need for perfection. When producing a policy, the outcome should be a tool which can be used as a basis for action.

THE CONTENTS OF A CONTINUING EDUCATION POLICY

To determine the major issues that need to be addressed, continuing education policy statements from twelve universities have been analysed, two from the United Kingdom (one 'new' university and one 'old'), one each from Finland, France, Portugal, Spain, and two each from the Netherlands, Switzerland and the United States. The issues identified were further explored in a workshop when revised policies were drafted for continuing education sectors/departments in universities which differed greatly in their history, size and role. The third source was discussions at the 1994 Continuing Vocational Education Conference on the Impact of Professional Development held at the University of Leicester.

Despite the widely separated universities and the lack of any inter-action between them, there is a marked similarity in the topics addressed in the continuing education policy statements examined. These topics are iden-tified in the list below, and Table 3.1 indicates which of these topics were specifically considered in the continuing education policies of each of the universities studied. Not surprisingly, however, in view of the very different organization and histories of the universities producing them and the very different conditions within which they work, the actual contents of the poli-cies and their formats are generally very different.

The discrete elements identified from the examination of these policies are:

- a definition of the students and subjects, that is the *markets*, to which continuing education is directed;

- the *external links* which the organization has (or aims to estab-lish);

- the *course formats* which they choose to provide, e.g. from half-day courses to several years of part-time study;

- the *locations* of the provision;

- whether or not *qualifications* (or credits) are offered;

- the policy on *fees* and the financing of continuing education;

- the *course organization* system adopted within the university to deliver the continuing education (including reference to struc-tures);

- the *staffing* policy, e.g. on the selection, training and remunera-tion of staff from inside and outside the university;

- *student support* (including guidance and other services for the wide range of continuing education students); and

- the system for the maintenance of the *quality* for the programme.

STRUCTURES FOR THE IMPLEMENTATION OF POLICY

The possible structures for the provision of university continuing profes-sional development were surveyed by Onushkin (1977) and four major

Table 3.1 Elements contained in the continuing education policies of the twelve universities studied

Country	Markets	External links	Course formats	Locations	Qualifications	Fees/ finance	Organization structure	Staffing	Student support	Quality	Research
Finland	•	•	•	•	•	•	•	•			
France	•	•	•	•	•	•	•	•	•	•	•
The Netherlands (1)	•	•	•	•	•	•	•			•	•
The Netherlands (2)	•	•			•	•	•	•		•	•
Portugal	•	•	•		•	•					
Spain	•		•		•	•	•		•	•	
Switzerland (1)	•	•		•	•	•	•	•	•	•	•
Switzerland (2)	•	•		•	•	•	•	•	•	•	•
United Kingdom (1)	•	•	•	•	•	•	•	•	•	•	•
United Kingdom (2)	•	•		•	•	•		•	•	•	•
United States of America (1)	•	•		•	•	•	•	•		•	
United States of America (2)	•	•			•	•	•	•		•	

Table 3.2   Advantages and disadvantages of different structures to provide university CPD

Advantages	Disadvantages
Special unit in university	
Can centralize and concentrate efforts, coordinate, plan and develop	More costly
More autonomy, bringing greater curricular freedom, ability to initiate, flexibility to meet clients' needs	More exposed to budget cuts
	Duplicates some facilities of university
	May become isolated from rest of university
	Creates administrative work
	Represents a permanent commitment
Greater specialization, e.g. on course design for adults	Possibly difficult to persuade other faculties to become involved in CE
Staff more enthusiastic and committed to CE	
Has special funding and staff	
Promotes interdisciplinary provision	
Existing unit in university	
Uses existing expert staff and facilities	Additional work for staff often busy already, often lack expertise in CE
Reflects CE experience back into full-time students' courses	Bureaucratic problems, lack of flexibility
Staff benefit from outside contacts (industry, professions, etc.)	Takes resources from full-time student teaching
Challenges/encourages staff	Risk of neglect of CE, or uneven distribution of CE in university
Can produce high quality	Risk of conservative teaching methods
External unit for which the university is responsible	
May have greater experience: new approaches reciprocal learning processes	Lack of control over: duration of courses timing of courses quality
May have more support from professional bodies, industry	More difficult to coordinate
Courses more likely to meet needs of clients	More effort needed for communication
Less expensive for university: less administrative work can use facilities of others	University staff and departments generally less committed
Flexible	
Supports intra-institutional cooperation	
University participation in a separate unit	
As for the external units for which the university is responsible	Lack of control
	Subordinate role for the university
	Difficult to build teams for courses
	Weaker links between university and clients
	More travelling for staff

Source: Adapted from Onushkin, 1977

structures were identified: a special unit in the university established for the purpose; provision by the existing units; an external unit for which the university is responsible; or participation by the university in a separate external unit. Adapting Onushkin's conclusions to present-day conditions, the advantages and disadvantages of adopting each of these structures in a university setting are indicated in Table 3.2. It is clear from Onushkin's work that there is no single ideal structure for all universities: the structure that will most effectively achieve the provision of the continuing professional education in a particular university will depend on a number of factors including the history of continuing education in the university, its present resources, the current policy for continuing education and the administrative structure of the university itself. It is by no means uncommon to find several of the continuing education structures, and sometimes all of them, existing simultaneously in a single university. The choice can be pragmatic, and designed to suit the precise activity. Certainly, too much structural purity may be restricting.

Whichever structure is chosen by a particular university, this needs to be operated in such a way that its benefits are maximized and its disadvantages minimized. Once the chosen system is in place and the responsibilities have been defined, the detailed decisions concerning the provision of continuing professional development can be made, guided by the objectives.

CASE STUDIES OF POLICY IMPLEMENTATION

The ways in which policies can be implemented are more easily demonstrated than described. The implementation is therefore presented here in the form of case studies to illustrate each of Onushkin's first three categories. (The fourth category is not under the control of the university and its resources are deployed by others. This category is therefore not considered further here.) All the case studies given here illustrate examples that have operated successfully for some time. It is important in reading these case studies to concentrate on their structure and to take the contents of the policies only as examples: the detailed content will necessarily vary from one university to another.

Case Study One

A Central Unit in the University: a Continuing Education Department

Aim: Through the provision of continuing education, to make available the scholarship, knowledge and skills of the university to the outside world.
Objectives: It is the policy of the Continuing Education Department that:

- the courses it offers should, as far as possible, meet the educational needs of adults. The courses provided should span the whole range of subjects offered by the university (including the particular subjects of the department itself) and cover its range of academic levels. Particular effort should be made to enable adults with a disability to attend these courses;

- it should strive to maintain excellence in all aspects of its continuing education and to apply its quality assurance system to the whole of its course provision;

- the form of the provision may need to range from a single session to a part-time course lasting two years or more; the teaching may take place during the day or in the evenings, during the week or at weekends, and in or out of university terms;

- there should continue to be the closest cooperation between the department and all the other departments of the university to ensure the provision of appropriate courses. The department should support the university's provision of post-experience vocational education and, to this end, work readily with all other departments of the university;

- where there is mutual advantage to be gained, the department should maintain a close relationship with a wide range of organizations in the United Kingdom, including local and national government departments, the Workers' Educational Association and organizations with a particular subject interest, including the appropriate professional bodies;

- the courses can take place wherever there are appropriate groups of students and suitable teaching accommodation, both within its own country and abroad;

- the department should expand its programme of courses relating to Europe and, to this end, should develop its link with other European universities and other appropriate bodies;

- the programme of courses leading to university qualifications should be expanded by working within a credit accumulation and transfer system;

- the programme of liberal adult education courses should be maintained;

- the programme of short vocational courses should be increased;

- the fee for each course should generally be set to cover the full costs of that course. In determining the fee, all the appropriate grants for the course should be taken into account; and

- all members of the academic staff should contribute to the development of their subject by research into either its academic or its educational aspects.

Policy implementation: Courses are organized by individual academic staff, each with support staff, responsible for a designated element of the continuing education programme. (Continuing professional development forms part of a much wider programme which includes liberal adult education and courses leading to university qualifications.)

The staffing complement has two senior academic staff as managers, twenty-six academic staff, two central administrative staff and thirty-five support staff.

Extensive, external contacts are maintained with international and national professional bodies, potential clients (including industries, other local and national employers), other suppliers of continuing education and many others.

The course programme consists of about 1000 courses each year with around 25,000 enrolments in essentially all the subjects of the university.

There is a wide range of course formats to suit student needs, some residential.

Courses are provided widely across the region and, to a lesser extent, throughout the country. Around 1 to 2 per cent are run in other countries each year, mainly elsewhere in Europe.

Some of the courses lead to university credit and, in a few cases, to degrees.

Fees are set to cover the full costs of a course. In determining the fee, all appropriate grants for the course are taken into account.

Quality is formally the responsibility of the Vice-Chancellor, devolved to the individual members of the academic staff in the department through the Director.

Formal monitoring is carried out, by questionnaires and with visits by trained assessors to a cross-section of the courses; informal monitoring is conducted by the responsible members of the academic staff who frequently meet students for informal discussions.

Case Study Two

Existing Units in the University: a Continuing Education Unit in a Professional Faculty

Aim: To make available resources of the School of Veterinary Science to update the veterinary profession throughout the country and to train veterinary nurses.

Objectives: As far as possible the Continuing Veterinary Education Unit will:

- provide courses in all the subjects in which the veterinary school has competence and for which there is a demand from the profession and from other institutions;

- collaborate with the professional body when appropriate in making this provision;

- set its fees to cover the full cost of the unit and additionally to fund the upgrading of the continuing education facilities in the veterinary school; and

- run courses of a quality to support and enhance the reputation of the Veterinary School.

Policy implementation: Course organization is the responsibility of the Continuing Education Unit within the veterinary school.

The staffing complement has one full-time organizer and a part-time secretary.

External contacts with the profession are formally conducted through the Continuing Veterinary Education Committee of the professional body, and with the profession more widely through past students. Contacts with industrial suppliers to the veterinary profession are maintained through previous speakers and students.

Suggestions for new course topics and client groups come from students on present courses, the academic staff of the veterinary school, proposals from clients and changes in legislation.

Advertising and promotion methods are direct mail and journal advertising, and future courses are mentioned in current course material.

The course programme covers all the subjects of the veterinary school for which there is a demand for courses.

The format extends from one-day courses for veterinary surgeons to blocks of about one week for others.

Courses are delivered at the veterinary school.

Transferable credits are available for undergraduates, and veterinary nurses are prepared for an external examination. No continuing professional development credits are offered at present.

Fees are set to meet market expectations (sometimes subsidised, partly with help in lieu).

Quality assurance is carried out through questionnaires and informal discussions with students.

Case Study Three

Existing Units in the University: Continuing Education by Part-Time Degrees in a Faculty

Aim: To provide educational opportunities to the maximum sustainable extent, paying particular attention to the economic and social well-being of the local and regional environment, through the high quality of teaching of part-time degrees by the faculty.

Objectives: As far as possible the faculty will:

- use the university's flexible modular degree structure at both the undergraduate and postgraduate levels to offer part-time degree programmes in all the subjects of the faculty;

- where there is sufficient student demand, provide part-time degree programmes by scheduling all the required modules and a range of optional modules in the evenings. Degree programmes may be offered solely as a part-time evening provision;

- collaborate with professional bodies when appropriate;

- apply university regulations and practice to course validation, quality, staffing and fees;

- provide part-time degree programmes on the university campus, and offer some Level 1 (first year) and Level 2 (second year) modules at further education colleges in the region using a franchising arrangement;

- admit students with a range of qualifications and experience, and apply the university's credit accumulation and transfer policy;

- enable students to transfer from the part-time to full-time study mode or vice versa. (Evening modules may be taken by full-time students.) Part-time students on evening degree routes may attend daytime modules, for example, to increase their choice of options.

Policy implementation: Course organization is undertaken by the faculty in accordance with university practice for all degrees.

A senior member of the academic staff in each discipline, the course tutor (with a deputy for extensive programmes) has responsibility for each part-time degree programme, and has administrative and clerical support.

Modules are taught by full-time staff of the university without additional payment, and occasionally by external tutors paid at the university rate.

The faculty and university have extensive contacts with employers, educational advisers, former students, schools and further education colleges in the region, and with the appropriate professional body.

Market research is undertaken through faculty and university contacts with past, present and prospective students, and with employers and regional organizations. Staff awareness of national trends in higher education and in the professions also plays an important role.

Promotion methods are advertisements and contributions in regional newspapers and on local radio, a university prospectus of part-time courses and brochures for each course. University publicity (in which the faculty actively participates) to recruit adult students includes a local 'tabloid' newsletter, a Saturday fair, and Adult Learners' Week events. Direct mail is used to promote courses to employers.

The course programme includes all the degree programmes of the faculty at the undergraduate and postgraduate levels for which there is a demand. (There were 220 student enrolments in 1994/95.)

Modular degree programmes at undergraduate and postgraduate levels are offered during the day or, where there is sufficient demand, in the evenings.

Provision is on the university premises, though some Level 1 and 2 modules on degree programmes are offered by further education colleges in the region under franchise.

Qualifications which can be obtained are: BA, LLB, Diploma in Higher Education; MA, and postgraduate Diploma. Transferable credits are also available.

All the university services are available for student support; faculty course tutors act as the students' personal tutors.

Fees are set following university regulations. No full-cost courses are currently offered.

The university's quality assurance system is applied. Course leaders have informal discussions with students (and their employers, where appropriate).

Case Study Four

External Unit to Provide Continuing Education for which the University is Responsible: A Limited Company Associated with a Professional Faculty

Aim: To make legal information and continuing education available to lawyers and others in the region by research, books, periodicals, conferences and courses.

Objectives: It is the policy of the company (which is limited by guarantee and associated with the faculty) that it will:

- facilitate research leading to publications or courses;

- compile and publish a monthly bulletin of legal developments, publish books and specialist papers for lawyers, produce publications on law for the public, and edit and publish a quarterly journal;

- organize conferences and courses on legal and multi-disciplinary topics for lawyers and other professionals in collaboration with the legal profession, and courses for the general public;

- work closely with the university, the legal profession, the court service and other relevant organizations;

- be self-financing overall, taking into account grants from sponsors and university support;

- strengthen the faculty and the university through its activities.

Policy implementation: The programme is provided by the company. There is a distinguished Advisory Committee (about 20 members) and a Board of Directors (about 8). The Managing Director, together with a Management Committee (of around 8), is responsible for day-to-day operations. The programme operates from the Law Faculty.

One senior member of the academic staff is seconded from the faculty, and between two and four professional staff are responsible for specific parts of the programme (one with a continuing education remit). The company employs two secretaries and at times since its establishment in 1979, researchers and marketing staff have been employed. Lawyers, civil servants and many law faculty staff contribute. Continuing education tutors come from the legal and other professions, the faculty, the university and elsewhere.

Formal external contacts are maintained with the legal profession through the Advisory Committee and the Board of Directors. In addition there are contacts with individual members of the legal profession, former students, government departments, other professions and banks and businesses through extensive networking in the community. Contact with the general public is maintained through events, publicity and via local organizations. For the 'internal market' of the faculty and university personal contacts and regular reports are the prime vehicles.

The company has clear 'niche' markets (geographic, legal practitioners, academics, students, and law for other professions). Market intelligence is sourced from staff generally, and from clients on courses both informally and by questionnaire. Contributions are also made by the Advisory Committee, Managing Director, the legal profession, from changes in law and practice and by analysis of current issues.

Direct mail is usually circulated free of charge by the legal profession or another body, and an extensive mailing list has been established. The publicity materials are professionally designed, and advertising is carried out at no direct cost through use of the company's own journals. Press releases and radio and television interviews offer further opportunities for promotion. The company has an extensive informal network of contacts, and enjoys the support of senior lawyers as 'champions'.

The course programme offers all legal topics for which there is sufficient demand (including some non-legal topics for lawyers).

The format comprises one- or two-day courses for lawyers (some in series) and one-term or three-term (at three hours per week) courses for other professions and the general public.

Courses are provided at the university, various legal offices, hotels and clients' offices.

No qualifications are offered through short course provision, though CPD points for solicitors can be obtained. Some non-lawyers are prepared for an external qualification for provision of approved training.

Fees are set to meet market expectations and programme objectives. There is an element of cross-subsidy from some courses/conferences to others.

Quality assurance is conducted through questionnaires/feedback from clients and informal feedback. The organizer or deputy is present at all short courses, and additional feedback is received from the Managing Director and Advisory Committee.

The faculty and university benefits from revenue to support publications, and the additional experience gained, research undertaken and income achieved by academic staff. The faculty enjoys an enhanced reputation for quality and reliability with the legal profession. It has a high research rating, and in 1994 the programme won the UK Queen's Anniversary Award for Further and Higher Education.

THE BENEFITS OF A POLICY

A policy for continuing education, as for the other activities of a university, focuses the efforts of the providers and allows them to work to better effect. Benefits flow both from the process of forming the policy and from its use. These clearly interact: policy formulation is a step towards implementation;

policy review and reformulation is a form of use. For clarity, however, we consider separately the benefits of forming and of using a policy.

The benefits of forming a policy

The process of forming a policy makes that policy explicit in each of the major issues identified. In this way it removes ambiguities which may previously have existed and, especially when widely disseminated, enables all sectors of the university to complement one another. A clear policy which has been derived pragmatically after extensive consultation enables realistic and appropriate policies to be adopted for continuing education to match the overall aims of the university. This helps to ensure the support of the vice-chancellor/rector and other senior personnel for implementation. The policy is further legitimized if, as often happens, it is approved by the appropriate committee.

The process of forming a policy serves to focus the minds of staff at all levels, whether with long service or new to the university. Communication is very important to the process and the views of all staff should contribute to the drafting. Student views and those of other relevant people and organizations should also be taken into account, together with developments outside the university. This is an informative exercise in itself. The policy should address the needs of all the users. The wide input will almost certainly lead to more appropriate objectives, help to inform and motivate staff, encourage them to take a broader view (with more awareness of the institutional, national and European dimensions) and also take a longer-term (perhaps three to five years) perspective rather than focusing exclusively on immediate concerns. The process of forming a policy is a valuable human resource management tool and is itself a step towards its implementation.

The benefits of using a policy

Using a continuing education policy has benefits externally (both in relation to other parts of the university and outside) and internally within the unit or department making the provision.

The benefits to the unit providing the continuing education of using a policy follow to some extent from those described above. It is of assistance in securing the support of senior university staff in implementing the agreed policy (since it will help to achieve the goals of the university's policy), in ensuring that appropriate and sufficient university systems and resources are in place, in removing obstacles, and in ensuring that the needs of continuing education are taken into account in broader university planning and development. It is a help both with public relations within the university and with effective operation.

Outside the university, using the policy enables the unit to work, where appropriate, towards externally determined objectives which reflect regional, national and European and other international developments designed to meet the needs of clients and their employers. External personnel and organizations which have been consulted are more likely to become actively involved in implementing the policy; this provides a good basis, for example, for constructing funding applications, and for further development. Dissemination of accurate, positive information leads to good public relations. Performance data, monitored against objectives, provides hard evidence to support future developments. Furthermore, the very diversity of continuing education provision in different European universities makes a short, clearly drafted statement of policy an asset. It also makes it easier to meet the requirements of external funders, for example, the Higher Education Funding Councils in the United Kingdom. Overall, the use of a policy enables continuing education providers to meet the needs of their clients, and their clients' employers, more effectively.

Particularly important benefits are gained from using the policy within units providing continuing education. First, it helps considerably when setting up the structures and systems to implement the policy (or to modify the existing structures and systems). Second, it aids detailed day-to-day decision-making. The objectives clearly set out the framework, known to all, within which all can operate. This in turn allows much greater freedom for staff to work independently, thereby increasing their job satisfaction. Third, the policy is the basis for the allocation of resources: staff, accommodation, facilities and finance. Fourth, reference to the policy will set the pattern of provision and can resolve many of the detailed questions that arise. Finally, the policy provides a basis for monitoring and reviewing the continuing education programme in an open way. The quality of a programme may be judged by how well it has achieved its stated objectives; each objective is a benchmark against which a judgement can be made. A fixed reference point of this sort is particularly helpful at a time of rapid change. Quality reviews, taking into account specific external and university developments, may indicate the need to update the policy; this should certainly be done from time to time.

Overall, a policy statement is a considerable aid to communication. The well-known statement concerning objectives undoubtedly applies: 'if you know where you are going, you are much more likely to get there.' To this can be added in the case of university continuing education: 'if others know where you are going, they are more likely to understand and assist you.'

REFERENCES

Commission of the European Community (1991) *Memorandum on Higher Education in the European Community*. Brussels: CEC.

Commission of the European Communities, Task Force for Human Resources, Education, Training and Youth (1992) *European Community Course Credit Transfer System: Presentation of the ECTS Pilot Scheme* (2nd edn). Brussels: CEC.

Commission of the European Community (1993) *The Outlook for Higher Education in the European Community: Responses to the Memorandum*. Luxemburg: CEC.

European Universities Continuing Education Network (1992) *Response to the European Commission on the Memorandum*. Bristol: EUCEN.

Onushkin, V. G. (1977) *The Role of Universities in Post-experience Higher Education*. Paris: International Institute for Educational Planning.

Otala, L. (1992) *European Approaches to Lifelong Learning. Trends in Industry Practices and Industry–University Cooperation in Adult Education and Training*. Geneva: CRE-ERT.

Seidel, H. (1994) *Universities: An Element of European Culture and a Mirror of Social Development*. Budapest: Proceedings of the Tenth General Assembly, pp. 126–32.

Chapter 4

How Credit Accumulation and Transfer Contributes to CPD

Hazel Knox

Given the present rapidly changing labour market and the increasing competition to be faced within a global economy, it is likely that in future people will follow a series of short careers during their working lives rather than having a 'job for life'. They will therefore require opportunities to change career direction and to update skills and knowledge as the labour market demands. Universities and colleges are well placed to cater for such needs as continuing professional development (CPD) for some, and indeed in the future for many, may equate with entering higher education for the first time. However, higher education institutions (HEIs) need to be sensitive to the fact that their traditional form of provision may no longer be appropriate. They must be responsive to the need for change.

Entrants to higher education seeking to continue their professional development will rarely be first-year, full-time undergraduates. Employees will wish to continue with employment where possible, to build on the learning they have already acquired as a result of prior qualifications and work experience and to follow a programme of study which dovetails with their individual requirements. Similarly, as employers will not wish to lose employees while they pursue further knowledge or qualifications, minimizing employee downtime will be high on their agendas. The advent of credit accumulation and transfer schemes (CATS) creates an appropriate vehicle to meet such requirements. CATS enables and empowers individuals to enter higher education at a level commensurate with their prior learning and to pursue further learning at a pace which fits in with the other demands on their time. The potential benefits of using CATS for CPD are manifest.

In Scotland, all higher education institutions are signatories to the Scottish Credit Accumulation and Transfer (SCOTCAT) agreement, whereby they mutually recognize the general credit accrued either from study at another university or college or from nationally recognized professional qualifications. Thus there is a national benchmark for the level of provision within universities and a formal structure within which individual programmes of study can be negotiated. CAT schemes are embedded within the quality assurance procedures of their host institutions, hence there is a natural system of quality control for the education offered.

There is the additional benefit to both the individual and the employer organization that any training or education successfully accomplished within CATS will result in nationally recognized credit which may subsequently be used towards a qualification if desired. Graduates, too, can benefit from CATS. They are not protected from the need for CPD just because they have already secured a degree! It is generally recognized that the value of a graduate's initial education decreases rapidly in relative terms as time passes, knowledge increases and technology advances. To maintain professional competence, graduates increasingly need to manage their future learning. CATS enables them to update their knowledge base in areas already studied, to add new areas of expertise or pursue postgraduate study on a flexible, part-time basis.

There is, of course, no requirement that the student enrolling in CATS should aim for a qualification. The flexibility of the scheme also caters for the CPD needs of the individual who simply requires expertise in a single subject area.

To sustain the ability to compete in the world markets of the twenty-first century, companies will depend largely on workforce competence. Employees may therefore be required to retrain or upskill rapidly as market forces dictate. Thus the higher education sector must be capable of responding, and responding quickly, to the needs of a society in which lifelong learning becomes the norm.

THE NEED FOR INSTITUTIONAL CHANGE

The introduction of a CAT scheme into a rather traditional higher education institution such as the University of Paisley requires a sea change in the attitudes of institutional policy makers, administrative and academic staff and, indeed, of students themselves. Credit accumulation and transfer undoubtedly provides opportunities. It is up to institutions and individuals to exploit them.

There is little doubt that the arrival of the CAT scheme at Paisley sent 'shock waves reverberating through its academic community' (Raban and MacLennan, 1995). The flexibility of CATS which puts the student into an active rather than simply a passive role means that many established practices and procedures have had to be re-examined and modified where appropriate. The process of empowering students and giving them ownership of their individualized programmes of study can be interpreted as posing a threat both to conventional administrative practice which has been designed to cope with cohorts of students progressing apace with one another on a prescribed course, and to the long-held protectionist views of academic staff who may feel that they alone know the content which should be prescribed.

The interesting and rather unusual characteristics of CATS growth at Paisley however, is that it took place within a persistently traditional framework. The centralized academic and administrative changes which normally precede this form of academic innovation within an institution did not happen at Paisley. Instead, a whole infrastructure was developed within the main university organization encompassing student guidance, academic programme design, accreditation of courses, marketing, admissions and student tracking. For the latter, a customized management information service, the CATS database, was designed. Essentially, the Centre for CATS and Continuing Education (formerly the CATS Unit) became 'a University within a University' (Knox and MacLennan, 1994). Changes are now beginning to take place to introduce more open, flexible programmes on a fully integrated institutional basis. As part of this philosophical shift, modular provision within a semester structure was introduced at Paisley in 1995. CATS has thus acted as the agent for significant institutional change.

An extensive programme of staff development seminars has been delivered by CATS staff. This has made a vital contribution to winning over the hearts and minds of the administrative and academic communities. Providing a regular platform for philosophical debate and for the exchange of information has been a successful strategy for securing the cooperation of staff which is critical for putting the principles of CATS into practice.

CATS AT THE UNIVERSITY OF PAISLEY

The introduction of CATS at the University of Paisley (then Paisley College) in September 1990 substantially increased the flexibility of institutional provision and presented the first 'real' opportunity for students to gain access to the university while remaining in employment. This is proving to be a powerful attraction. The future demands made of higher education will be met most effectively by offering such a markedly different form of educational provision to a new and rapidly growing client group, which will be mainly composed of mature adults who are studying on a part-time basis.

At Paisley, under the auspices of CATS, qualifications in combined studies ranging from Certificate of Higher Education to Masters level are available. Students can enrol on a full- or part-time basis, attend day or evening classes, and may study throughout the calendar, not just the academic, year. Each student's programme of study is individually validated, and may include prior learning, formal university study either on campus or locally delivered, work-based learning or independent project work. Thus a very flexible form of higher education is offered which in turn is responsive to the present needs of individuals and the rapidly changing needs of the market-place.

The importance of CATS cannot be overestimated for the individual students concerned. This is the vehicle which enables them to continue their professional development without necessarily having to give up the other personal, employment, financial and social commitments in their lives. It enables future career prospects to be enhanced or new careers to be planned. The case studies of students speak for themselves.

Allan left school in 1957 aged 16 and entered an engineering apprenticeship. Between 1957 and the time he enrolled as a CAT student in September 1990 he held a number of different jobs, completed a wide range of engineering courses including a part-time Higher National Certificate in Mechanical/Production Engineering and latterly had secured employment as a lecturer in engineering at a local further education college. After four years of part-time evening study, he graduated with a B.Sc. in Combined Studies (majoring in Manufacturing Technology with Business Administration):

'I'm on the staff of a very go-ahead college and was definitely encouraged to, indeed I almost felt forced to, pursue my education to degree level. I really enjoyed the opportunity to view education from the student side and felt the pressure to study and meet deadlines. I updated my knowledge. Gaining my degree will certainly increase my job security. I can now lecture at a higher level and I have the ability to apply for posts which require a degree qualification.'

Frances was a 27-year-old staff nurse with nine years of professional experience when she joined CATS in 1991. She was a Registered General Nurse, with additional midwifery and professional studies qualifications. After two years of part-time evening study she graduated in Health Studies:

'When I joined CATS I wanted to further my career in community nursing and also to meet my personal development goals. I always wanted to go into higher education, but didn't have the chance when I left school. Very little immediate contribution has been made to my career prospects – however, having completed my studies and gained my degree should have some benefit in the future should I apply for promotion. I enjoyed the learning experience and felt stimulated to learn. It encouraged me to read a lot more, both educational and recreational literature and I gained valuable experience in how to express myself in writing and in how to evaluate any material read.'

The Programme of Study followed by another student is shown in Table 4.1. This example amply illustrates how the inherent flexibility of CATS can be used in practice. Harry is a police sergeant who seized the opportunity presented by CATS to complete 'unfinished business' and gain the degree from which promotion at work had forced him to withdraw in 1989. The programme of study illustrated in Table 4.1 shows that academic delivery has been tailored to meet the needs of the individual. It is quite likely that this particular programme will remain unique to this particular student.

Table 4.1   Example of programme of study

Student: Harry

Prior credits
APL
Glasgow Polytechnic BA Social Science (0.5 first year passed)
UK Police Promotions exam

APEL
Portfolio submitted to Department of Applied Social Studies
Portfolio submitted to Centre for Alcohol and Drugs
Portfolio submitted to Department of Economics and Management

1992 Assessment
Social Psychology (day class)
Economics of Health and Social Services (evening class)
Personnel Administration (day class)

1993 Assessment
Management in the NHS (evening class)

1994 Assessment
Alcohol and Drug Abuse (evening class)
Project (work-based)

1994
BA Combined Studies
(Majoring in Social Sciences with Business Administration)

There has been significant growth over the five years of operation of the CAT scheme at Paisley, from thirty-two students in 1990/91 to approximately 2000 students in the 1994/95 academic session, which now represents almost 25 per cent of the total university student population. Experience at Paisley shows that flexible provision in terms of point of entry and exit, mode of study, location and time at which learning occurs, curriculum choice, type of learning undertaken and so on, is attracting a significantly different population of students to the university.

Traditionally, higher education at Paisley was accessible primarily on a full-time basis for school leavers and under-21s, frequently with a high proportion of males and with the majority of students entering at first-year level. By contrast, over two-thirds of CAT students study on a part-time basis while continuing in employment (85 per cent of the part-time students are in full-time employment). The mean age for a CAT student in 1993/94 was 30.4 years, 60 per cent were female and a small minority (18 per cent) entered at Level 1.

One of the most attractive features of CATS is that prior credit can be imported. The Paisley CAT scheme acknowledges both accredited prior learning (APL), e.g. Higher National or professional qualifications and accredited prior experiential learning (APEL), i.e. learning derived from workplace, community or other experience. The majority of students take advantage of this facility. Of the 770 students entering CATS for the first time in 1993/94, less than 10 per cent entered without prior credit. Approximately 28 per cent entered with prior credit from professional qualifications, 46 per cent transferred from other further or higher education institutions and the remaining 17 per cent transferred from another degree course within the University of Paisley.

As CAT students may be full- or part-time, may enter and exit at various stages and may opt to take 'time out' as other demands on their lives require, the question arises of how to define success in a credit accumulation and transfer scheme. The traditional concept of cohort progression rate, based on the proportion of students on a course progressing to the next stage of that course, is obviously no longer tenable. In CAT terms the accumulation of credit is not a prerequisite for continuing in the scheme and the assumption that all students are studying the same units and for the same overall amount of credit cannot be made.

One way to measure success is in terms of the number of credit points gained as a percentage of credit points attempted. Using this measure, the overall success rate has risen steadily over the first three years of operation of CATS, and reached 82.7 per cent in 1993/94. In general, part-time students performed better than full-timers, with no significant difference between the performances of day and evening part-time students. However, as would be anticipated, non-completion rates among part-time students were higher than among full-time students.

Such a success rate is gratifying, bearing in mind that the heterogeneity of CAT students makes them a very vulnerable population, given the other financial, employment, social and domestic demands and responsibilities in their lives. They are obviously motivated to study and fully committed to continuing their personal and professional development.

EMPLOYERS AND EMPLOYEES

Recent research, supported by BP Exploration, has evaluated the CATS operation at Paisley (Knox, 1996). In addition to conducting a thorough examination of archived data in the CATS database, an extensive range of questionnaires was designed to explore CATS from the perspectives of current and former students, recent graduates, local employers and academic staff.

Evidence from this research established the employment status of 1993/94 CAT students and the extent to which part-time students receive financial sponsorship from their employers. As Table 4.2 shows, over 90 per cent of part-time students are in work.

Table 4.2   Employment status of part-time students

Employment status	Percentage of part-time students (total 1070)
Working full-time	84.5
Working part-time	5.7
Unemployed	4.8
Not working (by choice)	5.1

Of the working students, more than one-third have all course fees paid by their employer, approximately 10 per cent get some assistance with payment of fees and the remaining 55 per cent are funding themselves. Many of those who are self-financing are enrolled for BA/BSc Health Studies. This part-time evening degree programme is a good example of the value of using the principles of credit accumulation and transfer as a vehicle for responding rapidly to a market need for professional development. The launch of Project 2000 created a demand among nurses for the opportunity to add an academic qualification to already secured professional qualifications without having to give up employment. The degree in Health Studies was purpose-designed to cater for the CPD needs of this significant group of people. The existing credit framework enabled both professional qualifications and appropriate prior experiential learning to be credit-rated, imported and used as the basis on which to build towards a degree award through study of modules delivered at the university. For many nurses the achievement of graduate status was possible after two years of part-time study.

The majority of students who are in receipt of financial support from their employers are studying for qualifications in Combined Studies. The sponsoring companies represent a wide range of local, national and international businesses. They include small firms, local radio, voluntary organizations, other educational establishments and large multinationals. The university itself sponsors many academic, administrative and technical staff. In total, nearly a hundred employers throughout the West of Scotland have staff studying through the University of Paisley CAT scheme. A small subset of these employers participated in a survey to evaluate what CATS can offer to meet the CPD needs of their employees.

In general, employers are very supportive, even if the initiative to continue professional development by entering higher education is taken by the employee him- or herself, as was reported to be the case by over 90 per cent of sponsored students. 'We didn't send him to university, he decided to continue with his education and we provided some financial support', said the Senior Executive Officer of an international organization with an employee enrolled as a part-time evening combined studies student. So although the initiative may not necessarily come from employers, they realize the opportunities presented by CATS to meet their CPD needs. Seventy-five per cent agreed with the statement 'the flexibility of CATS is a major advantage in planning staff development programmes with my employees'. Flexibility is certainly a key feature of CAT schemes and obviously appeals to employees and employers alike, as is shown in Table 4.3. There is agreement that being able to attend part-time and in the evening is most attractive.

Table 4.3   Attractive features of CATS

Flexible feature	Employees (%)	Employers (%)
Mode of attendance	66	61
Choice of subjects	47	48
Point of entry	45	45

Although the employers were from widely diverse backgrounds in terms of the size, location and type of business conducted by their organizations, there was consensus on the need for CPD. The overwhelming majority of employers recognized the importance of lifelong learning, of upskilling and of providing opportunities for their employees to pursue individual professional development.

In addition, many employers believe that CPD which involves upgrading academic qualifications among the workforce will contribute to the development of both the employee and the company. Employers can obviously see the benefits of an improved academic profile, and indeed for the majority of employers (over two-thirds) the primary motivation for sponsoring an employee through CATS was 'to gain an academic qualification'. The benefits of participation in HE are well recognized by employers, as exemplified in this statement by the head of research and development of a large pharmaceutical company:

'There is no doubt that CATs presents a valuable opportunity for people to raise skill and experience levels to the requirements of the twenty-first century. Higher education is one of the key ways to achieve a well trained and educated workforce who are motivated to succeed.'

Among the companies surveyed, the estimated percentage of graduates in their current workforces was reported across the range of 0 per cent (for example, in a small local company with only three employees, one of whom has enrolled as a part-time day student) to approximately 80 per cent (for example, in a local further education college). The mean percentage of graduates employed in these organizations was 16 per cent.

A significant number of employers were using the CAT scheme as a means of enabling their employees to access higher education without necessarily aiming for an academic qualification. Their primary motivation for providing sponsorship was to enable their employees to 'gain knowledge of a particular subject area'. Experience to date shows that the most popular areas chosen include quality assurance management, marketing, accounting and languages. The main reason given by the sponsored students for entering higher education was to 'enhance career prospects' (57 per cent) which they mainly equated with gaining a degree.

Caul (1993) argues that universities must do more than merely impart knowledge; they also have a duty to facilitate the intellectual and personal development of their students, i.e. to contribute actively to the 'value-added' components of higher education. There are, of course, major difficulties to be faced in the definition and measurement of value-added, difficulties which are sharply brought into focus when assessing the value added for part-time, mature students who are combining study with work.

Employees/students and employers were asked to rate the importance of the value-added factors listed in Table 4.5 in ensuring an effective employee. A five-point scale was used ranging from 'very important' to 'very unimportant'. By this procedure value added was essentially being defined by the respondents themselves. The rank order of importance of each of the factors is given in Table 4.4, with the percentage of respondents considering the attribute 'very important' in brackets alongside. Students were also asked to state whether or not they believed that the CAT student experience presented opportunities to acquire valued attributes (Table 4.5).

Predictably, few factors were considered to be unimportant. The factor considered 'very important' by two-thirds of each group of respondents was oral communication skills, with written communication skills rated 'very important' by over half of the students and 45 per cent of employers. Although 'specialist knowledge' was ranked third, it was considered 'very important' by less than half of the students and only one-third of employers. Interestingly, work experience and age were ranked low priority by both groups, although 21 per cent of employees compared with only 3 per cent of their employers considered work experience to be 'very important'. Given that the majority of CAT students are mature adults, the finding on age was encouraging as it was not considered important by either their employers or themselves.

Table 4.4   Value-added factors

Value-added factor	Employer rank order	Employee/student rank order
Oral communication skills	1 (68%)	1 (65%)
Written communication skills	2 (45%)	2 (52%)
Specialist knowledge	3 (32%)	3 (46%)
Independence	4 (24%)	8 (19%)
Social skills	5 (23%)	4.5 (25%)
Autonomous learner	6 (19%)	9 (15%)
Cognitive skills: analysis, synthesis, evaluation	7 (10%)	6 (26%)
Transferable skills	9 (3%)	4.5 (25%)
Work experience	9 (3%)	7 (21%)
Age	9 (3%)	10 (2%)

There was general agreement (Spearman's rank order correlation coefficient value 0.73) between employers and employees/students on the very important factors, with unanimous agreement that oral and written communication skills were top priority. Harvey (1994) reports similar findings in his extensive research into the desirable attributes of graduates as reported by employers.

Table 4.5 reports on whether or not CATS is perceived by part-time students as providing the opportunity to acquire those attributes which they consider to be important. Respondents could reply 'yes', 'no' or 'not sure'. The majority of respondents reported that the CAT student experience provides the opportunity to acquire specialist knowledge, independence, transferable skills and written communication skills.

Table 4.5   Value-added factors and CAT student experience

Value-added factor	Employee/student responding yes (%)
Specialist knowledge	78
Independence	58
Transferable skills	57
Written communication skills	56
Cognitive skills: analysis, synthesis, evaluation	49
Oral communication skills	47
Autonomous learner	46
Social skills	31

Less than half of each group consider they have the opportunity to acquire oral communication skills or social skills. The explanation of these findings may lie in a combination of university provision and the nature of the part-time student. As part-timers attend only occasional classes they may not get to know other members of their university peer group, which could hamper their opportunities to acquire social skills. The lack of opportunity to acquire oral communication skills may lie in large class sizes and that consequently little oral assessment features in the university curriculum. However, another factor must also be taken into account. Part-time students are most frequently mature, employed adults who may already have acquired good oral and written communication skills and may already feel that they are socially skilled. Hence such students may not necessarily look upon their student experience as an opportunity to acquire these attributes. Indeed, many respondents made comments to this effect on their questionnaire returns. This again emphasizes the different nature of the CAT student population.

CATS AND CPD

Credit accumulation and transfer schemes undoubtedly have the potential to cater for the continuing professional development needs of both employees and employers. They provide a framework within which flexible provision can be delivered, the most attractive aspects of which are the facility to import prior credit and the ability to attend on a part-time basis in the evening. The former avoids repetitious learning and significantly reduces the time required to gain an academic qualification; the latter enables individuals to maintain the responsibilities in their lives and may preclude the need to take time off work for study.

A unified credit framework, such as that agreed in Scotland (HEQC, 1995) ensures that employers know what they are 'buying' when employees enrol with CATS. Institutional quality assurance mechanisms are in place to ensure quality of provision, whether this is in respect of accreditation of prior learning or prior experiential learning, the delivery of formal university tuition, the completion of work-based projects, or the delivery of education and training commissioned for a particular purpose by an individual employer. Further, quality is assured whether sufficient learning is purchased to lead to an award, or small units of learning are purchased as and when required. Employers also acknowledge the intangible benefits of raising the academic profile of their workforce and appreciate the value-added benefits of the experience of higher education *per se* for their employees.

Transferability of credit means that CPD structured around higher education entry does not cease if the demands of the job require relocation or necessitate a temporary halt to study. Credit once gained remains intact, for possible future use. Pathways can therefore be plotted across time both within and between national and international institutions. Credit can thus motivate employers to look to higher education to meet their CPD needs as the flexible provision of CAT schemes opens up this possibility in a way hitherto unseen.

Credit also motivates employees. They too can anticipate benefits from an improved academic qualification and from the student experience itself. Further, if employer-led CPD ceases, the individual still has the credit accumulated for his or her personal use. Study can continue in subject areas of interest and credit used towards a future award.

After four years in operation, the success of the CAT scheme at the University of Paisley is demonstrated by the quantitative data of participating numbers and success rates together with the qualitative data of student evaluation and the support of students by their employers. The evidence confirms that the flexible provision of CATS is attractive to both students/employees and their employers. This further testifies to the value of using higher education to meet continuing professional development needs. There is much to be offered to employees and employers alike.

REFERENCES

Caul, B. (1993) *Value-Added: The Personal Development of Students in Higher Education*. Belfast: December Publications.

Harvey, L. (1994) *Employer Satisfaction*. Quality in Higher Education Project. Centre for Research into Quality, University of Central England in Birmingham.

Higher Education Quality Council (HEQC) (1995) *The SCOTCAT Quality Assurance Handbook 1995*. London: HEQC.

Knox, H. (1996) *More Than a Degree: An Evaluation of the Credit Accumulation and Transfer Scheme at the University of Paisley, 1990–1994*. Poole: BP Educational Service.

Knox, H. and MacLennan, A. (1994) Coping with the challenge of growth. In *Proceedings of the Innovation '94 Conference on Curriculum and Professional Development for Larger Numbers in Higher Education*, University of Wales at Bangor, 5–7 January 1994.

Raban, C. and MacLennan, A. (1995) *Credit Accumulation and Transfer in Context: The Paisley and Sheffield-Hallam Experience*. Sheffield: Pavic Publications.

Chapter 5

Comparability of Qualifications across Europe – a Possible Solution

Denise Hevey

Creating conditions for mobility of labour, particularly among professional groups, is viewed as of equal importance to the ideals of the European Union as creating a free market in goods and services. However, the problems of lack of comparability and transferability of qualifications have always acted as major obstacles. The history of trying to overcome these obstacles can be interpreted as falling into three policy phases: harmonization, mutual recognition (including the comparability initiative) and improving transparency.

HARMONIZATION

Article 128 of the Treaty of Rome empowered the then EEC to identify the common features of vocational and professional education and training across member states with a view to working towards harmonization. The harmonization approach focused on comparison of the routes to achieving qualified professional status and assumed that, through a process of negotiation between the relevant professional bodies of each member state, it would be possible to encourage a process of convergence, with the ultimate objective of achieving (more or less) standard duration and content for professional education and training for any target profession throughout Europe (resulting in a so-called sectoral directive). The sorts of features that were examined were: the entry requirements to professional training in terms of basic or post-basic education; the duration of any formal education and training courses and the types/level of institution in which they may be undertaken; the content of syllabi followed during the required period of professional education; the nature and duration of supervised practice opportunities, and so on.

However, what seemed like a simple idea turned out to be virtually impossible in practice. Professional formation routes were normally steeped in the tradition and culture of individual countries and suggestions for change could be interpreted as questioning their assumed excellence, which created strong reactions from long-established professional bodies. Thus, for example, in some countries professional formation was dependent not so much on attending courses as on an extended period of apprenticeship to an experienced professional. Another serious problem was posed by fundamental differences in the basic education and training systems of member states that provided different starting-points for professional formation. So, for example, in England and Wales an honours degree course normally takes only three years because specialization occurs very early in the secondary education process, culminating in three narrowly focused A-level subjects. In other parts of Europe (and even in other parts of the UK, notably Scotland) the final years of schooling are broader based and honours degree programmes take at least four years.

In the end, very few sectoral directives were finally agreed. One possibly apocryphal tale tells of the experience of architects working hard on harmonization for seventeen years before reaching agreement!

MUTUAL RECOGNITION (COMPARABILITY)

The harmonization approach was clearly proving to be long-winded and impractical, and twenty years on the political climate was starting to change. The initial idealism of the EEC towards convergence of all aspects of economic and social life was either wearing off or being thwarted by the addition of new members with more isolationist views, such as Britain. Recognizing that harmonization was unlikely to be achieved on a wide scale and that progress could not be left to the idiosyncrasies of individual sectors, an alternative policy was developed. This involved an exploration of systems for establishing equivalence and mutual recognition of the qualifications that already existed within member states.

Two major initiatives followed from a European Council Decision in 1985 (85/368). First was the establishment of the European Centre for the Development of Vocational Training (CEDEFOP) in Berlin. CEDEFOP was commissioned to undertake detailed comparisons of the roles and qualifications of skilled workers at craft and technician levels in a number of target industries and to represent their findings in tables setting out the points of similarities and differences across member states. The nineteen target industries ranged from agriculture to the electrical and electronics industry. It soon became apparent that this task was far more complex than had been first imagined. Not only did they discover differences in formal qualification requirements reflecting and arising from fundamental differences in the underlying education and training systems, but they also discovered differences in the way that work was organized in the different member states.

Put quite simply, some jobs do not exist in every country. So, for example, in some states, skilled workers are expected to be specialists in a single craft, and trades union agreements, terms and conditions of employment, etc. reflect this, whereas in others a worker may have varying combinations of skills and be expected to carry out a wide variety of tasks. This meant that an actual role or job title might not have direct equivalence in another member state, making comparisons of the qualification requirements to fulfil that role extremely difficult. CEDEFOP persevered with the production of comprehensive comparison tables of required qualifications for all nineteen occupational areas, but at the end of nine years of hard work the Council Resolution on transparency of qualifications was forced to conclude: 'there are doubts about whether the work on comparability provides the kind of clear information about qualifications necessary to promote the free movement of labour' (CEC, 1993). In practice, the resulting comparison tables were too difficult for the average employer or employee to interpret.

MUTUAL RECOGNITION (THE GENERAL DIRECTIVES)

The second outcome of the 1985 Council decision was the introduction in 1989 of a first general directive (89/48) on mutual recognition of qualifications across Europe. This first general directive came into force in 1991 and is concerned with labour mobility at the level of professional workers. Implementation of the first directive in the UK is the responsibility of the Department of Trade and Industry (DTI, 1992). It covers professional qualifications which require a minimum of three years' certificated post-secondary education (i.e. degree equivalent in UK terms) and is subject to state regulation. This potentially restricts its influence since, with a few notable exceptions such as medicine, dentistry, teaching and nursing, the UK has very few state-regulated professions. In contrast, the majority of professions in the UK are regulated on a purely voluntary basis by the codes of conduct of professional bodies, many of which (such as the British Psychological Society) are incorporated by Royal Charter. This means that they keep a register of chartered members but it does not give them the authority to prevent someone practising the profession who has been barred from membership.

Mutual recognition agreements under the general directives are operated through a designated 'competent authority' in each state which has responsibility for vetting the acceptability of professional qualifications proposed by individuals from other member states (DTI, 1989). The designation of the competent authority varies widely depending on the way the profession is regulated as does the range of professions which come under the directive. So, for example, although medicine is all-graduate and state regulated (and therefore within the scope of the first general directive) in all member states, teaching is not so consistent, and in the UK social work falls outside the directive on both counts. Nevertheless, around sixty professional and chartered bodies are recognized as competent authorities in the UK for the purposes of implementation of the first general directive. Chartered and professional bodies are increasingly part of pan-European networks which facilitate recognition arrangements and in 1992 they collectively dealt with 2755 applications for recognition of EC qualifications in the UK, of which 2050 were accepted without any additional 'adaptation requirements'.

There are a number of problems with the first general directive in addition to the complexities described above. First, despite a 1991 implementation date, at the time of writing two member states (Greece and Belgium) have yet to introduce the primary legislation necessary to incorporate the directive into national law and now face being taken to the European Court. Second, even though one's qualifications may be recognized in the target state, entry into the profession is still not guaranteed. Although it has always been considered legitimate for a competent authority to impose reasonable 'adaptation requirements', such as a language test or demonstration of knowledge of the relevant legal frameworks of the target state, some requirements still amount to a barrier to access. For example, in France and Spain, teachers are civil servants, and in order to get a job in either of those countries UK teachers would be expected to sit the highly competitive civil service entrance exams in the host country's language and relating closely to the host country's education system. Third, the majority of occupations remain outside the scope of this directive, but with the creation of the single market in January 1993, individual workers increasingly need occupational mobility.

In order to cope with the latter, a system of 'transitional directives' was introduced through which the DTI issues and handles certificates of experience for self-employed workers whose occupations are not regulated in the UK but are regulated in the member state(s) in which they wish to work. This involves the individual in providing details of previous experience and qualifications which show how he or she has met the requirements of the relevant directive. The DTI confirm information and check out references. The whole procedure should take no longer than four months to complete but it is nevertheless time-consuming and off-putting to all but the most determined applicants. Currently, enquiries to the DTI about certificates of experience are running at twenty to thirty per week with only half that number coming forward eventually with a completed application.

Despite the fact that the first general directive has not yet been fully implemented, a second general directive was introduced in 1992 to promote systematic mutual recognition agreements across Europe for wider categories of professional, technical and supervisory staff. This second directive covers occupations involving vocational and professional qualifications which require between one and three years of certificated post-secondary education and which are subject to state regulation. The majority of occupations at this level are not regulated in the UK because of government policy favouring deregulation. However, many craft and technical occupations (e.g. electricians) are regulated in other member states because it is regarded as essential for reasons of health and safety that they should be. Some industries (e.g. electrical contractors) are now setting up their own voluntary registration schemes in order to make it easier for their UK workers to move around in Europe.

Special provision has been made within the second directive for the recognition of UK National and Scottish Vocational Qualifications (N/SVQs) at levels 3 and 4, despite the fact that, being outcomes-based qualifications, they do not meet the normal input-based specifications of the directive. In the UK, responsibility for the second general directive lies with the Department for Education and Employment. The target implementation date has already passed but the complexity of the legal implications means that primary legislation has not yet been enacted in the UK and effective implementation is still a long way off.

In some ways the focus on comparability and transferability of qualifications across the EU has diverted attention from the inadequacies of existing vocational and professional qualifications systems which operate within national boundaries. The UK has made considerable progress towards achieving a comprehensive national framework for vocational qualifications, under the auspices of the National Council for Vocational Qualifications (NCVQ) and the Scottish Vocational Education Council (SCOTVEC). This can already claim to cover 84 per cent of occupations and further work is continuing on the outstanding, mainly higher level professional roles (NCVQ, 1994a). However, the experience of the twenty-four projects set up under the EUROFORM initiative to explore the development of transnational qualifications in a European context has revealed glaring gaps in the national systems of individual member states.

> Some countries do not have a comprehensive and nationally recognised system of accreditation and certification in the vocational training field ... In some member states, for certain new subject areas, it may not be possible to obtain certification within the member state. It may be necessary to obtain certification from a relevant national awarding body within another member state.
>
> (EUROFORM, 1993, p. 22)

This poses a fundamental problem for comparability. How can you work out equivalences for qualifications across states if the necessary educational and vocational qualifications for a particular occupation or professional role have not yet been standardized or agreed within a state?

INCREASING TRANSPARENCY

The debates around the second general directive have in some ways been overtaken by events. The Treaty of Maastricht introduced the principle of subsidiarity which implies valuing the differences between member states and a renewed antagonism to anything that smacks of bureaucracy and central control. Pan-European harmonization of approaches to education and training is definitely passé and pragmatic state-to-state or bilateral recognition is being favoured over the all-embracing solutions promised by mutual recognition agreements. That a certain disillusion with achieving anything on a pan-European basis is setting in may not be surprising in view of the problems of previous policies which can be summed up as follows:

- Harmonization has proved impossible primarily because of differences in basic education and training systems in different member states – the way people enter work – and is in any case no longer considered to be a politically desirable goal.

- Comparability has proved unworkable because of differences in job/role profiles – the way that work is organized in the different member states.

- Mutual recognition has proved less than fully effective because of differences in the speed of implementation and in the degree of statutory versus voluntary regulation – the way work is regulated.

- The transitional directives are a relatively time-consuming and ultimately inefficient way of sorting out immediate problems of transnational acceptability of qualifications on an individual basis and for one country at a time.

So, where does that leave us? One option is to ignore the complexities of establishing precise equivalences altogether and to tackle the problem at the most pragmatic level through the eyes of a prospective employer. Faced with wide-ranging, transnational education and training backgrounds, qualifications, employment and other relevant experience, the simplest way of improving the 'transparency' of candidate applications from an employer's perspective is to standardize the way in which information is presented.

> Genuine free movement of workers can only be achieved if
> people can present their qualifications and work experience
> clearly and effectively throughout the Community. Employers
> need to receive clear descriptions of job applicants' qualifications
> and experience if they are to judge fairly suitability for the jobs
> on offer. In order to do this, individuals can be provided (on
> request) with a document, recognised throughout the
> Community, in which they can detail essential information
> about themselves and their achievements. This document is the
> Individual Portfolio.
>
> (NCVQ, 1993)

In many ways this idea is similar to that behind the National Record of Achievement (NRA) which was introduced for all school leavers in the UK in January 1993. And it is no accident that the National Council for Vocational Qualifications, which pioneered the National Record of Vocational Achievement (NROVA), subsequently brought into line with the NRA, is currently responsible for coordinating European trials of the Individual Portfolio. The first priority is to reach agreement on the categories of information and order of presentation of information. In the trial document these cover:

- basic biographical information;

- full-time education and training history;

- employment history;

- certificated achievements since entering work;

- occupational skills and competences.

Early feedback on the trials of the individual portfolio has been largely favourable, indicating that a standardized approach to the presentation of information does indeed help employers to establish the suitability of job applicants from countries other than their own. However, regardless of how much this initiative may contribute to improving transparency, the fundamental problem of the need to establish equivalences for different forms of qualification on a pan-European basis will not go away. Far from abandoning the pursuit of a solution, the Commission has recently reiterated the importance attached to the original problem by relating it back to the purposes of a European Union and by extending its scope to include comparability and recognition of academic as well as professional/vocational qualifications.

> The most tangible aspect for the citizen of the Community of no
> internal frontiers is that of free movement. The right of resi-

dence, the right to work, whether as a salaried worker or self-employed, within the territory of a Member State other than one's own, and the mobility of students and young people, are the Community-established precedents from which the European citizen can now benefit … . The concept of free movement is thus at the root of the functioning of the European area for the professions and training, for which recognition of qualifications for academic and professional purposes is the principal mode of action.

(CEC, 1994)

This particular communication, based on the work of a trans-European expert group with a particular focus on higher education, goes on to distinguish four types of recognition:

- *de jure professional recognition*, which refers to the legal enforceability of recognition agreements for regulated professions under the sectoral directives and the first (and soon second) general directive;

- *de facto professional recognition*, which refers to the growing acceptance of equivalences of qualifications, approved by competent authorities, for professions which are not formally regulated in the host country;

- *cumulative academic recognition*, which refers to the ability of a student/trainee from one country to have his/her stage of training recognized as equivalent in order to complete professional qualification in a second country;

- *academic recognition by substitution*, which refers to the acceptance of planned study periods abroad as an integral part of the degree/diploma courses of academic institutions in a host country.

These four types of recognition have different bases and different policy objectives, but the purpose of this latest communication from the Commission is to stimulate debate as to how some sort of convergence, or in their words 'synergies', may be achieved between them with a particular focus on the higher education and professional level qualifications. Four types of action are suggested:

- the development of high-quality information sources describing the nature, content and duration of courses, teaching methods, etc. in equivalent discipline areas in each member state;

- the creation and support of trans-European academic and professional networks in different academic discipline/professional areas (many of these are already being established under the auspices of designated 'competent authorities' such as the British Psychological Society in relation to psychologists);

- joint adaptation of courses which encourage convergence and Europeanization of curricula as have been previously operated successfully through the LINGUA, COMETT and ERASMUS programmes;

- the assessment of quality in training programmes and assessment systems and the involvement of representatives of business and the professions in those assessments in order to 'strengthen mutual trust' in the standing of equivalent qualifications in each member state.

These suggestions fall short of offering any ultimate solution to the problem of establishing equivalences of qualifications, since they acknowledge the recurrent dilemmas of regulation versus voluntarism and of reconciling the right of freedom of movement within the EU with the desire of nation states to 'safeguard national identity' as reflected in the different and specific characteristics of their respective national education systems. However, in an interesting comment on the range of approaches needed to facilitate both academic and professional recognition, the communication states that the usual method of comparison of level, duration and content of training courses is inappropriate for professional recognition and goes on to suggest that recent developments have set new legal precedents: 'In this situation, *de jure* professional recognition is based mainly on a comparison not of training but of fields of activity.' This statement has far-reaching implications for the sorts of solutions that may be sought to the long-standing problem of establishing comparability of qualifications across the EU.

OUTCOMES AS A POSSIBLE SOLUTION

Since the establishment of the NCVQ in 1986, a 'quiet revolution' has been taking place throughout the UK system of vocational education and training (Jessup, 1991). This has involved the development of a single systematic framework of National (and Scottish) Vocational Qualifications (N/SVQs) spanning five levels, from Level 1 – relating to the performance of mostly routine tasks under supervision, to Level 5 – relating to higher level professional roles requiring the application of fundamental principles and complex techniques in analysis, diagnosis, design, evaluation and so on, and having a high degree of personal autonomy, accountability and responsibility for others. N/SVQs are modular in structure and are based on occupational standards, agreed by representatives of employment interests on a national basis, which define in outcome terms the expectations of competent performance within a given occupation or profession.

> Overall this represented a radical shift of emphasis away from the traditional concerns of the supply side of education and training providers for 'inputs' in terms of the length, content and process of training and towards 'outcomes' in terms of occupational competence – what individuals needed to be able to do and to know in order to meet the demands of employment. The effective decoupling of qualifications from approved training programmes had the added effect of enabling greater direct participation in training and assessment by employers.
>
> (Hevey and Smith, 1993, p. 6)

Implementation of the new system has been somewhat slower than expected because of the need to create the infrastructure for assessment within the workplace. It has also been plagued with problems centring on the training of assessors and quality assurance of workplace assessment and exacerbated by a change-over to outcomes-based funding for training. N/SVQs have met with considerable suspicion and criticism from the educational establishment (Hevey, 1993). They have been described as reductionist, based on failed behaviourist principles and have been accused of ignoring the role of knowledge and understanding (Smithers, 1993). While these criticisms may have been valid in relation to the early prototype versions of N/SVQs developed for lower level occupations, they can no longer be said to be true of more recently accredited qualifications at higher levels. The importance of analysis at the level of function rather than task and of the critical role of knowledge and understanding, especially at higher levels, has been highlighted in the most recent edition of criteria and guidance for NVQs (NCVQ, 1994b). Despite 'teething problems', the fundamental principles of the new competence-based system have been strongly reaffirmed in the CBI report (CBI, 1994), which called for the NCVQ to be given more money to market the new qualifications and more teeth to police the system effectively.

Work is now in hand in collaboration with professional bodies to develop national occupational standards for many graduate equivalent professions. The engineering sector, and within that, the Construction Industry Standing Conference (CISC) are perhaps most advanced in this respect, with several Level 5 awards having reached the pilot stage. The

Engineering Council recently issued revised guidance on the education and training of engineers (Engineering Council, 1995) which describes Level 4 N/SVQ as representing the competence outcomes expected of a newly qualified engineer (career threshold) which, together with evidence of their academic attainment and commitment to a professional ethic and code of conduct, would lead to chartered status. Level 5 N/SVQ in this model represents a career pinnacle and would only be achievable through a process of continuing professional development after several years' experience as a chartered engineer.

The N/SVQ framework, once complete, will provide comprehensive, competence-based descriptions of what people have to know and must be able to do in order to be judged competent in all types of vocational and professional roles in the UK. Such qualifications attest to the outcomes of education, training and experience and are entirely independent of modes or duration of study/training. Because they are based on published national occupational standards, they are fully transparent to both students/candidates and employers.

There is growing recognition in Europe, and particularly among the EUROFORM projects on transnational qualifications, that comparisons based exclusively on the input side of the qualification equation are problematic.

> If we look at it in terms of a continuum of development [that] in the past we paid a lot of attention to comparing training systems and to the 'inputs' of training; more recently, we have looked at the results of training and actually trying to document these, for example, through the mechanism of certificates awarded as a result of training. Now we are moving into the whole phase of 'outcomes', what can people do as a result of training, what they can do in terms of skills, in terms of the knowledge they have, in terms of the personal skills which they are developing.
>
> (Lyons, 1993, p. 27)

> If the primary need is for information about what a qualified person should be able to do, it is important that the outcomes of learning should be transparent. In other words, details of competences are a more important factor in determining the usefulness of a qualification and the degree of transferability of a qualified person than information about the learning process involved.
>
> (Handley, 1993, p. 6)

The UK's particular approach to competence-based qualifications has both similarities and differences with competence-based systems currently being developed in Australia, New Zealand and parts of the United States. In particular, the development of the system from the bottom up rather than from the top down has led to a degree of over-prescriptiveness which is only now being modified with experience of developing competence-based qualifications that allow for the exercise of professional knowledge and judgement. The UK system of N/SVQs and associated assessment methods is still evolving for use at higher education levels and may not be considered appropriate to the culture and traditions of other European countries. Nevertheless, a general move towards providing a transcript of the outcomes of learning, rather than just the inputs of formal education and training, together with developing mechanisms for describing and certificating the competences achieved through work experience, could provide the basis for a potential solution to the problem of establishing equivalence of qualifications while respecting the diversity of national systems across Europe.

> The single greatest advantage of the outcomes-based approach is its transparency for all concerned – whether employers, training providers, young people or experienced workers. It is possible that this advantage could be transferred without adopting the wider reforms undertaken in the UK. If other member states were to express the outcomes of their education and training in terms of what holders of awards are able to do and to what standard, the qualifications system would be made infinitely more transparent whilst the integrity of the different training and education systems would be respected.
>
> (Hevey and Smith, 1993, p. 20)

REFERENCES

Confederation of British Industry (CBI) (1994) *Quality Assessed – The CBI Review of NVQs and SVQs*. London: CBI.

Council of the European Economic Community (CEEC) (1985) Council Decision (85/368) of 16 July 1985 on Comparability of Vocational Training Qualifications.

Council of the European Communities (CEC) (1993) Council Resolution of 3 December 1992 on Transparency of Qualifications, reported in *Official Journal of the European Communities*, No. C49/1. Brussels: CEC.

Council of the European Communities (CEC) (1994) Communication from the Commission *'On Recognition of Qualifications for Academic and Professional Purposes'*, COM(94) 596 final. Brussels: CEC, 13 December.

Department of Trade and Industry (DTI) (1989) *The Single Market – Europe Open for Professions* (guidance for competent authorities). London: DTI.

Department of Trade and Industry (DTI) (1992) *The Single Market – Europe Open for Professions* (UK Implementation), 3rd edn. London: DTI.

Engineering Council (1995) *Competence and Commitment*. London: The Engineering Council.

EUROFORM (1993) Key issues identified by working groups in the development of certification in EUROFORM projects, *Qualifications in the Trans-national Context*, a report of the EUROFORM Workshop. Dublin, 12–13 May.

Handley, D. (1993) *Transparency and Transferability of Qualifications – Needs, Obstacles and Means*. Discussion paper prepared on behalf of the European Communities for the First European Forum on Vocational Training, Brussels, 8–10 November.

Hevey, D. (1993) *What Is Competence?* Paper One in Occasional Papers series. Milton Keynes: Vocational Qualifications Centre, Open University.

Hevey, D. and Smith, P. (1993) *Towards a European Qualifications Area – the UK Perspective*. Discussion paper prepared on behalf of the European Communities for the First European Forum on Vocational Training, Brussels, 8–10 November.

Jessup, G. (1991) *Outcomes: NVQs and the Emerging Model of Education and Training*. London: Falmer Press.

Lyons, M. (1993) New qualifications, certification terminology. *Qualifications in the Trans-national Context*, a report of the EUROFORM Workshop. Dublin, 12–13 May.

National Council for Vocational Qualifications (NCVQ) (1991) *Criteria and Related Guidance for National Vocational Qualifications*. London: NCVQ.

National Council for Vocational Qualifications (NCVQ) (1993) *Individual Portfolio and Guidance for Users*. London: NCVQ.

National Council for Vocational Qualifications (NCVQ) (1994a) *Annual Report*. London: NCVQ.

National Council for Vocational Qualifications (NCVQ) (1994b) *Criteria and Related Guidance for National Vocational Qualifications*. London: NCVQ.

Smithers, A. (1993) *All Our Futures – Britain's Education Revolution*, a *Dispatches* Report on Education. London: Channel 4 Television.

Chapter 6

Degrees of Support: Employer Commitment to Staff Development on Postgraduate Courses

Julia Carter

Over recent years there has been a trend among academics and policy-makers alike to stress the role of the employer rather than the education provider in the provision of training and professional development (Pedler *et al.*, 1989, Tuckett, 1991). Initiatives such as the NVQ movement and the establishment of (employer-led) TECs are examples of the increased importance attached, by government at least, to employer leadership in training. Behind this policy shift is an assumption that employers' responsibility for training and development will benefit the individual, the company and the British economy as a whole (National Training Task Force, 1993), though whether employers themselves are as committed to the wider aspirations of the policy is perhaps a moot point.

This trend and the emphasis on training and development is matched by a separate and parallel movement among individuals themselves to seek higher academic qualifications through a vocationally related Masters degree. Such degrees are typically offered part-time to students who are experienced professionals working full-time. They therefore provide an opportunity for continuing professional development (CPD) which an individual may take advantage of once or more during a working life in order to increase competence or enhance promotion prospects. The demand for such degrees has grown significantly in the past two decades as knowledge becomes quickly outdated and as individuals need to acquire new skills either within their own job or in order to make a career change.

These trends have prompted research to explore more fully the experience of students on a sample of part-time, professionally related Masters courses and to learn more about their employers' attitudes to their studies. Behind our interest lay an assumption that employers play a key role in selecting and supporting staff to attend such courses. We assumed that employers played a critical role in sending staff on courses, supporting their studies and then rewarding their achievement with promotion. Our research findings were to fundamentally question this assumption.

RESEARCH AIMS AND METHODOLOGY

The research centred on part-time students on postgraduate courses with a work-related focus and explored the involvement of employers with their employees' professional and personal development. Our approach included a questionnaire survey and follow-up group interviews with students on six postgraduate part-time courses. The courses selected were all concerned with management although they were located in a range of specialist disciplines including engineering, computing and arts. They were thus deemed to be particularly relevant to employment and were generalist, in as much as management itself is a generalist subject.

In addition to our survey and interviews with students we also conducted in-depth interviews with employers, matched by occupational sector and size with those of the students, although for reasons of confidentiality we chose not to use their actual employers. Interviews were conducted with ten employers representing, in the main, large businesses including public, private and recently privatized companies in the areas of banking, utilities, telecommunications, structural engineering, arts management, property management, computing, retail, hotels and insurance.

Our respondents were training and development personnel, although in some cases respondents had overall responsibility for human resources and, in very large organizations, a specific responsibility, within training, for management development. In our research we were seeking to answer a number of questions relating to the part which employers play in postgraduate studies that are heavily work-related, for example:

- what role do employers play in selecting staff to go on courses?

- which staff do they select and on what criteria?

- how do employers choose the course on which to send staff?

- how do employers evaluate courses?

- what is the relationship between organizational benefit and individual benefit?

- how do employers support staff – by sponsorship of fees, time off work, work place support and mentoring, use of company facilities for projects, etc.?

- what part does the individual (employee or student) play in the process?

- what are the rewards for employees who take such courses?

Our findings are reported under four headings: the students' position, company training policies and cultures, support for staff pursuing postgraduate courses, and the conclusions drawn from the research.

THE STUDENTS' POSITION

In reality we found that the overwhelming majority of students on our courses had taken the initiative to enrol with little or no encouragement from the workplace and often in active defiance of their employer organization. Despite the fact that the fees for Masters courses are relatively high, only a minority of students in our sample of courses (one-third) had their fees paid in full by an employer (though another one-third enjoyed some employer contribution). Significantly, very few students felt that their employers were supporting or backing their studies in other, non-financial, ways. Students reported that no allowances were made for the fact that they were holding down a job and studying, and many felt that their employers were not interested in their scholastic progress. Only a small minority believed that their new skills and learning were being recognized in the workplace or would ever be recognized by their present employer. One of the interesting issues to emerge from the study was the extent to which students' perceptions of their employers' attitudes (lack of support and encouragement) appeared to prevail regardless of whether there was an employer contribution to fees. Thus although two-thirds of students in our survey were receiving some employer help with course fees, nearly all of our respondents felt unsupported by their employer.

Nor were the employer attitudes (as perceived by the students) out of line with the students' own views on the role of the employer. The students we interviewed and the questionnaire responses we received suggested that students felt strongly that their studies were their own affair and not their employers'. Although they would have liked recognition for their learning and qualifications in the form of promotion and additional responsibility, most respondents appeared resigned to the inevitable lack of such prospects and for the majority, the main reason for gaining the Masters qualification was to obtain a new and better job elsewhere. Students would and did pressure their employers into contributing to course fees but they often argued for this, not on the grounds of the course itself or the new skills they and the company would acquire but rather on the basis of quite unrelated issues and from special positions of strength, for example, threatening to leave the firm if they were not given help with course fees and in one case agreeing to drop a claim of sexual harassment. Given the employers' motivations for contributing to course fees it is not surprising that their payment did not imply any real employer commitment to the course. Further, since the students had themselves exploited the situation, they had actively colluded in setting up the position they found themselves in.

There was a similar ambivalence over issues of non-financial support. Though a few students were disappointed at the lack of support and encouragement they received from their line manager, others were adamant that they would have resisted any involvement from the workplace and such students were keen to keep the degree separate from work as 'something for me'.

Similarly, although students sometimes felt overwhelmed by the act of juggling the competing demands of the workplace and their studies, they were often loath to delegate responsibility or to bypass the chance of tackling a major task since to do so would jeopardize their chances of promotion. Since we assume that those employees who enrol on professionally related Masters degrees are normally ambitious, it follows that they will seize every opportunity to shine at work and would resist any attempt by the employer to sideline them for the duration of their studies.

In summary therefore, although students often regretted the lack of support and interest they received from their employers, they would have resisted any close involvement which might have threatened their independence and autonomy. Some students claimed to have turned down opportunities to attend similar courses customized to the needs of their employer since they were looking for something which gave them a new and alternative perspective rather than a confirmation of the old.

COMPANY TRAINING POLICIES AND CULTURES

The employers in our sample, though matched by sector and size with those of the students', were not the students' employers. Such an approach would have been impossible within the framework of confidentiality which we promised the students. The sectors covered by the survey reflected the range of courses and the occupational areas of the students and were: banking, a utility, telecommunications, structural engineering, arts management, property management, computing, retail, hotels, and insurance.

In-house management development

The majority of employers in our sample had mandatory management development programmes. In the main this was related to company size, smaller organizations not having such schemes. However, other factors were also significant. The importance attached to management development reflected companies' own cultures and the emphasis these placed on management. There was considerable variation here between companies which were managerial in style and those which were more individualistic. In the latter category two types emerged, both of which placed emphasis on the individual but in different ways. The first was a traditional professional organization, an international consulting engineer partnership, where technical expertise was more highly rated than general management skills. The second was an insurance company, described by our respondent as 'having a deal-cutting culture', 'which placed emphasis on individuals and their prowess in the market rather than on any collective and corporate sense of a managed organization. In both the professional and the deal-cutter organizations, management itself was undervalued: our respondents pointed out that no one had been promoted to board level on the basis of their general management skills. It was therefore no surprise that management development was similarly undervalued – in the engineering consultancy this was relative to technical professional development, while in the second type of organization there was no clear appreciation of staff development overall, rather a belief that good employees came ready-made.

In the companies with management development programmes these varied considerably. Though all involved some participation in in-house training sessions, many organizations complemented this with open learning which allowed managers to integrate study with practice. In one company the management development programme was spread over five years and managers' participation planned to coincide with critical stages in their career. At least one organization had their management development programme accredited by a university and others were competence-based though not (yet?) NVQ accredited.

Beyond the level of basic management development the majority of organizations had distinct programmes to develop managers at differing levels, typically junior, middle and senior management. Where possible these were integrated into career or succession planning systems to ensure both an adequate preparation for the next career move and the recognition of an individual's goals and development needs.

In some organizations, development followed, or immediately preceded, promotion. In others, where an élite was identified early and destined for the most senior positions, there was considerable demarcation and stratification of management personnel with the highest grades (or those destined for that level) receiving the most careful and expensive development (see Connor et al., 1990). Only one respondent, a bank, mentioned the operation of a fast-track or high-flyer stream. This differentiated between managers even before they joined the company, through a dedicated recruitment process, and involved distinct induction and development. For this group the management development programme involved a five-year period of operational postings designed to develop the individual's skills and potential for senior management. During this period the manager was supported by additional appraisal and mentoring and participated in a special programme of in-house and customized external courses. Significantly, although managers were placed in a number of operating divisions, the responsibility for their development rested in the centre: 'I am responsible for the care of an élite cadre whose services the company is loath to lose' (Management Development Manager).

The majority of our contacts appeared uneasy about the high-flyer or officer class approach. Although they were unwilling to use such terms about their own organizations and even insisted, unprompted, 'we don't use the term', they frequently described an approach which seemed very similar, though it may have been less widely recognized and may have operated at a less formal level.

External courses

All but one of the employers in our sample had a policy to support staff to attend external courses. The type of course most commonly supported was one leading to a professional qualification in personnel (IPM) or accounting (CIMA). Students on such courses were normally offered course fees and day-release to attend and there was also an automatic assumption that the opportunity for such training went with the post. The same policies applied to professional courses at the postgraduate level: all but one of the employers were supporting staff to attend higher degrees in professional areas, such as librarianship and engineering.

Beyond this there were wide differences in the types of courses employers supported and the extent to which their cultures had led to detailed policies and pro-active strategies. Two organizations used special initiatives to encourage all forms of learning even at basic levels and supported enrolment on GCSE and A-level courses, BTEC National and even some general basic education. In one case this was actively promoted by a publicity campaign targeted at individual members of staff through posters in canteens and rest-rooms. In other companies the emphasis was on more vocationally focused external courses and at least one organization had produced a ring-bound catalogue of thousands of courses available nationally, which was circulated to departmental training managers.

Departmental training managers were, in nearly all cases, responsible for agreeing the funding (and release arrangements) for all part-time courses, regardless of level. Departments controlled their own devolved, global training budget from which they bought or provided internal and external courses. Internal training programmes, to which the department was committed (by head office), frequently accounted for nearly all of the budget, with vocational external courses taking second place and more general educational courses coming a poor third. (In two companies a small ring-fenced fund for 'education' was allocated specifically.)

The criteria used to agree sponsorship of courses were 'business- ' or 'job-relevance'. This was true for all levels of course; however, on lower-level, relatively cheaper courses where no release was required for attendance, there was, understandably, a more relaxed interpretation of the criteria. (At this level too it is arguably harder to disprove the business relevance of a basic, general qualification such as BTEC National in business and finance.) Applications to support study on expensive, advanced courses might therefore have been turned down by training managers in favour of supporting more individuals on less costly lower level programmes. Although all but one of our employers were supporting staff to study on postgraduate management and business courses, the total numbers were typically low (single figures per annum).

We suggest, however, that these figures may not be entirely accurate and reflect the funding procedures used within organizations. Though there was a range of slightly different arrangements, companies in the main differentiated between staff who were centrally funded, i.e. the high-flyers on full-time courses, and those who were locally funded and on part-time courses. This pattern related directly to the differentiation already noted between high-flyers and the rest. Since our employer respondents tended to be from head office it was likely that the information they gave us related only to the group they funded and ignored students on part-time courses being supported from local budgets. This further confirms the impression of a two-tier organization with staff on part-time study being somehow second-class. It is interesting to note that head office's ignorance of their development suggests that their achievement may also go unrecognized within the organization at large.

SUPPORT FOR STAFF IN PURSUING POSTGRADUATE COURSES

The criterion most commonly quoted for allowing an individual to attend a course referred not to the individual but to the course and its relation to the job or business: 'it must be business related', and 'it must help an individual to do the work better'.

This criterion was clearly open to many interpretations, and indeed that may be one of the reasons it was so widely used. The criterion of business relevance and benefit appeared to mean something slightly different in different companies. At the heart of the criterion was an attempt to recognize that there are a number of players involved in a sponsorship arrangement and that their interests may not always coincide. Three of the players were easily identifiable:

- the business or corporation (corporate interest and benefit)

- the department, division, trading company or group (departmental interest and benefit)

- the individual (self-interest and benefit)

In some companies the overarching criterion of business interest was an attempt to ensure that benefits accrued to the company overall rather than the individual (corporate versus individual benefit). In others the tension was perceived to be strongest between the departmental and corporate interests (corporate versus departmental benefit).

Corporate versus departmental benefit

Since, in many of the companies surveyed, the authority and funding for sponsorship were devolved to a local or departmental level there was a corresponding tendency to sponsor staff for local rather than corporate benefit. In some organizations this was addressed through joint funding, particularly for full-time courses, when the course fees were paid by the centre and the salary by the local department.

In other cases the authorization and funding were handled differently and, though the department recommended the sponsorship, it was approved by the centre regardless of payer. In one company, applicants were recommended by their local, departmental director and then interviewed by the director of another department to ensure corporate rather than departmental benefit.

Where an organization had a high-flyer stream whose members' development was the responsibility of the centre, sponsorship was a central rather than local matter.

A number of employer respondents spoke of the tensions which ensued between departments and the centre when staff who had been on courses were then not returned to their original departments. This was particularly acute in cases where the department had been involved in the funding of the study period.

Corporate versus individual benefit

Many of our respondents expressed serious doubts over the corporate return on investment in sponsoring an individual to study for a postgraduate qualification in business. This confirms the findings of Constable and McCormick (1987). The degree most frequently mentioned in this context was the MBA, though this may have been because it is the most expensive and best known and was being used as a generic term for all non-technical higher level qualifications.

The poor track record of MBA graduates in returning to, and staying with, their employers was also emphasized. One contact reported that all six employees sponsored by his company had subsequently left the organization. Other respondents appeared to be relying on more anecdotal or impressionistic evidence. This issue was often referred to as a re-entry problem, interestingly confirming the view already noted, that all MBA students were perceived by employers to be studying full-time, or perhaps suggesting that even part-timers became decoupled from their jobs and thus 'returned' to work on qualifying.

A few employers felt that employees' expectations were unrealistically raised by taking a postgraduate course and that they grew frustrated if their responsibilities at work did not match their expectations. Thus there was a mismatch in timing between the course and promotion possibility, as noted by Connor et al. (1990). There were also strong fears among employers that individuals might wish to pursue a qualification at the expense of the general good: 'The company is not happy with people who put a high value on postgraduate qualifications.'

Two employers spoke critically of graduate recruits who demanded higher amounts of continuing professional development than the organization offered. Similarly, an employer spoke of fears that staff assumed qualifications would bring automatic promotion. In both cases individuals' ambitions were perceived as running counter to the interests of the company overall. In an attempt to address this, one or two companies had further refined the business relevance criterion to one of job relevance: 'Help to do the job here and now is what it is all about.' This was clearly a more narrowly defined criterion which focused on the present and suggested the possibility of an objective interpretation. It was nevertheless not unproblematic. One employer illustrated this point with the example of an employee whose request for sponsorship for a French language course was turned down even though she was currently working on an international project with French colleagues.

In most cases, companies which had been 'bitten' by investing in MBA sponsorship of staff who had then left were now 'twice shy' of sponsorship. A few had made a policy decision not to support MBA (and similar) courses. However a number of contacts recognized that they were nevertheless caught between their own poor experience and their sense that such development is 'a good thing' and should have corporate benefit: 'We are keen to be seen to be supporting a good thing which may have corporate benefits but experience suggests that those with qualifications will leave.' Their policy thus sought to differentiate between staff motivations and to prevent the sponsorship of employees whose primary motive was personal development.

For employers then, the major issue regarding advanced courses was one of staff retention. Only a minority raised issues concerned with the courses themselves, their relevance ('We have doubts about the relevance of the course for which we are paying') and efficacy ('The job teaches you most, you are surrounded by talented people and are being stretched; from time to time you're doing your own thing').

This is a particularly sensitive area since it is often hard to evaluate a postgraduate course which does not have the type of skill-based outcomes that can be easily observed on the job. Only one employer had a system in place for the evaluation of high-level courses, though a second was developing one. This is an area of critical significance for educators and employers since it lies at the heart of the academic/workplace divide. Although innovative approaches to management development seek to bridge the divide there are still tensions and misconceptions which it might be fruitful for employers and academics to explore together.

Strategies

For the company respondents we spoke to, the MBA and other high level CPD courses presented problems. On the one hand, the organization recognized that the high calibre staff they wished to recruit and retain wanted to develop themselves. On the other, they failed to perceive any benefits of CPD for the organization and in many cases actually saw it as detrimental since it seemed to be encouraging heightened expectations in staff who were then likely to leave.

In a few cases companies had risen to the challenge and developed positive responses to the MBA. Such policy generally focused on the course itself. In one or two companies it had led to the development of an in-house MBA offered collaboratively with a university business school. Another company had focused on the course mode and adopted a policy only to support students on part-time and open learning (Open University) courses. In a third company, there was a policy only to participate in programmes which offered work-based learning. These strategies had perceived the problem as one of 're-entry' and sought to address it by preventing the student/employee from absenting him- or herself from the workplace and/or attending classes at another institution. This might appear to be a quaint misunderstanding to educators who would claim that the process of learning takes place regardless of location. However, it will be interesting to evaluate the success of this policy which may reveal a hitherto overlooked experience involved in attending a face-to-face course in another institution which contributes to the employee's sense of alienation from the workplace. Not only did this approach obviate the participant's re-entry, but it also addressed the issue of disruption to colleagues which one member of staff's attendance on a course can mean.

A few of the organizations had also focused on the company's handling of re-entry in particular and career planning in general. At least one respondent reported that the company was now sending staff on MBA programmes later in their careers than before. This enabled the graduates to be offered posts with more responsibility and challenge on their return. In a second organization, staff were being offered more counselling before, during and after their courses, with their next post agreed before the course began. Succession planning and similar attempts to make career planning more transparent in the short and long term were also strategies being increasingly used together with course sponsorship.

In two companies, increased use of a competency approach to the identification of management skills was being extended both to the task of identifying staff development need and to the evaluation of management courses.

In the remaining companies we found that there were few positive approaches to the issue of high level CPD; rather, a defensive approach pertained. In one case, graduate recruits were explicitly told at entry that there would be few if any opportunities for such development.

CONCLUSIONS

Our research suggests that, with a few exceptions, companies were not yet managing CPD satisfactorily at postgraduate level. The predominant tensions between the players – the business as a whole, the department and the individual – were, in part, a manifestation of this.

Another contributing factor seemed to be a lack of clarity of purpose. Though training and personnel managers had mission statements for their work, these rarely translated easily into practical guidance in situations such as those covered by our study. Staff development, through external postgraduate courses, necessarily challenges many of the employee's previous assumptions and practice. Since these are likely to derive from the organization, the individual will begin to question the organization and his or her relations with it, strengthened by an alternative, external authority to pit against the culture of the workplace. An organizational response to such a challenge needs to explore from a holistic point of view the re-entry problem and may involve a culture change within the organization which recognizes, values and exploits the contribution of continuing professional development and the challenges to current practice which it stimilates.

One employer in our survey recognized this and had a clearly defined role for education at all levels in the workforce: 'To prepare people for the unknown and the unexpected.' Most companies did not share this view; they were attempting less radical approaches which concentrated on minimizing risk (perhaps realistically). Perhaps they also failed to see the full complexity of the situation and its interrelatedness, aptly demonstrated in our interview with one employer.

Employer: If an individual wants to attend for personal reasons the company will not support them.
Interviewer: Why?
Employer: Because they will leave.
Interviewer: Why?
Employer: Because we do not manage their re-entry well.
Interviewer: Why?
Employer: Because we did not send them in the first place.

Although the challenge may have retreated with recession and slow down in staff turnover, it is only a temporary reprieve. Companies may well need to adjust their traditional attitudes to staff development which assume that the employer controls the selection and allocation of development opportunity. Such an approach, while it is based on policy assumptions mentioned in the introduction, may already be outdated. Since it involves an expectation of employer/employee relations which is now largely redundant, Maguire *et al.* (1993) already note a new emphasis towards 'individual commitment' apparent in national policy.

Nor is this phenomenon limited to the UK, as Otala notes: lifelong employment and mutual loyalty between employer and employee is vanishing in all countries, even in Japan. Downsizing, mergers and acquisitions take place frequently. Macro-economic instability shortens business focus and increases turbulence. Such changes limit the possibility and willingness of companies to take on the responsibility of employee competence development, with the result that employees themselves become responsible for their own career and competence (Otala, 1993).

Our research suggests that employees in the UK are moving towards or have already adopted this approach and see professional development as the responsibility of the individual. Otala characterizes this attitude as American and suggests that it is the only feasible approach in today's climate. However, our study would suggest that although it is in evidence among employees, acknowledgement of this trend is not yet found among

UK employers. It is the resulting mismatch in perceptions which leads employers to view with suspicion staff who are obviously aspirational and wish to enhance their career prospects through continuing education and development outside the company. Such expectations are seen as disloyal and perceived furthermore as somehow challenging the authority of senior management whose role it is to select for training and development within a context of essentially sponsored mobility. Employees are thus in a dilemma: if they are to behave in a manner which to them seems responsible they are likely to suffer in the short term since they are unlikely to be rewarded by the organization and are more likely to be penalized. However, if they remain passive and compliant to company expectations and yesterday's rules they are likely to suffer in the longer term when they may find themselves unemployed and unemployable within a wider culture where job prospects depend upon qualifications in a highly competitive labour market.

For the providers of advanced CPD too, there are lessons to be learned: too often Masters degrees are not seen as CPD. Both in terms of funding and organizational structures the two are often kept distinct, reflecting and confirming deeper divisions between 'academic' and 'professional' provision with a newer division into government funded and employer funded courses. The government programme of funding for non-award bearing short course provision, whatever its longer-term outcomes, has in the short term strengthened this divide and confirmed the existence of two distinct cultures and expectations. It is to be hoped that the recent inclusion of accredited courses within the framework of the government programme for pump-priming CPD will now lead to broader and more flexible provision which can embrace both short and award-bearing courses, and promote collaboration with employers through validation of in-house programmes, customized Masters degrees and the use of the credit accumulation and transfer scheme to create flexible qualifications. Such development will need to address employers' fears and doubts and will need to examine the 're-entry' problem which is viewed as central by the employers themselves.

Finally, it is important not to overlook the effect of the process. Distance and open learning delivery modes for part-time postgraduate courses, though attractive in a number of ways, preclude much of the course process and the shock of the impact of a new culture by removing student interaction, face-to-face contact with new and alternative authorities and, most obviously and symbolically, the journey over a distance to attend another institution. The learning experience is not entirely solitary, although it takes place at an individual level; nor is learning intended to be unproblematic: courses which cause re-entry problems can foment change and as such they are threatening. Programmes which reduce the critical culture shock may be superficially easier to manage and therefore more attractive to employers (and to students?); however, at what cost to critical reflection and true growth? If Otala is right and the future lies in individual control of personal and professional development, these issues will need to be explored more fully.

REFERENCES

Connor, H., Strebler, M. and Hirsch, W. (1990) *You and Your Graduates: The First Few Years* (IMS report No. 191). Brighton: Falmer.

Constable, J. and McCormick, R. (1987) *The Making of British Managers*. London: BIM and CBI.

Maguire, M., Maguire, S. and Felstead, A. (1993) *Factors Influencing Individual Commitment to Lifetime Learning*. Sheffield: Department of Employment, and Leicester: Centre for Labour Market Studies, University of Leicester.

National Training Task Force (1993) *First Annual Report*. London: NTTF.

Otala, L. (1993) *Lifelong Learning of Engineers in Industry*. Espoo, Finland: IACEE.

Pedler, M., Boydell, T. and Burgoyne, J. (1989) Towards the learning company. *Management, Education and Development*, **20**(1), 1–8.

Tuckett, A. (1991) *Towards a Learning Workforce: A Policy Discussion Paper on Adult Learners at Work*. Leicester: NIACE.

Chapter 7

Whither Goest Thou: Professional or Management Development?

Mike Scannell

Professional development in many professions and organizations has become synonymous with managerial development, whereby individuals are rewarded and promoted for good performance by a move up the hierarchical structure to a more managerial role. In time such individuals will assume a professional management role and will leave their original professional specialization behind them. This distinction, or lack of distinction, between managerial development and professional development is a cause for concern for many sectors. The process of de-layering, now being carried out by many organizations with the consequent reduction in middle management positions and in promotion prospects for the individual, has accentuated this concern. The chairman of IBM UK, Sir Anthony Cleaver, has stated (Gretton, 1994) that de-layering may have increased the efficiency of companies but it has also reduced both the motivation and the opportunities of middle managers trying to make it to the top. Drucker (1988) believes that the typical large business twenty years hence will have fewer than half the levels of management of its counterpart today and no more than one-third of the managers. There is therefore a ground swell of interest in the development of the individual who does not wish to move out of his or her professional role. The development needs of such an individual may be very different from someone who is aiming at general management. The suggestion is that different development plans will be needed according to the emphasis on either a professional or management role.

In the United Kingdom, education is one of the most widely used of our public services. School provision is the largest part of the education service, educating over nine and a quarter million pupils; employing about 538,000 teachers (full-time equivalent) and a great many other support staff, and costing around £31 billion in 1992/93. Education legislation of the 1980s introduced a number of fundamental changes for the education service in England and Wales. The changes as they relate to schools concerned, among other things, the *de facto* demise of the local education authorities, the introduction of local management of schools, the expansion of grant-maintained schools and the establishment of the National Curriculum. The hierarchical structure within the teaching profession itself has been subject to little change despite the many and varied changes that have taken place in education over the past fifteen to twenty years. Nevertheless, the concept of development of the professional as well as development of the manager applies equally to the teaching profession as to any other profession or organization.

Bradley (1990) calculates that the most expensive resource in schools is the teachers, and argues that 'We have been very slow to realise in education circles that teachers need and deserve support, reassurance and encouragement to go on extending their skills and exploring the frontiers of their knowledge.' Battye (1993, p. 141) further contends that

> In education we have so changed the perception of teaching that we have reduced its value to the lowest of tasks performed by a teacher. It is the labouring job within the classroom. We in fact reward our best teachers by releasing them on an increasing basis from the drudgery of classroom teaching so that they can carry out other, often increasingly banal, tasks.

As teachers are promoted, their pupil-contact time diminishes and their management roles enlarge. Many managers in schools have had little preparation for their managerial roles, especially for the extra responsibilities (e.g. finance) that have been brought about by recent legislation. At the same time, many teachers find the notion of management an anathema and decide to forgo promotion and remain in front-line teaching. The teaching profession was therefore selected as the starting-point for research into factors affecting career development.

THE METHODOLOGY

The main base of the research was a structured interview supplemented by three questionnaires: a skills audit, a thematic analysis of career intentions and a critical success factors methodology. The structured interview consisted of twenty-five questions relating to the interviewee's life and career, and was designed to be conducted during school time in one 50-minute free period. In practice, it was found that many of the teachers interviewed obtained so much from the interview in terms of reflection about their career, and provided such detailed answers to the questions, that the interviews often extended, at the interviewee's request, to a second 50-minute period, and in a few cases to a third period. All interviews were carried out at school in a private office. Each interview was on a one-to-one basis. Each teacher had previously been provided with documentation for the Skills Audit, the Thematic Analysis of Career Intentions and the Critical Success Factor methodology to complete and bring to the interview.

The Skills Audit, in which the teachers provided a measure of the strength of particular designated skills, was adapted from a similar audit for managers and included a number of skills considered particularly appropriate to teaching. These skills were selected following discussions with lecturers employed in the Education Department of the University of Luton.

The Thematic Analysis of Career Intentions, consisting of three sections, was derived from earlier research which showed that there are a number of possible career directions that professional people should be able to consider. Section one asked the interviewees whether they rated themselves as a general manager, an educational manager, a specialist teacher or a subject specialist. In section two each interviewee was asked to compare his or her relative strength in six pairs of abilities involving the following four areas: subject knowledge, student management, school management, administration. In section three each interviewee was asked whether they rated themselves as an expert in teaching, or a general manager who happens to be in teaching, or a hybrid between teacher and manager.

The Critical Success Factor (CSF) methodology was developed at the Harvard Business School for a different issue: the identification and definition of the information needs of top managers. A significant level of success has been reported for this technique covering both the private and public sectors. Because of the success of this approach and the apparent fact that it need not be constrained to information needs, the CSF approach has been also applied to the career development issues of senior managers. It has been well demonstrated that career planning is an important factor in managerial success, perhaps even overtaking the role of luck or being in the right place at the right time. The CSF methodology is used as a starting-point for career planning, as it forces the individual to recognize that different criteria for success do occur. CSFs should support and define the career aspirations of the individual. Where success is defined, the individual is much more able to achieve this than where success is allowed to vary from circumstance to circumstance: individuals define those areas in which good performance is necessary to the attainment of personal goals. Having defined personal CSFs each individual must also define how to manage them, and to set priorities to distinguish critical from non-critical factors; the whole process helps the individual to recognize what must be done for career success.

The structured interview and the three questionnaires were initially tested and retested on a number of teachers known to the researcher in order to check the validity of the approach and to provide a base for further investigation.

Six schools in three widely separated counties of England were contacted and agreed to participate in the research. As secondary schools are generally larger than primary schools and offer much greater and wider opportunities for career development and promotion, all the schools chosen were comprehensive, non-selective secondary schools. These were as follows:

a mixed middle school, pupils aged 9–13
a boys' high school, pupils aged 11–16
a girls' high school, pupils aged 11–16
a mixed comprehensive, pupils aged 11–16
a mixed comprehensive, pupils aged 11–18
a mixed upper school, pupils aged 13–18

The pupil populations of the schools ranged between 700 and 850 with the exception of the middle school, whose pupil population was slightly over 250. Ethnically the schools ranged from one where the pupils were 99.5 per cent British and white to one where the pupils were 87.5 per cent ethnic minority. Classwise, the catchment areas of the schools varied from urban working class to urban middle class to rural working class. Two of the schools had been awarded the Schools Curriculum Award, one was seeking Investors in People status. Two schools were heavily involved in initial teacher training, one through a local university, the other through an in-house training scheme. One school was combining its staff development programme with a local higher education institution to enable interested staff members to gain further qualifications. Of the heads of the schools, two were female and four were male.

To ensure that the interviews would elicit information relevant to teachers and their careers, the researcher spent up to four days per week for a period of eight weeks at one school actively involved in the life of the school. With the permission of the head of the school and staff, the researcher attended lessons, assemblies, staff meetings and school functions. In short, the time was used to get to know the staff, and for the staff to get to know the researcher. Mutual confidence and trust were established between many of the staff and the researcher, giving the researcher insights into the teachers' trains of thought, helping to shape the questions to be asked in the structured interview, and producing many volunteers to take part in the research. When the interviewing schedule began, the quality and depth of information given in the interviews between the researcher and teachers where a relationship had been established was noticeably higher than in those interviews where there was less of a relationship.

Twenty-five teachers at that school selected for researcher familiarization were then interviewed. This sample represented 50 per cent of the total teaching staff of the school. All the interviewees were volunteers. The findings from this group of teachers were presented to a further ten teachers known to the researcher, five senior managers and five classroom teachers, for their comments and criticisms.

The contact at each of the other five schools, either the head or a deputy head, was asked to provide six interviewees, two in each of the three categories of senior management, aspirants to senior management roles and classroom-focused teachers, as identified in the first stage of the research. The total sample consisted of fifty-four teachers (one withdrew due to illness), all of whom agreed to participate on a voluntary basis. The interviewees were not informed that they were part of any particular category.

The ages of the teachers ranged from 24 to 62, with three teachers in their twenties; forty-five in their thirties or forties; four in their fifties; and one in his sixties. (One teacher declined to give her age.) Most of the teachers had thus had time to develop their careers, although there were some late entrants to the teaching profession in the thirties to forties age group. The teachers were thus in mid-career, would have made career path decisions and would probably have a realistic appreciation of their career aims and ambitions.

THE FINDINGS

On the basis of the interviews, a taxonomic analysis was carried out on each of the teachers (sample size = fifty-four). They were classified according to their career achievements and aspirations. First, teachers could not, in general, be identified as general managers *per se*. At most, they saw themselves as teacher/managers. This conclusion is also supported by the thematic analysis of career intentions, in which some teachers regarded themselves solely as teachers, while others considered that they were teacher/managers. Only one regarded herself as a general manager.

Second, the twenty-five teachers classified as having a management orientation could be further divided into those possessing a senior management role (defined for the purposes of this research as head or deputy head), or those aspiring to such positions. Within the second group of aspiring managers it was evident that there were two further distinct groups, those who had apparent potential to become a senior manager and those whose careers appeared to have reached a plateau and who were unlikely to achieve such a role. This left a group of twenty-nine teachers who were classified as classroom-focused. Finally, classroom teachers could

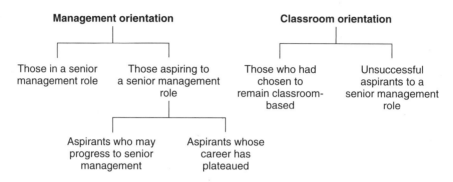

Figure 7.1   Taxonomy of career types

be subdivided into two sections: those who chose to be classroom-based, and those who would have wished to make progress towards management but had not been successful. This produces a taxonomy, at three levels, of career types for professional teachers (Figure 7.1). The taxonomy shows a clear asymmetry and is skewed towards management aspirations and lack of career opportunities for classroom-based teachers. Of the five categories identified, four show a current or at least an expired aspiration towards management. Only one shows a focus on the classroom. The relevant data were inspected for evidence of a distinction between those who enjoyed teaching/pastoral care versus those whose primary focus was upon the subjects taught, but none was found. It is, however, possible that by increasing sample size, evidence may be found of a subdivision within the category of those teachers who had chosen to remain classroom based.

Factors affecting the obtaining of a senior management position were:

- having a mentor, normally the head of the school of first employment, and normally on an informal basis;

- rapid early promotion, a normal occurrence at the start of their career for teachers now in their forties;

- changing schools;

- career planning;

- planned continuing professional development;

- number of courses and conferences attended ('courses attended' include both subject-related and management-related courses);

- having a high profile in education circles, i.e. networking – generally within the local education authority and outside the school of employment;

- quantity of hours worked.

Factors affecting *not* obtaining a senior management position were:

- rapid early promotion within school, thus satisfying early career objectives;

- a failure to recognize the need to change schools, resulting in a lack of varied experience, which inevitably will be a negative factor when seeking to obtain promotion later in one's career;

- little career planning;

- little continuing professional development. The continuing professional development that did take place was school-based rather than career-based, and courses and conferences attended were likely to be subject-based courses rather than management courses;

- having a high profile within the school, i.e. taking on additional responsibilities, often unpaid;

- falling school rolls, resulting in fewer deputy head posts being available;

- age.

Factors involved with those who wished to remain classroom-based were:

- the strong belief that teaching is based on pupil and classroom involvement and is not administration and school management;

- anti-change – especially the rapid change of the past few years which usually appeared, to those teachers at least, to be change for change's sake;

- the large amount of hours that are deemed to be necessary to be worked by those who are seeking management promotion. It is important to point out, however, that many classroom-based teachers will work the same amount of hours but not in the school setting. Many have second jobs, some connected with teaching such as evening classes in further education or personal tuition classes, while others have jobs not connected with teaching. Examples include taxi driver, professional gambler, church minister, and (as an unpaid job) parenting.

Factors affecting those who wished to progress up the management ladder but did not succeed were:

- status of subject, e.g. art, design, etc.;

- late entrance into the profession;

- age.

All classroom teachers, whatever their reason for so being, were affected by: lack of motivation from senior managers; lack of recognition; lack of status; lack of financial reward (an important but not a total factor in having a second job); lack of input to decision-making; and lack of thanks. This confirms Crowther's (1993) view that historically teachers have often felt relatively powerless regarding the decision-making processes which determine the nature of their work. Crowther quotes the US Carnegie Task Force (1986) which commented that 'Rules made by others govern their behaviour at every turn.... An endless array of policies succeed in constraining the exercise of the teacher's independent judgement on almost every matter of moment.' For the classroom teachers who took part in this research the above applies both with respect to government policies and to their own school policies.

The Skills Audit showed that the senior managers, as a whole, rated their skills consistently higher than the aspirants who in turn rated their skills higher than the classroom-based teachers. The senior managers and the aspirants both rated their highest skills as managing people and interpersonal skills, while the classroom-based teachers gave the highest rating to their specialist subject knowledge.

From the Thematic Analysis of Career Intentions, the three groups saw themselves as educational managers rather than general managers, with the rating in both classes being highest for senior managers, then aspirants, then classroom-based teachers. Conversely, the classroom-based teachers rated themselves higher than the aspirants and even higher than the senior managers in being a specialist in their chosen subject, and in being a specialist teacher. Specialism in the chosen subject rated higher than specialism in teaching for all three groups.

The senior managers showed a bias towards student management, school management and administration as against subject knowledge and a bias towards school management over student management. The aspirants showed a bias towards student management over subject knowledge and student management over administration. The classroom-based teachers considered their strengths to be in subject knowledge over both school management and administration, and in student management over administration. In all the other pairings of abilities, relative strengths were considered to be almost equal. The senior managers and the aspirants thus leant towards management as against students and subject, while the classroom-based teachers leant towards subject and students as against management.

When rating themselves as either an expert in teaching or a general manager who happens to be in teaching, or a hybrid between teacher and manager, only one interviewee rated him- or herself as a general manager and was the only person involved in postgraduate studies who did not have an education connotation – in this case an MBA.

The Critical Success Factor methodology was completed by only half of the teachers interviewed, possibly indicating that teachers have difficulty in formatting objectives or do not generally tend to set themselves objectives or plan for the future. Of the teachers who did define their critical success factors, those either in or seeking a senior management position tended to concentrate on career and management factors, while classroom teachers were more concerned with development of classroom skills.

THE ROLE AND FUNCTION OF CPD

One of the teachers interviewed summed up the motivation of his colleagues as follows: 'I recently attended a heads of department course run by the local education authority. All the course members were aged early to middle forties. The major topic of conversation was retirement.' What are the causes of such demotivation?

Brown (1993) states that recent union studies, and other stress-related research reports, show a remarkable degree of unanimity in regard to those factors which teachers report as stressful. The factors include: heavy work-load; lack of resources; poor school management and organization; poor communication at all levels including meetings; constant demand for change for no good reason; rate of change; little involvement in decision-making; greatly increased bureaucracy, and lack of staff development. Many of these factors were, as noted earlier, confirmed by the teachers interviewed during this research.

Newby (1988), however, considers that stress can be caused as much by understimulation as by overload. Goddard (1990) quotes Drucker writing in the *Wall Street Journal* that under present conditions 'people will stay in their present job another 30 years or so. We will have to redesign manager-ial and professional jobs so that even able people will still be challenged by the job after five or more years in it.' Slocum *et al.* (1987) refer to plateauing as the slowing down and the inevitable end of promotions and state that plateauing must happen to almost everyone. It is normal, and it has little to do with failure or success. Unfortunately, most people regard promotion as the only reward that really counts.

For most teachers in the forties age group, promotion will be a thing of the past, if it was ever wanted in the first place. Few teachers will be able to change to a new career, especially if they wish to earn the equivalent of their salary as a teacher. Retirement for most will be a minimum of fifteen years and a maximum of twenty-five years ahead. For the demotivated and plateaued teacher it is likely that performance over that final fifteen to twenty-five years will suffer.

Newby proposes two options available to counter mid-career demotivation. The first option is simply to 'let them go' cushioned by early retirement payments, an option generally not available to teachers in the forties age group. The second option is to improve the rate of return from the individual. The key to this is in remotivating the demotivated. Within work, this is provided by changes in job activities that impose a significant learning requirement on the individual. The goal must be to overcome stagnation and over-conformity and to create new challenges and targets.

Many of the factors that cause stress are outside the control of individual teachers and the profession as a whole. But within the control of both is the concept of continuing professional development (CPD), which is defined by Tomlinson (1993) as the systematic maintenance, improvement and broadening of knowledge and skills, and the development of personal qualities necessary for the execution of professional, managerial and technical duties throughout one's working life. Tomlinson argues that we need to have lifelong professional development for teachers as managers of learning, which is systematically planned throughout their career. He cites the Handy (1987) and Constable and McCormick (1987) reports on British management which suggested the need for individual managers to take action to own their own careers, and to positively seek continuous training and development to get the learning habit early in order to recognize when new knowledge and skills are required and to seek them out. Teachers need encouragement to approach their own education and training this way.

The introduction of compulsory CPD to the teaching profession may well raise the cry from within the profession that it is just another exercise designed to add to the teachers' already heavy workload. That most teachers work long hours cannot be denied. The average hours worked by the teachers interviewed, over and above their contracted hours, totalled nearly twenty hours per week, with the range varying between six and thirty-one hours per week. Much of the work was preparation of lessons and marking of assignments. Little time was spent on personal development. Few of the teachers interviewed allocated time for reflection on their careers. Most admitted that their development tended to be reactive rather than proactive. Promotions gained were often a case of being in the right place at the right time rather than part of a career plan. Teachers' feedback on the interviews conducted often stated how productive and enjoyable it had been to spend time thinking about themselves, their lives and their careers. A number of teachers reported how useful the interviews had been in assisting their appraisal process. Some of the teachers interviewed stated they spent no time on continuing professional development; others were unable to quantify any time spent, although a few stated that the process was continuous.

Some professions are now insisting on CPD as a prerequisite of membership. The Chartered Insurance Institute (1994) will be requiring all its chartered members to undertake CPD as an integral part of their overall professional development. The Institute of Personnel Management (1991) states that all corporate members will need to produce evidence of CPD activity in the long run, and encourages all members to undertake CPD activity straight away. The Engineering Council (1991) aims to promote CPD so that it contributes to business performance, individual career advancement, the image of the profession and international competitiveness. Every engineer and technician is required to develop and maintain a high level of competence throughout his or her career, and is responsible for taking appropriate action to update and develop knowledge and skills relevant to his or her current job and career path, and to anticipate future requirements. Similar strategies have been adopted by other professions.

If the teaching profession were to also promote CPD for all its members, it is more than possible that many of the additional hours worked by teachers would be reduced, or the time spent more productive. Examples might be a reduction in time spent attending meetings, or for in-service training days to be more applicable to teachers' requirements. Comments given describing such days as 'days spent tidying cupboards' or 'yet more bloody IT' might then become a thing of the past. Most professions request that thirty-five hours a year be spent on CPD. For this small investment in time, individual teachers, and the profession, could reap much benefit, and probably reduce the heavy workload which is a feature of teachers' lives. The study of teachers' career development and aspirations in the six schools confirms the paucity of personal and professional development within the teaching profession, both for management and classroom teachers. The personal and professional development needs of teachers require further consideration, though of necessity taking into account the lack of funding available for any large changes to the existing system. The recommendations presented below could all be implemented at comparatively little cost, yet would quickly lead to greater professionalism for the individual teacher and a rise in status for the profession as a whole. The costs that are involved would be more than covered by increased efficiency and production.

Thody (1993) surveyed a sample of eighty professionals in middle management positions in primary, secondary and tertiary institutions in England and Australia. She found that 'what was surprising about their qualifications was the dearth of those concerned with management qualifications.' Most secondary schools in the United Kingdom have an annual budget of between £1 million and £3 million per annum, a figure much higher than the majority of businesss in the country. Yet we expect schools, these large 'businesses', to be managed by people with little or no financial training. A similar position exists with respect to people-management skills, recalling that classroom teachers, as indicated above, suffer from lack of motivation, recognition, input to decision-making and thanks.

The first recommendation, therefore, is that formal training for senior management posts be established, to the extent that no teacher would be appointed to such a position without having obtained credits in designated modules, somewhat similar to the police having to pass sergeant and inspector examinations before there is any possibility of earning promotion. Examples of modules might include leadership, team-building, communications, decision-making, delegation, finance. Modular credits could be built up over a number of years by distance learning, evening classes and attending week-long summer courses. The modules would also be of value to those teachers who had no intention of progressing to a senior management position. All teachers are managers to a greater or lesser extent. Knowledge of management and financial skills will, at the very least, improve communication between the various levels of teachers.

For professional (as opposed to management) development the following recommendations are made:

- Jobs to be rotated every five years within the same establishment, e.g. head of year to become head of department. In some schools this has already taken place, although more because a particular teacher has been unhappy in a post rather than as a strict result of job rotation. At present, for this to happen it requires two teachers to agree to swap jobs and for the suggestions to come direct from the teachers involved.

- Teachers to rotate schools every five years within a local education authority, the switch to be between schools probably, but not necessarily, of a similar kind.

- Older teachers to be allowed to take early retirement but to be retained by the same school on a part-time consultancy basis. Take as an example the case of a teacher who took early retirement at the age of 55. He now supplements his pension by supply

teaching, covering absences of permanent staff, on an approxi-
mate one-third basis. His total income from his pension and
supply work is the equivalent of his salary if he had remained a
full-time teacher. His stress level has reduced dramatically and
he is totally reinvigorated. He was employed full-time in a
secondary school as a head of faculty and personally specialized
in geography and geology. However, as a supply teacher his work
has included teaching a class of 6-year-olds in a primary school
and teaching biology to a class of 13- and 14-year-olds in an all-
girls high school. Given the greatest will in the world, there is a
danger that he is in effect child-minding in his supply teaching
role. As an alternative, he could have been retained as a consultant in the school from which he retired, where he had worked
for over fifteen years, on one-third of his salary to work one-third
of his time. A young teacher could have been employed full-time
on two-thirds of the retired teacher's previous salary. The total
cost to the school would thus be the same. The consultant
teacher could act as a formal mentor to the new teacher (and
other teachers) and 'supply' teach when necessary, with the
added benefit of knowing both the pupils and the absent teacher,
and thus being able to teach at a much higher standard than a
supply teacher brought in from the cold; act as a teacher substi-
tute to allow full-time colleagues to work together or to observe
each other in the classroom; organize in-service training and
many other jobs, thus relieving senior management for more
teaching duties and pupil-contact time, and by retiring early
would enable young teachers to obtain promotion more quickly.
Not every teacher seeking early retirement would be suitable for
such a consultancy position but a careful and correct appointment, not necessarily someone retiring from a senior
management position, could only produce great benefit to a
school at no additional cost.

- Appraisal to be bottom-up as well as top-down and to be of a
general nature rather than the specific items which constitute
teacher appraisal at the present time. This would be a public
acknowledgement of the value and experience of the classroom
teacher, and if conducted properly, could only lead to better
communication and team work within each school.

These four recommendations do not require great changes in the teaching
profession as it exists today. More radical changes, such as those proposed
by Hargreaves (1994) with the concept of the 'master teacher', should also

be considered. What is important is that teachers and management do not rest on the *status quo* but actively seek to solve the career progression and motivation difficulties which are besetting the profession.

REFERENCES

Battye, D. (1993) A most undesirable occupation. *Education*, **182** (8), 141.
Bradley, H. (1990) Foreword. In R. Bollington, D. Hughes and M. West, *An Introduction to Teacher Appraisal*. London: Cassell.
Brown, M. (1993) Cutting down on the stress. *Management in Education*, **7** (1), 22–3.
Carnegie Forum on Education and the Economy (1986) *A Nation Prepared: Teachers for the 21st Century. The Report of the Task Force on Teaching as a Profession*. New York: Carnegie Corporation.
Chartered Insurance Institute (1994) *Continuing Professional Development. Register of Training Providers (Applicants Guide)*. London: CII.
Constable, J. and McCormick, R. (1987) *The Making of British Managers*. London: BIM and CBI.
Crowther, F. (1993) How teachers view themselves. *Management in Education*, **7** (4), 14–16.
Drucker, P. F. (1988) The coming of the new organization. *Harvard Business Review*, January–February.
Department for Education (1994) *Education Statistics for the United Kingdom*. London: DFE.
Engineering Council (1991) *Continuing Professional Development. Framework for Action*. London: Engineering Council.
Goddard, R. W. (1990) Lateral moves enhance careers. *HR Magazine*, **35** (12), 69–74.
Gretton, I. (1994) Stepping up your career. *Professional Manager*, **3** (1), 16–17.
Handy, C. (1987) *The Making of Managers. A Report on Management Education, Training and Development in the USA, Germany, France, Japan and the UK*. London: National Economic Development Office.
Hargreaves, D. (1994) *The Mosaic of Learning: Schools and Teachers for the Next Century*. London: Demos.
Institute of Personnel Management (1991) *The IPM Policy on Continuing Professional Development*. London: IPM.
Newby, T. (1988) Mid-career plateau or launchpad. *Executive Development*, **1** (2), 8–10.
Slocum, J. W. Jun., Cron, W. L. and Yows, L. C. (1987) Whose career is likely to plateau? *Business Horizons*, March–April, 31–8.
Thody, A. (1993) *Developing Your Career in Education Management*. London: Longman.
Tomlinson, H. (1993) Developing professionals. *Education*, **182** (13), 231.

Chapter 8

The Contribution of Flexibly Delivered Postgraduate Post-experience Programmes to Continuing Professional Development in Interdisciplinary Fields

G. E. Chivers

In the mid-1960s I gained my first experience of adult education by working part-time at a technical college. I was responsible for teaching O-level maths (the main intermediate school qualification) to two groups of mature students (in their early twenties and early thirties), many from the Post Office, who needed the qualification to enable them to progress in the clerical grades of the Civil Service. Many of them had previously taken and repeatedly failed the O-level maths exams, some while at school, although the majority had left school at 15 years old, having sat no O-level exams. All the students were being funded by their employers to attend the college, the younger ones during the daytime as 'day-release' trainees, the older ones in the evening.

Although I tackled the task of teaching the students with enthusiasm (in something of a 'blackboard jungle' atmosphere with the younger ones at times) I found the situation incongruous to say the least. Many of the students also saw the situation they were placed in as laughable, while some seethed with resentment at what they saw as a ludicrous barrier to their career progression, and a total and utter waste of their time. Few of the students needed to utilize any mathematics in their work beyond elementary arithmetic, while none could foresee any future job which would require them to utilize the algebra or geometry which we were required to cover. The fact that most of the students actually passed the O-level maths exams that year, including those who had repeatedly failed before, pleased me, but did not change at all my view of the limitations of the vision of the employer and the college concerning post-experience learning for workers.

If we consider this crass example of a mismatch between the learning needs of workers and the actual provision of learning opportunity, it will reveal much that we can see as desirable about current developments in continuing vocational education towards accredited learning programmes. First, the students were in the classroom at their employers' wishes only; none would have been studying maths of any kind were it not for their work circumstances, and the rules set by their employers at a high level concerning qualifications for career progression. Second, no attempt whatsoever was being made to relate the required learning to the actual needs of their current or prospective work activities. Indeed, it was clear that much of the O-level maths curriculum could have no conceivable relevance to their work. The geometry, which represented one-third of the course and led to a full written examination paper, was especially seen as irrelevant, and not surprisingly most students made little attempt at first to follow my teaching in this area. Short of working out more effective routes for postmen to deliver letters, there was a real difficulty in attempting to illustrate ways in which geometric theorems could be applied to their work. Other matters which caused concern included the fact that the O-level maths book in use had clearly been written for young boys, and was quite unsuitable for these mature learners, who were predominantly women. Often students were absent from class due to work or family commitments, which meant that in a linear subject like maths it was difficult for them to make up lost ground and subsequent classes could become incomprehensible. There was no provision for one-to-one tuition in the programme to deal with such situations, or to offer extra assistance to students who were struggling with particular topics. Some students who had failed the O-level exam with monotonous regularity were by no means weak at maths in class and produced satisfactory homework. They clearly found it difficult to cope with the examination format of the final learning assessment, gaining no credit for course work achievement at that time. However, the interest and motivation of the students to learn greatly increased whenever I could show how the learning could be useful in their work, or in life generally.

It was apparent that the students were having to put a great deal of effort into learning this maths, doubtless at the expense of learning in other areas of real benefit to their employers. It all seemed such a waste of time, effort and money.

THE DEVELOPMENT OF CVE PROVISION

There is no doubt that much has changed in higher and further education and in the minds of employers since the 1960s. But leaving aside those professionally involved with continuing vocational education (CVE), has the world really changed so much? Perhaps not as much as we like to convince ourselves, to judge by the report of James Carmichael of the then Glasgow Polytechnic in 1992. In his study of *An Employer Perspective*, he wrote:

> Many of the organisations concerned had worked with educational organisations, universities, colleges and FE colleges and found that the courses were presented in an inflexible and inappropriate manner. Representations were made to them about changes, but in certain cases they were rejected or ignored.
>
> 'We asked them to change the course, to add some things we would have found useful, and they said they would adjust the course, but when they came back to us and showed us the course outline, it was just the same as before!'
>
> Where this happened, sooner or later, the organisation found another provider that was willing to be flexible, and simply moved their business to them.
>
> (Carmichael, 1992, p. 4)

In regard to courses for management at mid-level or higher, the Carmichael study showed that employers wanted courses which had a practical element to allow learners to 'operationalise theoretical studies, and go back to tutors with questions and problems'. A training manager is quoted as stating: 'There is little use in putting people through standard courses in classrooms. Courses ought to start from where they are: they should be built into their work experience through projects and the like.'

Carmichael (*ibid.*) goes on to quote employers' representatives as stating that:

- 'If the course content was not irrelevant, in many cases little attempt was made to demonstrate relevance.'

- 'The manner of presentation was too "dry" or "academic" in style.'

- 'The tutor sometimes seemed unable or unwilling to respond to questions and points raised by the students.'

- 'Tutors seemed unaware of the needs of the learners.'

- 'Colleges seemed to have little understanding that employers wanted to work with them in real partnership.'

Carmichael finds employers in his study to be aware and enthusiastic about recent developments in higher and further education, which open up possibilities to offer flexibility in learning, and to recognize the importance of learning in the workplace. However, his report points to the long journey we still have to make before we have the responsiveness to the needs of worker-learners and their employers, right across institutions, that CVE professionals would wish. We have made substantial progress in this respect in regard to non-accredited CVE short courses. However, the move towards accreditation of CVE, placing it in the higher education 'mainstream' and taking it further away from the control of CVE professionals, does raise concern about a reversion to traditional 'academic' approaches and values in learning programme development, delivery and assessment.

It is important in this context to bear in mind that the provision of higher level post-experience learning for qualifications, which is vocational in orientation and is often funded by employers, is not new. In particular, the (former) polytechnic sector in the UK has a long and proud tradition of offering part-time vocational degrees via this approach, often following on from initial vocational studies which provide an access route. Not infrequently such study programmes have been organized in conjunction with, or on behalf of, professional bodies. Professional bodies themselves have offered courses leading to their own awards via part-time study to those at work, sometimes involving distance learning by correspondence.

Until recent years the older universities have in general not been a major source of part-time vocational qualification course programmes for those in employment, with the exception of the management area where many part-time diplomas and MBAs have come on stream. Where technological courses have been offered in part-time mode they have often been in traditional disciplinary areas and follow the day-release and evening pattern of attendance. In specialist areas the likelihood of significant numbers of part-time attenders has been reduced by the need to live within reasonable travelling distance of the higher education institution concerned (especially in regard to evening modes of attendance). Very few such courses have been offered off-campus.

This situation contrasts considerably with the American scene. In 1980, Oveson reported that fifty-six universities in the USA were offering substantial numbers of postgraduate 'degree credit' courses, both on-campus and off-campus, for engineers alone. Indeed, his statistics indicated that the fifty-six universities were offering 3486 credit courses in post-graduate engineering with 30,756 participants enrolled. Interestingly, over 50 per cent of these courses were offered off-campus, and almost 40 per cent were taught using (substantially if not wholly) the media of the day: video cassettes, video tapes, television, electronic blackboard and telephone. Moreover, these figures do not include engineers studying for credit in other areas such as management. The UK now seems to be following closely the American pattern of higher education development, albeit with a long time-lag, and it would be surprising if part-time postgraduate vocational study for credit does not become a major feature of the higher education in this country by the end of the century.

THE CASE FOR POSTGRADUATE VOCATIONAL QUALIFICATION COURSES, DELIVERED BY FLEXIBLE METHODS, TO MEET THE NEEDS OF MANAGERS AND PROFESSIONALS

The educational system of England and Wales has long prioritized special-ization and a narrow disciplinary focus, and indeed has established a pernicious science–arts divide. In contrast, within the world of work societal and technological changes are creating demands for new types of profession-als who are at ease with all the dimensions of the workplace – human, organizational and technological. As professionals and managers go forward in their careers they generally take on broader responsibilities which require them to cope with problems that do not recognize disciplinary boundaries. Rapid changes in the workplace are generating demands for new types of expertise which are not reflected within the traditional disciplines. Examples from my own experience include energy management, occupa-tional health and safety management, environmental management in industry, training and development, information technology management, and quality management. Doubtless many other fields of vital importance could be added to this list, all requiring an interdisciplinary approach, and drawing on core knowledge and skills right across the arts–science spectrum.

In his Europe-wide study of senior managers' attitudes towards company learning, Coulson-Thomas (1992) reported that respondents indi-cated over seventy different subjects that they would wish to see included in a formal MBA type programme. In only three cases, namely marketing, human resources and strategy, were the same words used on three or more occasions to describe a subject area. To those of us involved with CVE short course provision the fact that employers seek learning programmes which are very specific, but none the less multi-disciplinary in nature, will hardly be news. However, this diversity of need is as yet poorly reflected in the university provision of post-experience, postgraduate qualification courses. Coulson-Thomas reports cryptically that 'There would appear to be a variety of requirements that are not being met by standard or off-the-shelf programmes.'

This brings us back to the initial case example of O-level maths and Post Office workers. There were doubtless a whole variety of quantitative methods that would have been valuable for GPO clerical workers to learn, especially those aspiring to become managers, but they were hardly likely to be congruent with the contents of an O-level maths textbook. In the same way, the management development needs of experienced managers at work are hardly likely to be covered by non-specific MBA programmes, nor the IT development needs of all engineers to be covered by any particular computer science postgraduate qualification course.

In a study of the role of professional bodies in the development of credit-bearing continuing professional development (CPD), Vaughan (1991) pointed out the role of universities in this respect:

> Higher Education should consider: developing a range of modular awards aimed specifically at the CPD market, especially MSc degrees in technical specialisms and occupation-specific MBAs; being open to collaboration with Professional Bodies acting in the role of broker, joint-provider or organiser; being pro-active in demonstrating to Professional Bodies the potential advantages of Credit Accumulation and Transfer, especially for non-graduate access; streamlining the use of APEL; targeting Professional Bodies with non-graduate admission requirements; and using the publicity networks of Professional Bodies to recruit professionals to new modular CPD courses.

If a statement had been added about flexible delivery modes here, he would have encapsulated much current thinking about the way forward.

CASE EXAMPLES

The two case studies below offer a practical guide to the generation of more flexible, interdisciplinary CVE provision at postgraduate level. They represent significantly different areas of CVE provision, but share the common features of flexibility in delivery mechanisms to suit the needs of adult learners in employment; a firm relationship with and encouragment for learning in the workplace, linked to appropriate assessment methods; commercial success in that the programmes recruit successfully, and ongoing course review and development.

Health and safety management

At Loughborough University, over a five-year period from 1974 to 1979, a substantial programme of short courses was established in the field of occupational health and safety. These courses had a bias towards topics of concern to scientists, engineers and technical managers. Over time a number of course delegates began to appear on more than one course, and the idea of deliberately linking short courses into a coherent study programme for a postgraduate award of the university came to mind. However, it proved difficult to progress a proposal for an award through the university committee system, and as an interim step the Royal Society for the Prevention of Accidents (RoSPA) was approached to offer a qualification

– the RoSPA Licentiateship in Health and Safety Management – for professional level health and safety managers. A programe of five one-week short
courses and home study to be assessed by RoSPA examinations was agreed
to fit the Licentiateship award, and the programme was organized and
marketed on this basis.

Recruitment to the Licentiate programme in the first instance was slow
until an approach was received from ICI Fibres at Harrogate. This division
of ICI was seeking a recognized qualification for its health and safety
managers (full- and part-time). The qualification was to be delivered via
university-level teaching, since all the potential delegates were graduates
and several held doctorates. A first run of the course programme went
ahead with a mix of course members from ICI Fibres and from other companies. In general the course programme was considered satisfactory, but the
RoSPA examination system was regarded as unsuitable for post-experience
learners at the level of seniority involved.

While this first year programme was taking place, the assistance of ICI
Fibres was secured to lobby for the provision of a university award for the
study programme. This proved very effective, not least because ICI stated
that if a postgraduate diploma were awarded, they would send on the next
run of the course programme all the heads of health and safety for each division of ICI. A revised course proposal was finally agreed by the University
Senate, the major change being the replacement of the examinations with
five coursework assignments, one for each short-course study week,
together with a company-based project and project report.

The Diploma in Occupational Health and Safety Management recruited
well from the outset and ICI did indeed place all of its senior managers in
this function on the course. The course programme, offering health and
safety law, physical hazard control, occupational health and hygiene, behavioural sciences and high-level risk management modules, has been held
annually until the present. The lectures, tutorials and small group work are
supported by very extensive sets of up-to-date course notes for each module.
Recruitment has been strong each year, with modest publicity leading to
between twenty-five and thirty delegates, many following up word-of-mouth
recommendations from past course members. Delegates are able to study at
their own pace, and while many complete the course in one year, the weekly,
modular format allows students to decide their own timescale and a two-
year pattern of completion is common. Course members have been drawn
from an ever-widening pool of organizations, and there is now strong representation from the service sector.

A proportion of smaller companies is represented, although the majority
of those attending are still drawn from large, well-known organizations.
Drop-out from the programme has always been surprisingly low, and very

often for non-academic reasons such as job change, illness or family circumstances. The programme requires a substantial amount of reading and in-company investigative work for assignments and the major project. However, basing the coursework on company concerns means it is frequently possible to integrate learning with normal company work. Clearly, the writing up of coursework assignments and the project report involves a great deal of extra work, and a task which many course members find difficult at first. However, the motivation of course members is invariably high and with firm tutor support throughout their studies, and often some support in the workplace, learners rapidly improve the standards of their coursework assignments.

The tutor team for this course programme has from the outset involved a mix of academics and non-academics, and this has been much appreciated by course members. Interestingly, numerous tutors for the current course programme are previous delegates.

The precedent set by this first example of a postgraduate/post-experience study programme based on short courses has been followed up by the introduction of programmes in security management and hazardous waste management, also leading to postgraduate diplomas, and also based on linked short courses. All these programmes operate on self-financing fees (nearly always paid by the employer), covering their full operational costs. The team of full-time tutors has been built up substantially over the years in view of this financial success, and there is now an extensive programme of research and development projects underway at any one time.

Continuing Education

The original Sheffield University course in Continuing Education, leading to a Masters or Diploma, was intended for mid-career professionals, and organized on a full-time and a part-time basis (evenings only). The course covered topics across both continuing education and further education, and course members ranged from those wholly concerned with teaching adults to those largely concerned with teaching young people in the 16- to 19-year-old range.

A review of the course programme revealed that:

- there was not sufficient commonality of concerns between those involved with teaching post-experience adults and those teaching young people to warrant bringing them on to the same course programme;

- in trying to attract those involved with post-compulsory learning in the further education sector, the course competed with expertise offered by another department of Sheffield University, which had strong teaching and research areas related to immediate post-compulsory education;

- the evening study format, based substantially on lectures by expert speakers, did not lead to active participation by the course members, who were invariably tired from their day's work and often a long journey to Sheffield;

- the focus on formal educational institutions as a source of course members had limited the course agenda, and there was scope to recruit adult educators working in a much wider range of informal as well as formal circumstances, ranging from voluntary organizations to the prison service;

- course assessment was based on traditional academic essay writing around theoretical and generalized themes, not involving consideration of workplace practice;

- employer involvement in the programme was low-key.

For these and other reasons it was decided to substantially change the course programme. First, responsibility for coverage of the post-compulsory area was transferred to the Division of Education, which set up a new and distinct Masters/Diploma programme in post-compulsory education.

Second, the course aims and objectives of the Masters/Diploma in Continuing Education were reorientated towards an all-out focus on adult education, and the course content was substantially revamped in terms of curriculum and format. Much more emphasis was placed on the development of practical skills relevant to the workplace. Course sessions were now to include far more group work with less emphasis on the expert speaker. The full-time study mode was left on the agenda, not least because of a trickle of interested applications from overseas. The part-time, three-year course was taken completely out of the evening study mode and a one day a week approach adopted. This was not seen as a formal 'day-release' approach, since the majority of course members worked flexibly, often substantially in the evenings, and did not need to negotiate a day off from work in the conventional sense. Indeed, relatively few part-time students have ever received time off from work, or a significantly reduced teaching load, in view of their involvement in the course.

At the outset the full- and part-time courses were offered separately, but as full-time numbers soon dropped away the two groups of learners have usually studied together. This has been done by teaching the first year part-time students on Tuesday, and the second year part-time students on Thursday, the full-time students taking all their classes on these days, with the remaining weekdays left for one-to-one tutorials and private study. In their third year those students progressing beyond the Diploma level have undertaken a major project, usually based on an important issue for their organization, and have written a 20,000- to 25,000-word dissertation. Success with this work, which is supervised by full-time university staff, leads to the award of the Masters in Continuing Education.

Although many students do complete the Masters course in three years, it is not uncommon for students to extend their studies over four or sometimes five years due to work pressures, job change, illness, etc. Some students wish only to progress to the Diploma stage, while in other cases students are advised to terminate with this award if they are not considered capable of achieving the requirements of the major project and dissertation. The programme encourages applications from non-graduates with substantial experience in adult education, and a number of non-graduates are accepted as course members each year. Those non-graduate students who wish to achieve the Masters degree are nevertheless registered for the Diploma initially, and transfer later to the Masters level if their course progress is deemed sufficiently good to justify this. Although we see this as a sensible precaution, there is in fact scant correlation between the academic qualification background of the students and their longer-term course performance. If anything, by the end of the programme non-graduates tend to slightly out-perform graduates, probably because they are required to have more years of relevant experience, and to some extent the course assessment picks up on their prior experiential learning.

The Continuing Education taught programme is modular in format and is now credit rated. Course assignments are requested for each module, but as the modules are not of equal length and vary greatly in their aims, the nature and extent of the course assignments vary significantly. Unlike the case study of Health and Safety Management, the Continuing Education programme is composed of compulsory 'core' modules, and a choice of optional modules to enable the mature learners to exercise judgement over the most appropriate study programme to meet their own interests and the needs of their employers.

More recently a third mode of study has been introduced, so that it is now possible to study the course entirely by distance learning (although a number of optional day schools are included in the distance learning package). The materials are text-based and are in effect the conventionally taught course converted into distance learning format by the course tutor team. This is now the most popular mode since the recruiting base is the whole of the UK rather than reasonable daily travel distance from Sheffield.

Mixed mode study is available and some part-time students opt to complete some modules in conventional part-time mode and others by distance learning. The availability of topics in distance learning mode means that students on the conventional part-time course who choose a relatively unpopular option can be accommodated via the distance learning materials more easily and cost-effectively than organizing one-to-one tutorials for a whole term.

Cases for the formal accreditation of prior learning, including prior experiential learning, are considered as a matter of policy. However, relatively few numbers of our students seek to be exempted from modules of the Continuing Education programme on this basis, either because the content is all rather new to them or because they have never studied the material at demanding postgraduate level. Where the employer is paying the fee, course members may want to cover the entire course to get full value from their study time. Increasingly, students are being required to pay some of the course fee themselves, while numerous newer students are paying the whole fee. This is sadly inevitable given that most students are drawn from the more impoverished of the public services, such as local authority adult education and social services departments. A large number of students are recruited from the health services, which are in somewhat better financial position to pay the fees, while the Prison Service, the Church and some voluntary organizations are still able to pay the fees (or part of the fees) of their course delegates. Where course members are paying the fees in full, plus the costs of books, travel, and subsistence, it is not surprising that they are particularly demanding in terms of both efficiency and benefits. They may start to press for more course exemption based on accrediting prior learning so that they can complete the course more quickly at lower cost. However, APEL is not without costs which we expect students to cover, and every effort is made to ensure that the standing of the final award is not diminished in any way.

The course fees for the programme are set below self-financing levels, although above current conventional postgraduate fee levels at Sheffield, and the course is partly resourced by the Higher Education Funding Council for England (HEFCE). The CE programme is proving more popular than ever, with recruitment for the current academic year so strong that we may be forced to turn applicants away in the interests of maintaining quality. This may be a reflection of the fee levels, but this is probably not the main reason, since the course is rather more expensive than equivalent competitor courses. More important may be the increasing concern among adult educators to become qualified in the field, and conventional courses are less practicable to take up than our very flexibly delivered study programme. There is good evidence that word-of-mouth recommendations by our past graduates play an important role in recruitment.

LEARNING FROM MY OWN EXPERIENCE

The years of experience of the course programmes described above, and of teaching on a range of CVE qualification courses for other organizations, have led me to develop a number of rules of thought about how best to structure and resource such programmes and market them to employers.

Many of the rules are in line with those developed for organizing short courses, ranging from an emphasis on group work to employing non-academics as course tutors, and from avoiding academic jargon in course brochures and notes to providing attractive course rooms with modern visual aids. In regard to the newer features of assessment and accreditation, I have always felt that conventional approaches leave much to be desired, especially examinations. Much of the real work put in by any learner on a qualification course is geared around the assessment methods, so it is important to pay full attention to these. If we agree that we want courses to be relevant to the workplace, the course work assignments must be drawn from workplace issues. If we see workplace practice as an important part of the course, we must know what learners are doing at work and place value on their experiential learning in accreditation terms. In most cases it must be possible for the learner to conduct new conceptual learning in the workplace where it can be immediately related to practice, and where work colleagues can become involved in the learning. It should be relatively easy for the employer to understand the relevance of the course work assessment to the company's concerns. Ideally, each course work assignment should be in a form which is valuable to the organization, and project reports and dissertations the resolution (in whole or in part) of major company concerns. These personal approaches have now received widespread support from academic colleagues.

Coulson-Thomas (1992) found in his survey that there was little support among employers for examinations, either as a means of selecting programme participants or of assessing how much they had learned. Performance on work-based projects was the preferred method of assessment, at least for management education and development programmes. The most appropriate location for learning in general was thought to be the place of work, and there was considerable support for:

- tailored, company-specific programmes

- courses with a project component

- modular programmes

- an issue-based approach (which implies interdisciplinarity)

- an emphasis on the learner managing her or his studies
- open and distance learning approaches
- portability of credits

Much of this listing, although specifically concerned with management development, accords with my own views concerning university level accredited CVE more generally. I do have reservations about qualification courses that are tailor-made for one employer. In my view it is difficult for young academics to stand up to senior managers of a powerful company in regard to issues of course content, assessment format and the passing standard for individuals, where the one company has financed the whole course development and delivery. In these days of short-term contracts for CVE academic staff the company is in effect underwriting the salaries of the academics involved, and the implications for academic standards are self-evident. Fifty-six per cent of Coulson-Thomas's sample were in support of joint assessment and validation between the academics and the company staff. I have elsewhere extolled the virtues of this approach in principle, in the context of assessing work-based learning where representatives of the employer can play an important role (Chivers and Nixon, 1992). However, based on my experiences in this area, and in involving able industrial trainers in assessment on a qualification course for unemployed managers, I am bound to express scepticism about the commitment and judgement of non-academics in the assessment area at postgraduate/post-experience level. Staff need a great deal of development and experience before they can dispassionately and fairly assess the learning of mature workers whom they are also trying to help through the course programme.

CONCLUSION

Within the field of CVE one of the most significant recent developments has concerned the issue of assessment. In the early days of government pump-priming funding for CVE, university qualification courses, even those involving experienced workers and supported by employers, were virtually disparaged. Development funding was not available to support the growth of CVE courses leading to any kind of qualification.

More latterly, the introduction of credit rating for modules of learning has undermined the rigid divide between qualifications and non-qualification courses. Development funding tied to non-accredited courses found itself swimming against the tide, since learning programmes could be initiated as free-standing short courses and later have credit attached to them. More significantly than this, however, the Employment Department, which had at an earlier stage also campaigned against the rigidity imposed on vocational learning for qualifications by further and higher education requirements in regard to curriculum, learning delivery and assessment, began to turn in favour of learning accreditation. Admittedly, the nature of the learning and accreditation system advocated by the Employment Department, based on competences and NVQs, was hardly congruent with conventional academic approaches, but it nevertheless became impossible for the Department for Education to hold out against support for qualification courses in the CVE field in face of Employment Department policy.

The European Commission's human resource development programmes were started in the 1980s and showed support for qualification and non-qualification CVE programmes alike, provided these were clearly favoured by employers and showed prospects of becoming self-financing for those in employment. Provided that institutions are prepared to be flexible about such matters as fee levels and entry qualifications, and provided that staff are imaginative, market-led and prepared to undergo the staff development needed to cope with interdisciplinary courses offered in flexible ways to post-experience learners, the market is clearly strong. While recruitment to any CVE course is sure to suffer during a severe recession, it is notable that recruitment to the CVE qualification courses presented above as case studies has remained largely satisfactory, while lower recruitment to stand alone short courses has sometimes damaged their viability.

There can be little more satisfying for any university teacher than to see his or her post-experience learners achieve much treasured qualifications, particularly those learners who are non-graduates on entry. To date my proudest moment has involved attending the degree ceremony for Tim, a student whose dissertation I supervised. This student, now a senior manager in a local college, was receiving the M.Ed. in continuing education, having started working life as an apprentice bricklayer after leaving school at minimum leaving age with few exam passes. I know my colleages are equally proud of Eric, who has obtained the same degree with a view to teaching adults to read. Eric did not begin the course until retiring from a lifetime's work in the insurance industry as a salesman. He had no relevant academic qualifications and found every stage of the course demanding, but his tremendous determination and hard work took him through.

Higher education should have much to offer people like Tim and Eric, who in return can offer valuable service to the community. Universities are beginning to provide opportunities for accredited adult education, but much remains to be done in the vocational field. Many of our academic colleagues remain sceptical about interdisciplinarity, about a workplace focus, about the intellectual demands of our CVE courses, about the standard of our learners, and the quality of our part-time teachers and learning materials.

On a personal note, I can state categorically from experience of all types of higher education qualification course over a thirty-year period that postgraduate CVE qualification courses in interdisciplinary fields are the most demanding and the most worthwhile that I have been involved with.

REFERENCES

Carmichael, J. (1992) *Accreditation of In-house Training: Courses and Accreditation of Prior Experiences – An Employer Perspective.* Stirling: University of Stirling.

Chivers, G.E. and Nixon, K. (1992) Some reflections on the issues involved in assessing and accrediting work-based learning at higher education level. *Conference Papers of the 6th National PICKUP Conference for Higher Education.* Nottingham: University of Nottingham.

Coulson-Thomas, C. J. (1992) Integrating learning and work. *Education and Training,* **34** (1), 25–9.

Oveson, N. K. (1980) *Continuing Engineering Education in the United States of America, Advances in the Continuing Education of Engineers.* Paris: UNESCO.

Vaughan, P. (1991) Executive summary to *Maintaining Professional Competence.* Hull: University of Hull.

Chapter 9

Managing Impact at a Distance: Professional Development at the Development and Project Planning Centre

Tom Franks and John Cusworth

Professional development has been one of the main activities at the University of Bradford's Development and Project Planning Centre (DPPC) since its founding in 1969. The Centre was set up at about the time of the establishment of the University itself because the then Vice-Chancellor saw development as one of the main international issues of the day and thought that a new university within the UK should be seen to be addressing the issue. In its early stages the focus of the centre was specifically on training in project planning and analysis, since this was the area in which there was a perceived deficiency among developing country nationals. The training was primarily utilitarian in its function, being designed to upgrade these skills so that the aid process could operate more efficiently. Since its early days the scope of activities in the Centre has broadened, first into project management as an addition to project planning, and second along divergent paths into, on the one hand development policy and on the other, management development. The latter progression into management development has led naturally to a reassessment of the nature of the Centre's training activities and a much greater emphasis on the concept of professional development of the individual, in contrast to the utilitarian approach of the early days.

Professional development training is not the only type of activity undertaken at DPPC. There is also a flourishing postgraduate programme, comprising several development-orientated Masters' courses, a doctoral programme and an active departmental research programme. In addition the Centre undertakes a programme of consultancy, both in the UK and overseas, much of which is also orientated towards professional development training. Nevertheless, the professional development programme remains the major part of the Centre's operations, contributing around 75 per cent of its revenue annually and involving a considerable part of the Centre's staff resources.

Since its establishment, the Centre has run about 190 professional development courses, typically covering a twelve-week period, with a total of around 4000 participants. The participants have to date come from more than a hundred countries, covering all continents but predominantly from Africa and South and East Asia, reflecting aid links between the UK and developing countries. Predictably there is at the moment an increasing number of participants from the countries of Eastern Europe and the former Soviet Union, with certain of the Centre's professional development activities being specifically targeted at the transitional economies. Whether from the east or the south, a typical participant is aged between 35 and 40 years, with a first and higher degree from a home country university, and often with some additional training experience. He or she normally works for a government department or in a parastatal organization, though an increasing number of private-sector employees are gaining access to official training funds, in a reflection of a shift in development paradigms.

It can thus be seen that this type of professional development activity is set firmly within the aid business and its style and content has evolved to fit the context of aid. DPPC and its sister institutions, of which there are many in the UK, have therefore traditionally worked within a well-established format of twelve-week courses, originally designed to fit the UK's policy that most training funds should be directed towards courses of this length so that participants should both have time to assimilate the course material and to benefit from extended exposure to the UK. This format is also subject to change as development processes change – even within the UK there is now a large number of training awards of shorter duration for specific purposes – but for the moment, twelve weeks remains the normal length of a course. However, in an effort to accommodate participants from non-UK agencies who are funded for shorter durations, many of the DPPC courses are now modularized so that participants can benefit from attending only parts of them.

Other recent developments within the Centre's operations include a pilot twelve-week course which allows for appropriately qualified study fellows to opt into a formal assessment scheme that results in their being awarded a university postgraduate certificate as opposed to the normal certificate of attendance that is issued to non-assessed fellows. The merits or otherwise of this approach to professional development are discussed more fully later in this chapter.

STRENGTHS AND WEAKNESSES OF THE PROFESSIONAL DEVELOPMENT PROCESS

The type of professional development training that has evolved at DPPC has always had many strengths, though some weaknesses are also apparent.

First and foremost among the strengths is the opportunity such training provides for participants to gain additional professional knowledge and skills in a short time and within a supportive learning environment. This is represented through the skills and experience of the centre's staff, most of whom have extensive operational as well as academic experience, a specialist library dedicated to development topics and a mass of case studies, handouts and interactive teaching material. A second major benefit derives from the diverse and international experience which such training permits. This not only widens study fellows' appreciation of the range of problems and possible solutions in aspects of their working life but also encourages them to think more broadly of their work, its role in development, and ways to improve in the future. Participants sometimes articulate the reverse of this position – 'because this happens in country X, it is not relevant to what happens to me in my country Y' – but are generally persuaded of the educational and developmental benefits of learning about different situations and approaches.

Related to this aspect of professional development at a distance is the fact that the training takes place away from the workplace and in an academic institution. In practical terms this is necessary because of the length of the courses. It is difficult to envisage how such courses could be run at or near the workplace: many of the participants are commonly under a great deal of pressure at work (public institutions in many developing countries are being continually reduced in size, without a corresponding reduction in workload), and would be unable to devote themselves fully to a twelve-week full-time development programme. Being physically removed from the workplace over a long distance means that they can concentrate fully on the training experience and everything that goes with it. In addition DPPC has the advantage of being located within a university. This allows fellows access to other university departments and to facilities such as the main university library in addition to its own very well-stocked development library. This gives the participants the chance to follow through intellectual approaches to the practical problems of development more widely; the professional development experience can then be seen not merely as a process of upgrading skills but as also addressing matters of knowledge and attitude which make it potentially an education as well as a training.

These twin advantages of internationalism and separation from the workplace are recognized by Brinkerhoff and Goldsmith (1992, p. 380):

> strategic options [include] long-term overseas training. For technical institutions, the formation of a critical mass of trained personnel can promote institutional sustainability. A major

reason is the development of high performance organisational cultures, besides the introduction of new skills.

The advantages are also evidenced by the commitment of participants to the training process. The great majority of the participants take the courses very seriously, even when conditions in their own countries are not propitious for their subsequent application on their return, and they are prepared to put in long hours to get the best benefit they can. This seems to hold true even in situations where there is almost complete political and social breakdown, where it would be reasonable to expect a degree of detachment and inattention. For example, four participants from the Yemen attended courses at DPPC during the period of the civil war there. It was surprising just how committed these study fellows were to their courses despite all the anxiety that they experienced due to the situation at home.

The advantages of professional development at a distance are nevertheless offset by a related set of weaknesses. These weaknesses all stem from the basic inability of the trainers to be on hand to follow up the professional development process. Once the participants return to their place of work they no longer enjoy the support of trainers and colleagues on the course but instead must work on their own to try to put into practice whatever they have learned. Often this is not easy.

An evaluation of DPPC training was undertaken with a group of participants in Bangladesh (Franks, 1992). The evalution took place in Dhaka, and was attended by around twenty participants who had taken part in professional development courses in Bradford previously, some of them up to eight years before. All had enjoyed the training experience in Bradford and felt very positively about it, though of course they had suggestions for improvement. Typical remarks were that 'the courses were well designed with respect to content as well as relevance to developing countries' yet at the same time they 'provided an opportunity to see how things are done in a developed country'. Main areas for improvement included greater emphasis on case studies relative to lectures and the need to inform study fellows in advance of the course of its content and programme. The post-training experience, however, was often not so successful. While many participants still looked on it quite positively with comments such as 'my confidence and efficiency were increased' and 'I was able to use the methodologies satisfactorily', all had found it difficult in one way or another. Two main reasons seem to emerge from the questionnaires and discussions. The first was a lack of real opportunity to try to put into practice their newly acquired skills and knowledge. Most found this difficult even if they returned to their previous work situation. Often, however, civil service procedures resulted in transference to a new post which had little relationship to the previous post held and for which the professional development training had been intended. Ironically this sometimes happened while the participant was actually undergoing the training, so that there was no chance whatever either to use the training themselves or to pass it on to others for whom it might be appropriate. Naturally this caused a great deal of frustration. The second reason for dissatisfaction was a lack of support from superiors and colleagues in trying to utilize and build on the professional development training. This manifested itself in ignorance, indifference and sometimes hostility, all understandable reactions in those who were not fortunate enough to undergo the programme, but nevertheless regrettable if the training was to be of value in human resource development.

Underlying both these responses are deep-rooted organizational dysfunctions which a professional development programme must help to combat over the long term. These dysfunctions stem from the nature of the public sector organizations from which the majority of participants come, with their reliance on traditional hierarchical structures and bureaucratic procedures. Handy (1981) describes the culture of such organizations, and his observations are extended by Franks (1989) to the specific case of developing country bureaucracies. Typically such organizations place emphasis on role rather than person and assume that systems will function effectively and mechanistically. Promotion and responsibility are therefore made with little reference to the individual's talents, experience and training, resulting in inappropriate transfer and a failure to make good use of professional development programmes. Similarly, the assumption of effective functioning means that bureaucracies punish failure but do not reward success, thus providing further powerful motivation for returned participants to keep a low profile and not to try any improvements or innovations for fear of failure and sanction. In many ways, therefore, professional development programmes have an important but difficult task, because the whole concept of professional (and, by extension, personal) development fits rather uneasily with the Weberian concept of bureaucracy, worthy as that may be in public sector organizations where equity, accountability, sustainability and openness are important attributes.

CURRENT PRACTICE

The DPPC approach to professional development has evolved to try to build on the strengths and to counteract the weaknesses described. First, use is made of the participants' commitment to foster an environment which is conducive to adult learning. Emphasis is placed on sharing experiences, and the use of case studies and seminars to develop open and flexible approaches to problem-solving. Effective group working is a prerequisite for this process to be successful, since it is the participants who bring the experiences with them and who need to be able to put them across successfully to their colleagues. In the early stage of courses considerable effort is therefore made to promote productive group work through the use of such exercises as 'broken squares', 'legoman' and the like, as well as a careful programme of introductions and scene-setting. Emphasis is also given to creating an awareness of the different values that people are guided by as a means to developing a learning environment that is dominated by mutual respect and support.

Most professional development courses follow a pattern broadly along the lines that are described by Analoui and Cusworth (1991). This is based on the precept that learning in the context of professional development is best founded on a 'process' approach which involves a sequence moving from 'ice-breaking' through understanding individuals' frames of reference and value systems, self-awareness exercises, development of learning objectives, guided learning, monitoring of progress to structured planning for return to the workplace. Course design is something to which individual course directors pay much attention. However, in addition to the academic structure and content of courses the learning process at Bradford is supported by associated activities designed to facilitate social interaction and openness among the community of study fellows. Newly appointed staff from more traditional academic departments have expressed their surprise at the frequency of social events associated with most courses. This deliberate policy fosters close relationships among both fellows and staff and helps to break down perceptions of hierarchy that most study fellows bring with them by way of memories from their previous formal education. Furthermore, many fellows are quite senior people in their own institutions and it is important that they do not gain an impression that they are returning to a university environment on the same basis as undergraduates. This could create problems regarding status which would almost certainly inhibit the learning process.

A further aspect of adult learning is the inclusion in most courses of an individual study programme. This is accommodated through the regular setting aside of course time for the individual study (which has a pragmatic benefit in making time for staff meetings and other activities), resulting in the production and presentation of a paper on some aspect of the course of specific interest to the individual. The specification of the individual study paper is that it could not have been written by the participant while in the workplace, so that new sources and references must be used, and the participants are in particular encouraged to make full use of the Centre's library and other sources of information such as local institutions and businesses. Individual study therefore takes on something of the nature of an academic paper and, while the standard of the papers submitted is very variable, it does foster the concept of lifelong learning which is very much part of the vocabulary of professional development.

Many of the management courses within the Centre's portfolio make extensive use of approaches to self and personal development described in Pedler (1986). Cross-cultural differences are naturally a matter of interest, and sometimes concern, when working with those from developing countries, but the type of approach described by Pedler seems in general to make sense to the majority of participants, and allows them to strengthen their ideas of self and personal development in a way which can contribute to their professional development. Part of the problem of the bureaucratic culture lies in the perception that members of the organization must develop their professional skills and knowledge to the greatest possible extent because this is required for the smooth functioning of the bureaucratic machine, but that they have no autonomy over their own careers and working lives. The processes of management and self-development described in Pedler help to counteract these perceptions and will, it is hoped, lead in the long run to more rounded and capable individuals.

Likewise, communication skills have become an integral part of the professional development experience. Many of the courses include extensive sessions on communication within interpersonal skills as an integral part of management development. Even the courses which are not explicitly management-oriented generally include some time on presentations and communication. This has two benefits, first within the course itself in aiding the process of sharing experiences and working in groups, and second back at the workplace in giving participants confidence to be able to put across ideas to colleagues, superiors and outsiders. It is noticeable how presentation skills among professionals in the UK have improved over the last few years, as they begin to realize that technical skills alone are no longer sufficient if they are to take a full part in social and political processes. A similar movement is now being experienced in developing countries and many of the participants now recognize, albeit sometimes reluctantly, the need to be effective presenters as part of their professional skills.

This emphasis on presentational skills is not, however, simply confined to verbal presentation. Many courses include modules on report and memorandum writing which reflect the need for senior professionals to communicate effectively on paper. This is particularly so in an age where information technology has been introduced in almost all working environments. In fact all courses now include modules on basic computing skills primarily designed to assist participants to gain confidence in their ability to operate in a work environment increasingly dominated by the IT revolution. This appears to be of particular benefit to female study fellows who are often inhibited in many developing country institutions from becoming involved with information technology at levels other than keyboard operators.

Finally, extensive use is also made of 'returning to work' modules, in which the participants explicitly confront the problems that await them in the post-training experience. This is done through a mixture of seminars and discussions, but use is also made of theoretical approaches such as the concepts of transition (Adams *et al.*, 1976). By this means false expectations can be dispelled and a sense of realism established. 'Returning to work' is not, however, only concerned with lowering expectations. An important part of the professional development process at DPPC is to draw on international experience and a body of academic theory and yet at the same time make it relevant to the situation in the workplace. Returning to work modules can therefore also be used to explore this relevance and to encourage participants not to distinguish the training experience (relevant only to the lecture room) from real life.

FUTURE TRENDS

In beginning to think about the future, it is salutary to remember that the whole concept of professional development is itself comparatively new. Indeed, only in the recent past has it been taken up on a widespread scale even within the UK; for instance, professional institutions such as the Institution of Civil Engineers have started to utilize the idea only within the last few years, and in developing countries the concept is newer still. Thus DPPC and its sister institutions have only recently begun to use the words 'professional development programme' instead of 'training courses' or similar, and are therefore still in the process of introducing the ideas to their customers and clients. Overseas, therefore, professional development faces an uncertain but interesting future, both in the developing and transitional economies. The market is large but very competitive; many new professional development needs are being identified and new providers are constantly entering the market including local and regional centres offering high quality programmes.

One important strand in this changing situation is the growth in project-related and project-funded training. Increasingly, development projects have training funds attached to them, sometimes as a large proportion of the total project costs. These funds are earmarked for professional development and training which is specifically targeted at project staff and for project activities, thus avoiding what has been called the 'scatter-gun' approach of earlier training initiatives identified with more general programmes of ministries. Project-related training should help to overcome the problems of transference and lack of positive follow-up identified by participants such as those at the Dhaka seminar, and help to improve the management of the professional development process in these situations.

This projectization of training programmes is associated with a broader change in development priorities that includes an emphasis on institution building and, more recently, organization development. Sustainable development is now associated with strong institutions operating in a relatively open and democratic system of government and economy. The strength of any institution is largely dependent on the calibre of the people working within it and therefore, increasingly, certain institutions are targeted for support by governments and funding agencies. Alternatively, specific levels of officials across a range of institutions are targeted in an attempt to build a cadre of professionals who, while operating in different institutions, are able to work effectively together through formal and informal networks by having a degree of shared experience through a common process of professional development. Each of these will necessitate different approaches to the design of their respective professional development programmes in the future.

A second strand is the as yet unresolved trade-off between short, highly focused professional development courses and the demand for longer courses with a formal qualification, such as Masters' courses. The value of qualifications is not in doubt: the value of long academic courses is more questionable, given the problems of transference and acceptability which pertain even with short courses. One way of addressing the problem is to apply professional development approaches to postgraduate programmes. Another is through the certification of professional development courses, an approach which is already being tried at DPPC on a pilot scale. In this case one of the portfolios of DPPC's standard twelve-week courses has been included within a university certification scheme, involving different entry requirements and an extensive assessment procedure. The advantages and disadvantages of this approach are yet to be fully evaluated. On the one hand, certification provides a measure of quality control, a powerful set of incentives for the participants and an element of standardization of qualifications. On the other hand, the need for assessment constrains the flexibility that is such a potentially valuable aspect of traditional professional development courses, in which the director and course members can steer the event in new directions as seem appropriate at the time. Formal assessment is, moreover, very time consuming, both within the course itself and for the participants' out of course time.

The aspect of certification raises the twin concerns of quality control and assessment. The professional development process, because of its flexibility and client orientation, needs to be particularly aware of the need to adopt and maintain high standards – within the UK there appear to be welcome signs of this awareness, as evidenced by the report of the Universities' Association for Continuing Education (UACE) (de Wit, 1993). Likewise there is a need to refine the process of assessment, to make the whole procedure more meaningful to the participant. In this regard self-assessment seems to have particular potential, because it can apply to *all* participants. Whatever their level of understanding at the start, or whatever aspect of the training process happens to interest or be relevant to them, self-assessment can show them that learning has taken place. This in turn leads to the type of autonomous learning individual which professional development seeks to produce.

Besides new markets and new procedures, institutions such as DPPC are becoming increasingly involved in new approaches to the whole process of professional development in developing countries. At the present time, this commonly incorporates a phased approach, as shown in Figure 9.1, encompassing an initial planning visit, training in the UK, a visit to a third country, and a final round-up and evaluation visit back in the client country.

The planning visit is used to set up the elements of the professional development process, to make sure that it is relevant to the needs of the client institution and its professionals and to engender a positive learning attitude in the participants. The training period in the UK can follow a variety of patterns, most of which have been successful in many different situations; these range from academically oriented programmes to programmes which consist of a number of attachments to suitable host institutions in the UK, or a combination of the two. For instance, a recent programme designed to train women for senior positions in the Bangladesh Civil Service took place partly at DPPC and partly through attachments to suitable locations with central and local government. Thus UK funded professional development training increasingly also includes a period in a third country: this idea has been around for some time but was given firm shape in a report to the UK's Overseas Development Administration

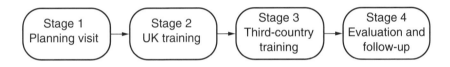

Figure 9.1   Professional development overseas

(Iredale, 1992), which strongly advocated the idea of third country training (3CT). As in example, the Bangladesh women's programme is spending some time in Malaysia in order to investigate parallel or complementary approaches to women's development. On a larger scale DPPC and a sister institution in Birmingham are involved in a programme for Kenyan senior officers which involves exposure to administrations in other parts of Africa, as well as a visit to the UK. This programme contains several of the key innovations currently being adopted, and the experience of running five such courses since 1989 has provided the Centre with an opportunity to evaluate some of them. The value of careful forward planning and the need to identify precisely the training requirements are essential steps in the process. 3CT can prove most effective in introducing new ideas to study fellows but there is a clear danger that unless the 3CT is properly focused on the real needs of the fellows, the process will become no more than an expensive example of development tourism. In addition, such courses require a consolidation or follow-up phase during which lessons learned may be evaluated against the actual working context of the study fellows.

The follow-up phase, which may take the form of a visit to the country by the trainers, draws the whole experience together for the participants, encouraging them to reflect on the process and relate it back to their working situation. Ideally, the follow-up visit takes place some time after the overseas visits have been completed and the participants have had time to be assimilated back into the working environment. This could be between three to six months later, at a time when reinforcement of the ideas of the professional development process can be particularly useful. The phased approach, while having the obvious disadvantage that it is a more lengthy and costly undertaking, has advantages in seeking to combine the best of the traditional approaches to professional development (which are largely based on the opportunity for the participants to detach themselves from the day-to-day preoccupations of their working and living environment) with the opportunity for the course director to be more actively involved in the management of the process and in particular to try to counteract some of the worst influences of the post-training experience. In this way the director comes to assume in part the role of an organization development consultant in seeking to bring about positive organizational change.

As an example of developing this approach, the Centre has over the last two years established close working relationships with the organizations from which a number of study fellows have been drawn. The idea is to involve senior management in the process of management development by targeting them for specialist training in the first instance or at least involving them in the selection of staff designated for training and in determining the purpose and nature of the training. Once they have developed an awareness of the need for managing change within their organizations they are more likely to become actively involved in the whole process of management development within their organizations and so foster a climate within which newly developed skills and knowledge acquired through training can be more effectively utilized.

Such positive organizational change is surely one of the main goals of the professional development programme in developing countries. Other approaches are being tried and there are many successful measures being implemented locally. The role of institutions such as Bradford University is likely to continue to be concentrated on the broader educational aspects of overseas exposure and training, and the strategies just described provide a fruitful way to progress for the time being.

REFERENCES

Adams, J., Hayes, J. and Hopkins, B. (1976) *Transition: Understanding and Managing Personal Change*. London: Martin Robertson.

Analoui, A. and Cusworth, J. (1991) Making management training more effective: towards an interventionist approach. *Teaching Public Administration*, **11** (2).

Brinkerhoff, D. W. and Goldsmith, A. A. (1992) Promoting the sustainability of development institutions: a framework for strategy. *World Development*, **20** (3), 369–83.

Franks, T. R. (1989) Bureaucracy, organisation culture and development. *Public Administration and Development*, **9**, 357–68.

Franks, T. R. (1992) *Seminar for Bradford Participants* (mimeo). Dhaka: The British Council.

Handy, C. B. (1981) *Understanding Organisations*. Harmondsworth: Penguin.

Iredale, R. (1992) *The Power of Change*. London: ODA.

Pedler, M., Burgoyne, J. and Boydell, T. (1986) *A Manager's Guide to Self Development*. Maidenhead: McGraw-Hill.

Wit, P. de (1993). *Approaches to Good Practice in Quality Assurance in University Continuing Education*, UACE Working Paper No. 3. Birmingham: Universities Association for Continuing Education.

Chapter 10

Workplace Enquiry as a Strategy for Personal and Organizational Development

Roger Aspland

Provision for continuing professional development in the field of management education currently appears to lack a clear sense of coherence and continuity. The need for the development of management expertise is well recognized, and the increasing range of providers including in-house training departments, commercial training and consultancy providers, professional organizations, government sponsored agencies and higher education testify to the growth of professional development activity. However, there appear to be a number of different philosophies informing this development and, in an increasingly competitive environment, a lack of debate across agencies about principles and practice for effective and sustained professional development.

Elliott (1993) describes three alternative philosophical perspectives – rationalist, 'social market' and practical science – which may underpin the design and delivery of professional development. Each of these perspectives holds different implications for the relationship between theory and practice, and for the process of continuing professional development.

THE RATIONALIST VIEW

This view has been perhaps most fully realized in the traditional practices of higher education, reflected not least in assessment procedures. The principal characteristic of the rationalist perspective is the assumption that good practice derives from the conscious application of theoretically sound principles. The means of professional development entails the acquisition of established theoretical understandings. Equipped with such knowledge, the rational autonomous professional can then seek to apply them in the workplace.

THE 'SOCIAL MARKET' VIEW

This view is informed by the production–consumption ideology of contemporary society, and has rapidly gained ascendancy over the rationalist view in many training programmes during the past decade. It is characterized by defining development in terms of specified behavioural outcomes, frequently identified as competences. Such competences are usually drawn from the atomistic identification of the skills and knowledge needed to undertake a particular role or occupational function. Since theory relates to inputs rather than outcomes, its role within this view is purely instrumental; neither is the process of learning especially significant. What is required is that the learner demonstrates competence against the specified criterion behaviour.

Within this social market perspective the concept of continuing professional development broadly equates with training in an additional repertoire of skills and knowledge commensurate with new, more varied and demanding occupational roles. The direct linkage with observable/measurable outcomes renders this approach particularly attractive to purchasers, heavily reinforced by the economic and social meta-values of efficiency and value for money.

Given the specification of required knowledge and skills, professional development activity may be located either within or outside the working context, though there is a heavy if not unproblematic emphasis on the capacity to demonstrate competence within the workplace for assessment purposes. Development of the social market view impacts heavily on the role of higher education in the provision of CPD. The traditional HE role as creator and disseminator of theoretical knowledge becomes largely redundant.

THE PRACTICAL SCIENCE VIEW

This view has been evolving over the past two decades, stimulated by the phenomenological movement in the social sciences, and given added impetus by influential ideas on experiential learning (Kolb, 1984) and reflective practice (Schon, 1987) which have been picked up by many organizations concerned with CPD. This view seeks to reformulate the relationship between theory and practice. Unlike the rationalist view, it is argued that practice is not derived from formal theory; neither is theory simply translated into behavioural outcomes. The practical science view argues that professional practice is derived from situational understanding. This principle implies that practice is developed through a holistic interpretation and analysis of the specific 'real world' circumstances of the workplace. The generation of more generalized theory is grounded in, and develops from action taken on the basis of situational understanding. The essence of this approach is to seek holistic rather than partial understanding. Such understanding can only be developed in the context of actual workplace experience. Within this view the emphasis therefore shifts from applying theory to practice, to that of developing theoretical insights based on practice and experience.

Of course established theory can play an important part in developing awareness and analysis of some features in a given situation, but only inasmuch as it might provide lines of enquiry or hypotheses worth testing in practice. It is necessary also to recognize the essential technical knowledge and skills required in the effective conduct of professional roles. The three distinctive philosophies can therefore be seen as complementary rather than mutually exclusive.

The major arguments for seeking an accommodation between these approaches must rest on the twin issues of relevance and transferability. The 'rational' view of theory-driven professional learning, with content usually determined by the provider, struggles and often fails to establish itself on either criteria. Primarily it suffers from an inability to encompass the sheer complexity and multi-dimensionality of work situations. While competence-based social market approaches have a direct relevance to occupational technologies, they are by their very nature locked into currently identified skills and knowledge, and largely untransferable to meet emergent, value-laden and often conflicting needs of uncertain situations. Their major limitations relate to those areas of professional functioning which are dependent primarily on the exercise of judgement rather than technical competence.

Used exclusively, both the rational and social market models present potential difficulty in seeking to develop flexible and adaptable professionals capable of exercising judgement in uncertain situations. In representing learning as the acquisition of established knowledge and skills there is a danger of, first, reinforcing the view that for each situation there is a 'right' course of action, and second, generating a sense of dependency on 'experts' as providers of solutions rather than a disposition towards problem-solving and self-development.

A 'PRACTICAL SCIENCE MODEL' FOR PROFESSIONAL DEVELOPMENT

Schon (1987) uses the term 'professional artistry' to describe the capacity displayed by expert practitioners in dealing with unique, complex and problematic situations. He argues that in creating appropriate responses, experienced professionals do not engage in abstract rationalizations nor recall and apply theoretical propositions. Rather, they appear intuitively or reflectively to compare current situations with those in their past experience to produce adaptive responses. This process both recognizes the significant features of situations and synthesizes them into a holistic awareness. 'Professional artistry', the exercise of wise professional judgements and decisions in uncertain situations, rests on the situational understanding which they embody.

However, such professional artistry does not spring up ready formed, nor for most people does experience alone necessarily ensure its development. Indeed, experience is also the nursery of the routinized actions which enable us to carry out our day-to-day work quickly and efficiently, but also lock us into habitual patterns of behaviour which are very difficult to change. The aim of CPD programmes grounded in the practical science view is systematically to foster and support the development of professional artistry. This aspiration centres on the conscious development of reflective practice through experience of workplace situations.

The model of professional development which we have cultivated in our programmes accepts that much professional behaviour involves practical action in situations which are both unique in their specific characteristics, and inherently problematic, unstable and value laden. In such situations decisions about action must be based on judgement rather than technical competence, since any number of alternative courses of action may be available to the practitioner. It is for this reason that the focus for the practical science model of CPD rests squarely in the study of actual workplace situations and problems in which the learner is involved.

Making intelligent decisions about action entails the development of situational understanding. Dreyfus (1981) has developed a helpful schema of the stages by which holistic situational understanding and decision-making might develop, from early occupational experience of the novice through to the expert performance of the skilled practitioner. His ideas stem from a dissatisfaction with the rational/scientific process of formal modelling of management activity. Much management education, he argues, fails to recognize let alone accommodate the unstructured nature which characterizes the context of decision-making about action.

Dreyfus suggests that situational understanding involves four mental capacities, each of which undergoes a qualitative change in capability as expertise is developed, moving from a simple to a more sophisticated form. The capacities are as follows:

Component recognition – in which the simple form involves attending to the objective non-situationally specific attributes of a situation; that is, those things which remain relatively constant and predictable within a general task environment. For example, when driving a car non-situational components may be such things as awareness of speed, gear or specifiable rules about procedures and places for overtaking, etc. The more sophisticated form requires recognition of the occasionally occurring features in specific situations, such as a child chasing a ball on the pavement. This situation may involve a complex set of judgements involving the age of the child, the nature of the child's activity and whereabouts of the ball, traffic conditions, the available avoidance possibilities, etc. While the former objective attributes are susceptible to formal modelling and routinization, handling the latter situationally specific components can only be learned by experiencing a range of real situations. What is important is the recognition that both sets are necessary for effective performance.

Most situations in the professional/managerial task environment involve both non-situational and situationally specific components, both stable and uncertain elements.

Salience recognition – relates to the significance of the various situational components relative to achieving a particular purpose or goal. The capacity to discriminate between those components of a situation which are important in terms of goal achievement and those which are not represents a second stage in the acquisition of practical expertise. The learner needs to develop understanding of what it is in any given situation which needs to be taken into account.

Inasmuch as some salient components may be objective and non-situational, rational/mechanistic models of decision-making may be a basis for appropriate action. But where salient components are unpredictable and situationally specific, the capacity to take effective action is dependent again on the cumulation of experience in order to make intelligent judgement.

Holistic recognition – the development of component and salience recognition in its preliminary stages requires the deconstruction of workplace situations through an analytical approach to experience. The variables are then reconstructed into a synthesis of the whole situational context as a basis for decisions about intelligent action. In parallel with Schon, Dreyfus argues that increasing experience provides a series of holistic mental 'templates' against which the current situation can be matched, and that this takes on the characteristics of an intuitive, rather than an analytical process.

Decision-making – even when the capacity for an intuitive understanding of situations has developed, decision-making may still involve a conscious and rational consideration of possible alternative courses of action. The final element in the practical wisdom evident in expert performance reflects a shift from rational to intuitive decision-making. 'Expert' decision-making implies that the choice of action flows intuitively from a holistic understanding of situations.

Dreyfus uses the development of these four capacities to map a series of progressive stages of development from 'novice' to 'expert performer' (see Table 10.1).

Table 10.1   Capacities for situational understanding

Stage (experience)	Component recognition	Salience recognition	Holistic recognition	Decision-making
Novice	non-situational	none	analytic	rational
Beginner	situational	none	analytic	rational
Competent	situational	present	analytic	rational
Proficient	situational	present	intuitive	rational
Expert	situational	present	intuitive	intuitive

IMPLICATIONS FOR CONTINUING PROFESSIONAL DEVELOPMENT

We need not be too concerned with the apparent precision with which Dreyfus characterizes stages in the development of expert performance. However, the concepts embodied in the development of situational understanding are useful in informing thinking about the CPD process, not least the debate between the 'social market/competency' model and the 'practical science' view of professional learning.

It could be argued that the behavioural competency model might be most appropriately geared to the 'simple' form of the four mental capacities, in particular offering a basic capacity to function within a given task environment at the novice/beginner end of the continuum. Given that basic capacity to function, the emphasis of CPD progressively shifts to the requirement systematically to learn from the basis of experience of the situations in a particular task environment.

In our attempts to apply this notion of professional development in a number of different course contexts it is not difficult to recognize the need to match programme content and structure to the developmental stage of the learners. In particular it is easy to underestimate the extent to which the capacity to exercise judgement in situations is dependent upon a degree of individual competence and confidence in basic operational knowledge and skills. But a simple sequential notion involving, first, the acquisition of formal aspects of knowledge and skills, followed by an increasing expectation of flexible applications geared to situational variables, is problematic. First, as can be seen from the 'learning to drive' analogy, in most complex activity the elements which can usefully be acquired as formal routinized techniques may actually be relatively few. Second, even these elements are usually contextually dependent, and their applications involve some degree of situational understanding which needs to be developed simultaneously. Third, learning is never discrete, but is always dependent on the previously acquired knowledge and experience, whether structured and intentional or informal and accidental. It is not always easy to anticipate and accommodate the variety of prior learning, experience and individuality which people bring to the development process.

But perhaps the most serious problem in presenting basic skills and knowledge as technical/formal relates to the development of a mindset and expectation of dependency upon prescribed technical answers to situations, rather than a tolerance of ambiguity and the development of adaptability and autonomy. The CPD student is often left in a vacuum. On the one hand, the culture of the manager's working context usually reinforces what Garratt (1987) calls an 'action fixated non-learning cycle' in which action rather than reflection is valued, and 'being right' is assumed. On the other, the traditional-style provision of CPD purveys 'expert' skills and principles to be learned and applied. Both of these tend to encourage students to accept 'right' ideas passively and uncritically. Neither adequately prepares them to function more effectively in a workplace where practical experience is made up of the problematics of 'real' decisions about action. When such learned dependency is established as a mindset it can create great difficulty – both for the learner and the provider of CPD – in seeking to develop flexibility and the exercise of judgement.

Against this background the process of action-oriented workplace enquiry forms the central element of the programmes which we have been developing over recent years. Adopting this as the substantive focus allows a number of characteristic features for our various programmes:

- developing the skills and analytical capabilities for situational understanding;

- developing communicative and relationship skills required to exercise influence;

- potential for impact of learning within the work organization.

DEVELOPING SITUATIONAL UNDERSTANDING

Many contemporary programmes of CPD, especially those offered in higher education, contain elements of reflective practice often associated with the production of some form of assessed written work. A major problem for course designers exists in the tension between structured course content – that conceptual knowledge and competence relating to the occupational function – and the process of systematic and rigorous enquiry and analysis necessary for the development of situational understanding. The standard design solution usually reflects a pragmatic balance between substantive content and the student-led process of workplace enquiry. Students are invited to convert this directed content into a situational enquiry by way of workplace evaluation, case study or possibly action research project. While some guidance is usually offered in the conduct and write-up of these enquiries, such projects are perhaps usually subsidiary to the progress of the content syllabus.

In our experience this formulation, while going some way to address the issue of relevance and practical impact, often fails to establish the capability in handling qualitative workplace enquiry which is necessary for the establishment of personal and professional confidence in situational understanding, and in developing theoretical insights grounded in experience. In our current programmes we are attempting to shift this balance by focusing more systematically and rigorously on developing the skills and techniques of workplace enquiry and analysis.

The various techniques for gathering qualitative data through interviews, questionnaire, structured and unstructured observation, audio and video recording and the compilation of research diaries and field notebooks are well established. For experienced researchers the use of such tools takes on a commonplace quality which belies many of the difficulties experienced by the novice. Not only does the use of such tools require practice if they are to be handled effectively, but they reflect a qualitative way of thinking about situations which suspends one's established ways of looking and thinking, and imbues the researcher with a sense of curiosity, to see the familiar in an unfamiliar light. This latter point may be crucial. Many reflective studies undertaken as part of CPD programmes begin with a preordinate research question or problem which the students bring from their work context. Data gathering is then designed and implemented to illuminate that problem. However, this process largely assumes a degree of certainty as to the nature of the problem or the appropriateness of the research question which limits at the outset the willingness and capacity to review situations holistically. In our experience it is highly desirable to undertake a broadly based reconnaissance phase of observation and data gathering as a basis for identifying the specific focus for a planned enquiry. While most experienced managers believe that they are aware of the inter-personal dynamics and problematics of their workplace, this is not necessarily borne out in practice once an enquiring stance is adopted. Typically students are exposed to some degree of destabilization in their accepted understandings.

> 'I was amazed, and slightly ashamed at what began to emerge once I started to listen and think about what people were saying, just in ordinary conversation. I thought I knew my staff quite well and that they felt really open about talking to me.' (headteacher, MA course)

> 'Starting to look carefully at how [interdepartmental communi-cation] actually worked was a real eye-opener for me. I began to see the organization in a completely different light. We have all this structure of meetings and regular briefings, but in fact that's not where things get decided at all.' (departmental manager, MBA course)

What begins to emerge is a different form of data from that which typically constitutes the formal concerns of managers. Rhodes and Thame (1988) make the useful distinction between hard and soft ideas and information which managers use in thinking about their work. They argue that much of the managerial culture and operation is concerned with hard elements – with facts, figures, structures, formal principles and procedures as rational influences on action. These hard elements constitute the accepted 'stuff' of formal or rational models of management. General reconnaissance, and more systematic qualitative enquiry involving people and social processes in the workplace, serve by contrast to highlight the soft aspects of organiza-tions concerning people's experiences, ideas, feelings and values, which are often ignored or dismissed as uncomfortable irrelevance in formal models. But it is often these soft qualitative components of situations, and their salience, which constitute the real problematics of work situations, identifi-cation of which leads to a degree of provisionality in interpreting situations. Reconnaissance and gathering data is therefore fundamental to component and salience recognition, developing situational understanding which breaks the bounds of habitual ways of knowing and doing, and encouraging the formulation of worthwhile lines of structured and systematic enquiry as a basis for making intelligent judgements about action.

An additional benefit of such enquiry frequently reported by students relates to the response of workplace colleagues to the process of qualitative enquiry. Workplace enquiry can operate as a catalyst for new forms of communication and relationships.

'No one had ever thought to ask these people what they thought or felt about the way the thing worked. There was a degree of cynicism at first, but people began to offer ideas and information ... to seek me out and tell me things.' (senior accountant, MBA course)

'The message for me in quite simple terms is, that by doing this research, ... that is intervention. If I hadn't been doing this, intervention wouldn't have been happening. People wouldn't be phoning me up, and sending letters, and asking questions about it at interviews, and sending me articles.... The organization is becoming more aware.' (health service manager, MA course)

The literature on workplace enquiry gives comprehensive coverage to the techniques for data gathering. However, the development of holistic and generalizable situational understanding requires more than awareness and availability of new, softer forms of data. The data themselves, while often offering considerable insight and stimulus for reflection, do not automatically generate generalizable understanding. Building mental templates which are transferable to other situations requires a capacity for analysis and the development of theories and hypotheses grounded in and emerging from the data.

For the experienced academic and organizational researcher the interpretation of qualitative data may demonstrate a quality of sophistication and artistry which it is difficult for the beginner to emulate. While raw workplace data may be of considerable intrinsic interest, its meaning is not necessarily self-evident. The process of ascribing meaning to data involves both analysis and interpretation. It is for this reason that we are concerned to develop students' experience in the use of a number of analytical tools which allow them systematically to view the data from a variety of perspectives, and to create alternative patterns of interpretation. Beginning with simple exercises and moving through reconnaissance phases into the main enquiry, we seek to expose our students to experience and practice in a range of analytical techniques. Initially the concern is largely to encourage a sense of curiosity and enquiry about taken-for-granted workplace phenomena – to render the familiar unfamiliar. The techniques can subsequently be adapted as appropriate to the student's own data and research interest. These techniques include the following:

- open coding
- word and phrase analysis
- metaphor analysis

- pattern analysis

- dilemma analysis

- critical incident analysis

- force-field analysis

The use of such techniques encourages a critical approach to the study of situational data. A major problem for studies involving reflective practice is that they often confine the researcher to a superficial and 'common-sense' interpretation of their data which is largely dependent on existing assumptions and understandings. They can easily lack the necessary rigour to explore fully alternative interpretations or to create new meanings. Developing new perspectives on workplace situations depends centrally on the capability to create meaning from evidential data.

Analytical tools form the central part of the process of identifying situational components and salience. They open up the possibility of reviewing one's own position, especially in terms of the assumptions and values which underpin the everyday perceptions of workplace issues. We believe they also develop confidence in the process of enquiry, and in taking a pro-active stance towards practical problems.

DEVELOPING INTERPERSONAL COMMUNICATION AND RELATIONSHIPS

It is well recognized that one of the major benefits which students derive from CPD courses is the opportunity to meet and exchange ideas and problems with others in similar situations. Undertaking workplace enquiry can be a lonely and isolating experience, and sharing experience with a supportive group offers a number of practical benefits. In developing our programmes we have placed particular emphasis on small group work, in which the individual student may present an analysis of some aspect of his or her enquiry and receive critical feedback from peers. This group work has many of the features of action learning but the discussion is focused by the presentation of data collected in the workplace. The most obvious advantages are access to alternative perspectives on issues derived from other people's experience and enquiries and the pooling of knowledge, not least in terms of relevant reading and research findings. As one student puts it,

'Classic kind of stuff being on a course with a group of people; people who are informed about the issues, and care about the issues. I found it stimulating, sparky, in a way that I don't get any kind of spark from the people I'm working with – because they're not into the issues at all.' (business manager, legal partnership, MA student)

And

'For me some of it has been about being challenged by other people about my practice, and having to justify it. Especially the underlying assumptions that are current in your organization that are never challenged.' (senior personnel manager DSS, MA course)

Once the basic focus for enquiry has been established through reconnaissance, and students have begun to acquire some experience and confidence in the techniques of enquiry, the use of small supportive learning groups, initially with a facilitator, becomes a major feature of the structured elements of our programmes. However, the major benefits to engaging in small group work relate to developing the capacity to exercise influence in workplace situations.

As we have argued, the general thrust of workplace enquiry projects involving situational understanding reflects the need for managers who are capable of exercising intelligent judgements in complex and uncertain contexts. While this is clearly important in terms of the challenges and problems facing individual managers, it is equally important that managers acquire the capacity to influence their organizations.

Much has been written on the needs for organizational learning (see for example, Pedler *et al.*, 1991), and many organizations have, through choice or necessity, experimented with structural and procedural forms intended to enhance communication, flexibility and responsiveness (see Hales, 1993). However, such structures and procedures may be a necessary but insufficient condition for enhancing organizational development. What is needed is a more general shift in the learning culture of organizations. This may involve:

- redefining established perspectives and expectation to embrace an understanding that management decisions and actions are based on judgements about situations, and are therefore tentative and provisional, rather than right in some absolute sense;

- establishing an ongoing dialectic between colleagues which seeks out and values differences in perspectives and ideas as an opportunity for collective learning.

Such a cultural shift can only be achieved through being enacted in the relationships and interactions of people in the workplace. It requires new interpersonal skills which are more dependent on the capacity to influence others, and less dependent on formal role or power.

Much of the potential value of the insights gained from workplace enquiry is often limited by a sense of powerlessness on the part of the student to influence others in the workplace. While many organizations espouse the rhetoric of the learning organization, in practice they are often unable or unwilling to suspend established patterns of power relationships leading to frustration and fatalism in those committed to change. While this continues to be a serious problem, small learning peer groups of students create an opportunity to acquire and practise the communication and inter-personal skills of influencing others, free from the established assumptions and constraining power hierarchies of the workplace.

We have considerable evidence that engaging with small stable groups of critically supportive peers contributes significantly to both personal and professional development, as in the following extracts from an evaluative dialogue among an MA group:

> 'It's given me a lot more confidence in feeling I could handle myself in a more senior role ... because I've got this real hang-up about [my] level of ability.'

> 'It's being in a group like this and people valuing what you've got to say, or contradicting it, makes you challenge yourself.'

> '... it's from working in this group in particular that if you think a bit more carefully how you want to come over, and what your objective is when you are about to say something, you can actually channel how you say it through thinking about your audience and being more persuasive and influential.'

> '... thinking before you speak and how to make your interventions powerful ones. I don't think I've learned how to do it, but I've got a handle on the fact that it's an issue.'

The insights and understandings gained from workplace enquiry and analysis, when combined with the skills of presenting argument and influencing others, is recognized by students as central to their effectiveness.

> 'It's encouraged us to be reflective about what we're doing and why we're doing it, which I think are life skills. But the major business skills people listen to you because your thoughts are well engineered, they're well put across and persuasive; they are difficult to attack and so on. And that's a great benefit.'

IMPACT ON THE ORGANIZATION

To date, our work encourages us to believe that a 'practical science' model of professional development fosters both relevance and transferability of learning in CPD programmes. It is important to recognize, however, that transferability involves a reciprocal process between the student and the organization in which knowledge and skills require an appropriate context for their development. While we are confident that our approach contributes effectively to the individual autonomy and judgements of managers in their organizational roles, the evidence of wider impact on their work organizations is more equivocal. On the one hand, some participants claim major impacts through this approach:

> 'Working in this way has revolutionized my whole approach to managing the factory. It has made sense of things which have been concerning me for years.... Since I started talking to people [at work], asking them about their views and so on, I can really see the point of doing things which I'd heard about and thought, yes, that's interesting.
>
> 'I've already begun to make changes based on some of these ideas. And I feel more confident that I can deal with new problems.' (factory manager, multinational company, MBA student)
>
> 'I've learned a great deal about my school, our staff, and myself by researching. I think we are all already beginning to feel the benefits.' (primary headteacher, MA course)

Against this level of impact must be set the laconic if not untypical comment on impact as 'bugger all!' Such comments must be set in the context of bringing about meaningful change as being a process over time. Unlike perhaps some more instrumental forms of training in operational skills and competences represented in the social market approach in CPD which can have relatively immediate impact on performance, the practical science model aspires to the development of practical wisdom, built on experience over time. The expectation of short-term impact on either the student or the organization may be misplaced. It is also difficult to evaluate organizational impact of workplace enquiry beyond the short term. Nevertheless, there appears to be a high degree of variability in the extent to which this approach to CPD affects organizational learning.

The degree of organizational impact is of course in part a function of individuals, not simply in terms of their managerial position and ability, but also relating to their beliefs about the cultural possibilities to influence change in their organization. This latter appears to relate to what Klemp (1977) calls 'cognitive initiative', the sense of being capable of changing situations for the better rather than being a helpless victim of events. In this respect we have found it increasingly necessary to ensure that the nature and expectations of our programmes are well understood in advance by potential students, and have where possible included consideration of this disposition in selection procedures.

However, our experience would suggest that the potential impact of practical science approaches to the professional development of managers is also heavily dependent on the underlying culture of the work organization, and its perceptions of the developmental needs of individuals. Since most students are sponsored onto programmes by their organizations, and elements of the organization are themselves generally the focus of workplace enquiry, the relationship between the course, the organization and the student becomes a critical factor for the success of this approach. A number of issues need to be addressed in developing this type of programme, and we are coming increasingly to recognize the need to develop careful and detailed collaboration between the providers and sponsoring/host organizations through the process.

- Initial publicity and explanatory material for both students and sponsors, ideally supported by personal contact, needs to make clear the underlying philosophy of the approach and aims of the programme to avoid misunderstanding and inappropriate expectations. In particular, sponsoring organizations need to recognize that workplace enquiry seeks critically to examine and question established values, assumptions and practices. As such it has uncomfortable as well as beneficial potentials.

- Where workplace enquiry projects involve elements of organizational development (as opposed to development of individual professional practice) there is a need to carefully negotiate a focus for enquiry which will contribute value to the organization and to ensure organizational support, ideally at a high level. One danger however is that of the organization dominating or taking over the enquiry process to its own ends at the expense of critical elements of the enquiry/learning process. The student is often in a relatively weak position to resist such hijacking, and close liaison involving the external provider is desirable to minimize difficulties.

- Any attempt to empower professionals with the skills and understanding to influence organizational development must be matched with responsive organizational structures and procedures. Opportunities must be available for participants to exercise influence, even where this crosses established boundaries of responsibilities and power. At its most effective, suspending existing power relationships and engaging in organizational dialectic around an enquiry project can be a most potent form of organizational learning. However, experience suggests that such opportunities cannot be taken for granted. We believe that, in addition to programme-based tutorial and learning group support, it is desirable to involve senior personnel within the host organization in both the managerial and practical support for enquiry-based projects.

In general, for workplace enquiry projects to have beneficial impact on organizations requires collaborative investment from within organizations, as well as from student participants and CPD providers, at the programme design stage and throughout the process. While the rhetoric of 'the learning organization' increasingly permeates managerial thinking, its actual development is long term, often politically sensitive and organizationally risky. Careful collaborative working with organizations therefore constitutes our current priority in developing the principle of workplace enquiry as a process for professional development.

Despite the increasingly competitive and commercialized world of CPD provision and the prevalence of the social market philosophy, our experiences over recent years encourage us in pursuing a practical science approach, rooted in workplace enquiry, as an effective means of personal and professional development. However, as providers we need to ensure a degree of humility in recognizing difficulties and problems for organizations in accommodating workplace enquiry, and to work collaboratively with them both in articulating their organizational needs, and in accommodating the learning process.

REFERENCES

Dreyfus, S. E. (1981) *Formal Models vs. Human Situational Understanding: Inherent Limitations on the Modelling of Business Enterprise* (mimeo). Schloss Laxenburg, Austria: International Institute for Applied Systems Analysis.

Elliott, J. (ed.) (1993) *Reconstructing Teacher Education*. London: Falmer.

Garratt, B. (1987) *The Learning Organisation*. London: Fontana/Collins.

Hales, C. (1993) *Management through Organisation*. London: Routledge.

Klemp, G. O. (1977) *Three Factors of Success in the World of Work: Implications for Curriculum in Higher Education*. Boston, MA: McBer and Co.

Kolb, D. A. (1984) *Experiential Learning; Experience as the Source of Learning and Development*. Englewood Cliffs, NJ: Prentice Hall.

Pedler, M., Burgoyne, J. and Boydell, T. (1991) *The Learning Company; A Strategy for Sustainable Development*. New York: McGraw-Hill.

Rhodes, J. and Thame, S. (1988) *The Colours of Your Mind*. London: Collins.

Schon, D. (1987) *Educating the Reflective Practitioner*. San Francisco: Jossey-Bass.

Chapter 11

The Reflective Practitioner: A Key Role for University Providers of CPD

Roseanne Benn and Clive Nicholas

In Britain, it is now some ten years since the Department of Education and Science decided to switch a significant proportion of funding for university adult education from liberal adult education to pump-priming post-experience vocational education.

During this period universities have increasingly become providers of continuing professional development (CPD), largely through the medium of short courses which provide practitioners with intermittent periods of learning. Although the importance of short courses in CPD is reaffirmed in this chapter, some of the limitations of this form of provision are examined in the context of adult education theory. Against this background the theory of the reflective practitioner is explored, suggesting that this might form the basis of more effective learning and that the provision of CPD through reflective practice is an area in which universities have a key role to play.

CPD THROUGH SHORT COURSE PROVISION

The term 'short courses' is used here to describe vocational, post-experience, employer-funded, self-financing courses provided by universities for practitioners in commerce, industry and the professions which are typically of one day to one week in duration and do not lead to an award. Short courses of this nature are used for a variety of purposes which can include specific problem-solving for individuals and organizations; updating knowledge and skills; acquiring new knowledge and skills, or awareness-raising designed to broaden knowledge or change attitudes.

Dewey (1990) saw learning as a transaction. If the concept of learning as a transaction is applied to short course provision as defined above, then it is clear that there is more than a straightforward transaction between tutor and participant. Also involved are the employer, who is funding the participant's involvement, and, in a much wider sense, government, which is interested in the contribution a better educated workforce can make to economic growth and thereby to the general level of well-being in society as a whole. It can be argued that what essentially brings these players together in the market-place is a transaction which is both financial and intellectual and involves the transmission of knowledge, skills or ideas to the learner in a relatively limited period of time.

✱ Thus in short course provision we see a fascinating juxtaposition of the financial, the intellectual and, indeed, the pragmatic (i.e. the need to be able to apply what is learned directly in the workplace). Embracing this mix of factors is a time constraint. This time constraint is driven principally by the limited time available for participants to engage in such activities and the need in the commercial world for short-term focused learning driven by immediate business needs.

The requirement for learning to take place in what is sometimes an extremely short time presents a range of issues which need to be examined in the context of adult education theory. This is all the more interesting when it is considered that much of the theory of adult education tends to largely examine adult learning either implicitly or explicitly in the context of a substantially longer time frame.

LIMITATIONS OF THIS APPROACH

Short courses involve the transmission of knowledge from tutor to learner. The use of the word 'transmission' is deliberate here in the sense that time and monetary factors exert a pressure to provide course participants with a neat value-for-money learning package. In contrast to this very utilitarian approach, writers such as Allman (1983, p. 120) have suggested that effective adult learning involves more than mere transmission of knowledge:

> Adult learning involves thinking in the increasingly complex ways that adults have the potential to develop. In fostering learning, knowledge can be viewed as either an open or a closed system. When viewed as open it is something to which learners can add or which they can alter through critical and creative thought. Even when perceived as a closed system it is viewed as something which the learner can use to solve problems or even to create new systems. As a consequence, education is not about transmission but rather it is selection, synthesis and discovery through the process of dialogue.

↪ Based on concepts such as the importance of dialogue, adult education theorists emphasize the need for a learner-centred approach and the significance of partnership in effective adult learning, particularly in negotiating the curriculum and methods of delivery.

This partnership may start at a very early stage in the process of curriculum development in defining learning needs. Knowles (1978), when discussing the diagnosis of needs in the context of andragogy, the art and science of helping adults learn, indicates the importance of self-diagnosis of needs for learning and argues that this process consists of three phases:

- constructing a model of the competences or characteristics required to achieve a given model of performance; it is in this model-building phase that the values and expectations of the teacher, the institution and society are amalgamated with those of the learner into a composite picture;

- providing diagnostic experiences in which the learner can assess his or her present level of competences in the light of those portrayed in the model;

- helping the learner to measure the gaps between his or her present competences and those required by the model, so that he or she experiences a feeling of dissatisfaction about the distance between where he or she is and where he or she would like to be and is able to identify specific directions of desirable growth. This experience of self-induced dissatisfaction with present inadequacies, coupled with a clear sense of direction for self-improvement, is in fact a good definition of motivation to learn.

Those involved in the organization and teaching of vocational short courses will recognize in Knowles's three phases similarities with the concept of training needs analysis which is regarded by many as a key factor in the development of short course curricula. However, in practice, it is not always possible to engage in such detailed diagnosis of the needs of learners and, indeed, the precise needs of course participants may not begin to emerge until the course has actually begun. There are several reasons why this might occur. If the course is 'open' (i.e. it is marketed to a wide range of potential participants from different organizations), then in devising the curriculum the tutor has had to make certain assumptions about the needs of learners. Although these may be clearly reflected in the course description, it is possible that participants will make different assumptions or read more into the course than the tutor originally intended. Participants may simply have been sent on a course by their employer without seeing the course description themselves and without really knowing why they are there. Where a course is 'closed' (i.e. it has been tailored specifically to meet the needs of a single organization), resources may not permit a detailed training needs analysis. The course may be devised on the employer's perception of needs which may differ from that of the employee. Thus tutors are presented with the dilemma of the needs of participants diverging somewhat from the planned curriculum.

If, as is usual, there are not specified entry requirements to a short course, needs may vary significantly because participants will come together with a wide range of status and experience. Mixed status among course participants may present difficulties in defining real needs. People may be tempted to express expectations which are based on what they perceive to be appropriate to their status rather than their actual needs, while others may distort their expression of needs in order to avoid displaying their limitations. It is possible that there is simply not enough time for the tutor to explore such behaviour to identify the true needs of participants. Over a longer period learning activities can be tailored to the needs of individual learners but this may be impracticable in the context of short course provision. Similar considerations apply to differences in the experience of course participants. In addition, it is likely that adult learners will have different learning styles based on their previous experience of education and the nature of their work. Learning styles may range from active learners who are confident, challenging and information-seeking to passive learners who will be prepared to accept without question what is provided by the tutor. Honey and Mumford (1982), for example, have identified the following styles of learning:

- *Activists* who like to get involved, now. Enthusiastic, gregarious, open brainstormers who may prefer novelty to quality.

- *Reflectors* who stand back, observe others in action, collect data, chew it over, are cautious and quiet, and, when they act, do so with a broad picture in mind and with some awareness of implications ... but it may then be too late!

- *Theorists* are systematic and logical, serious and objective, suspicious of subjectivity. They like to work from basic principles and test suggestions against these constantly, and become bothered if things don't fit neatly with their constructed, expected and rational reality.

- *Pragmatists* are essentially practical; they like to test ideas through experimentation and are less prone to extensive prior discussion. They respond to problems as challenging opportunities to do something.

In short course provision, given the constraint to time, it is often difficult to accurately identify individual styles and perhaps even more difficult to adjust and vary learning activities to accommodate such differences in learners.

It is therefore clear that there are difficulties in short-course provision in balancing what is considered good practice in relation to the theory of adult education when constrained by time. This dilemma can perhaps be illustrated by reference to Knowles's (1970) distinction between the 'content approach' and 'process approach' to curriculum development which he summarized as follows:

Content approach

- Someone decides in advance what skill or knowledge is to be transmitted.
- The tutor arranges this body of content into logical units.
- The tutor selects the most efficient means of transmitting this content.
- The tutor develops a plan for presentation.

Process approach

The tutor prepares in advance a set of procedures for involving the learners as follows:

- establishing a climate conducive to learning
- creating a mechanism for mutual planning
- diagnosing the needs for learning
- formulating programme objectives to meet the identified needs
- designing a pattern of learning experiences
- conducting these experiences with suitable techniques and materials
- evaluating the learning outcomes and re-diagnosing learning needs

Although most short course tutors would probably aspire to the latter approach, it is likely that they will be pushed towards the former by the need to deliver a defined curriculum in a limited period of time. In a survey carried out by the authors, short-course tutors were asked what they thought were the differences between curricula for short courses and for sustained study. Their responses included comments such as:

'There is room for greater negotiation of content in longer courses, thus reflecting the group's needs.'

'Short courses tend to cover topics in less detail but over a broader area and therefore rely upon limited methods of delivery. Field visits, project work, tutorial type work are largely lacking. Sustained study can include alternative teaching methods (e.g. library-based work, study-centred learning) and will tend to include more supporting, background information. Sustained study can offer specialization within a topic area. Short courses are usually self-contained.'

'Short courses are likely to involve less student-centred learning, less project work, less study "ownership" than courses of sustained study.'

Short courses have an important role to play in vocational education in providing knowledge, skills and ideas in a concise form that has been designed by the tutor to endeavour to meet both the requirements of employers and the needs of participants. However, by their very nature (i.e. that they are short and therefore time constrained), there are limitations to their effectiveness as a medium for adult learning. The need for dialogue rather than transmission, the need for a learner-centred approach based on process, the need for ownership of learning, all lead us to suggest that more sustained and self-directed study has much to contribute to effective learning and that universities are environments which are well placed to facilitate and encourage this mode of learning.

NEED FOR A NEW APPROACH

The limitations of short course provision are not the only problematic areas in institutional provision of CPD. The amount of new knowledge generated each year in the field of each profession, combined with a belief that everything must be covered, has arguably resulted in an unbalanced initial professional curriculum. This compulsion to enhance and update information has carried over into much continuing education for professionals (Paprock, 1994). Writers such as Tough (1971) and Rogers (1969) argue that the adult learner of the future will need to be highly competent in deciding what to learn and in planning and arranging his or her own learning. An entirely new situation arises where the goal of education is the facilitation of change and learning and the only person who is educated is the one who has learned how to learn. Eisner (1985) extends this argument by suggesting that not everything needs to be, or indeed can be, learned in an educational institution. Hence it is imperative that CPD utilizes real life and work experience and learning as part of a lifelong process. There needs to be a strengthening of the CPD curriculum to develop the ability to adjust to the new conditions inherent in a rapidly changing technological society and the propensity to modify, alter or change elements of professional practice or the professional community. In this context one of the most interesting theories of learning to emerge in recent years has been Schon's concept of the reflective practitioner (1982, 1987).

THE REFLECTIVE PRACTITIONER

The majority of educators, influenced by the nature of their own training, frame their decisions about knowledge and its transfer in the positivist viewpoint (Peters, 1994). Schon (1982) argues that uncertainty, uniqueness, instability and value conflict – all factors ever present in twentieth-century life – are troublesome to this epistemology of practice and hence that another approach is needed. In institution after institution and programme after programme, the value of the learner's experience is acclaimed but then ignored as a basis for the design and management of training activities. Schon exposes this discontinuity, arguing that in order for the professional to be effective, he or she needs to be practitioner, researcher and theorist all at the same time. This requires the increased valuing and legitimacy of knowledge that is knowledge-in-use and reflection that is reflection-in-action of professional actions, premises and paradigms, focusing on how practitioners can learn to think *whilst* practising in such a way as to enable more effective future action (Barnett, 1992).

Schon argues that being a professional involves the application of not only propositional knowledge, but also a more dynamic form of knowledge. Here the professional is able to think constructively in context and reflect in real time, not after the event, on the understandings which have been implicit in his or her actions, understandings which he or she surfaces, criticizes, restructures and embodies in further action. The assumption here is that the skilled professional has at his or her command a repertoire of strategies and techniques, the capacity to think creatively in context and the abilities to apply formal knowledge. These facilities are available to the practitioner at all times and are used at will to provide intelligent action. This leads to the conclusion that professional activity is more than the application of knowledge and more than technique. It is an extremely complex mix of thought and action, of knowing and doing. Hence any continuing professional development must be more than just the acquisition of further knowledge, important though this is. It should also provide the participant with the opportunity to develop further the more complex skills of, in Schon's terms, knowledge-in-use and reflection-in-action. Critical reflection is fundamentally critical self-reflection, allowing individuals to step back from their involvement and view this in the context of a wider framework, to evaluate and to consider alternatives. Through this kind of open critique, individuals reach a position of intellectual independence in which they are enabled to see through the apparent 'given-ness' of a proposition and its theoretical anchoring and so gain a measure of freedom from entrapment by any conceptual schema. It allows the professional to identify operative paradigms and to consciously move between them (Barnett, 1992).

This concept offers an insight into the way that skilled practitioners are able to carry out informed interventions in situations which they encounter in professional practice. It summarizes the complexities of the situations in which professionals find themselves called upon to act, indicates that they are able to call upon a range of strategies to deal with these situations, implies that they are able to evaluate these strategies and that they maintain an internal running commentary on their actions.

It is arguable that the essence of professional education should lie in the professional developing the capacities of a reflective practitioner, with the acquisition of further technological knowledge and skills being of necessary but secondary importance.

HIGHER EDUCATION AND THE REFLECTIVE PRACTITIONER

Higher education is valued by our society as a major means through which participants learn to bring powers of high level reflection to bear on their experiences. Different sectors of society including government, employers and higher education institutions would argue that higher education leads, or should lead, to higher learning and this calls for a higher thinking. This level of education should enable the meta-discourse which allows students to engage in critical dialogue with themselves at all times, i.e. that develops and strengthens exactly those skills that ensure the reflective practitioner. Higher education thus has a critical role to play in CPD; hence both the concept of the reflective practitioner and the involvement of the universities are central to CPD. However, the adoption of this reflective practitioner approach to CPD has fundamental implications for the universities in terms of the curriculum and learning methods. The space that self-reflection calls for points to significant levels of student autonomy and independence in thought and action and hence a teaching ethos which expects students to be responsible for their own learning. It is crucial that teaching styles should not be didactic but discursive and exploratory and that the student's experience, past, present and future, should be a real and central part of the curriculum.

A REFLECTIVE PRACTICE MODEL

John Peters (1994) has developed a model for learning founded on reflective practice. It is based on four steps of acting and theorizing:

1. Describe the problem, task or incident that represents some critical aspect of practice needing examination and possible change.
2. Analyse the nature of what is described, including the assumptions that support the actions taken to solve the problem, do the task or resolve the incident.
3. Theorize about alternative ways to approach the problem, task or incident.
4. Act on the basis of theory.

Peters suggests that this approach has something to offer in the development of participants as reflective practitioners. It would therefore seem appropriate to incorporate aspects of this approach in the development of university-based CPD.

STRATEGIES FOR UNIVERSITY-BASED PROVISION FOR CPD

Two CPD programmes recently developed at Exeter University demonstrate the application of reflective practice (while still retaining the value of short course provision). Normally both programmes will involve the student in a year or more of part-time study.

The University is collaborating with City and Guilds to provide the opportunity for professionals to obtain the City and Guilds senior awards of Graduateship and Membership. These qualifications differ from traditional university degrees as they are competence based, requiring the practical application of professional skills, knowledge and understanding in employment. In order to obtain these awards, experienced professionals need to demonstrate the same skills and competence required for a reflective practitioner. For the Membership, for example, the candidate must be: effectively supervising others in the application and development of established practice; applying and critically appraising new development; assessing social and economic implications of their work; managing innovation and change; gaining the confidence of professional peers, and communicating clearly and effectively. Assessment is by a combination of learning and professional practice illustrated in a portfolio. The content of the portfolio is negotiable but could, for example, contain evidence of courses attended together with an assessment of work-related experience(s) normally through a project report. This reflection on professional practice in a systematic, self-directed manner under the supportive supervision of a member of the University is intended to develop just those characteristics that Schon noted in the reflective practitioner.

A prospective MA in Professional Development takes these ideas and concepts to a further stage. The programme is aimed at experienced professionals and is designed to be appropriate in structure for the professional updating of those in full-time work. Negotiated pathways should ensure that both the individual needs of students are recognized and that the students take responsibility for their own learning. Learning from experiences both past and present is considered to be the best example of reflection-in-action. Hence by building on prior learning and experience, professionals will be encouraged to identify and describe assumptions underlying their practice and to make changes in some of these assumptions. Students will also be encouraged to examine operative paradigms and if necessary shift between them. Through workplace experimentation, group dialogue and an examination of academic literature, they will be encouraged to develop their own socially constructed theories of their professional work. At all stages, emphasis will be laid on critical self-reflection and critical internal dialogue.

The academic structure consists of three modules:

- A core module which deals with the nature of reflective professional practice as discussed earlier. This module will also consider study skill development and an overview of research methodologies. It will be group-based.

- Short-course provision of the type described in the first part of this chapter. By incorporating these within a wider structure, the professional practitioner will be able to both benefit by the transmission of information and skills and locate this learning within the personal learning framework developed in the core module.

- A dissertation based on the student's professional experience which draws out the learning achieved. This is negotiable with the student but may utilize the organizational framework for reflective practice. A practical example of this, in the field of education, is for a primary school head. Here the professional might review the context in which they are working; identify good practice through discussion, literature, relating practice and theory and reflection on practice; identify the learning experienced in implementing school change; consider the ethics, values and moral issues involved, and review outcomes in terms of school development and their own learning and understanding.

IN CONCLUSION

This chapter has identified some of the strengths and weaknesses of concentrating university CPD in short course provision. An examination of the theory of the reflective practitioner suggested that a different curriculum and approach might be more effective in encouraging the skills and abilities necessary for any professional to operate successfully in these times of rapid change. The importance of the role of higher education in the development of these higher learning skills leads to the conclusion that universities need to be centrally involved in the provision of CPD but that for some institutions the ideas of reflective practice will bring with them the need for new and different provision. The universities need to take this on board and design programmes firmly embedded in the concept of the integration of workplace practice with student-led, independent learning. Acknowledging the restriction of time, they normally need to involve the student in a year or more of part-time study. These criteria, together with the existing successful short course programme, will provide a flexible and accredited range of offerings that will enable professionals to continue their lifelong learning in a systematic and productive way. It may also be that the introduction of these ideas may change not just continuing education but also mainstream undergraduate and postgraduate provision. This would be most appropriate. As Barnett (1992) argues, we are all reflective practitioners now.

REFERENCES

Allman, P. (1983) The nature and process of adult development, in M. Tight (ed.), *Adult Learning and Education*. London: Croom Helm.

Barnett, R. (1992) *Improving Higher Education: Total Quality Care*. Buckingham: SRHE and Open University Press.

Dewey, J. (1990) (quoted in R. Kidd) The learning transaction, in M. Tight (ed.), *Adult Learning and Education*. London: Routledge.

Eisner, E. W. (1985) *The Educational Imagination: On the Design and Evaluation of School Programs*. New York : Macmillan.

Honey, P. and Mumford, A. (1982) *The Manual of Learning Styles*. Maidenhead : Peter Honey.

Kidd, J. R. (1973) *How Adults Learn*. Cambridge: Cambridge Book Company.

Knowles, M. S. (1970) *The Modern Practice of Adult Education: From Pedagogy to Andragogy*. Cambridge : Cambridge Book Company.

Knowles, M. S. (1978) *The Adult Learner: A Neglected Species*. Houston : Gulf Publishing.

Paprock, K. E. (1994) A conceptual framework for developing adaptive competency for professionals, in R. Benn and R. Fieldhouse (eds), *Training and Professional Development in Adult and Continuing Education*. Exeter: CRCE, The University of Exeter.

Peters, J. M. (1994) Instructors-as-researcher-and-theorists : faculty development in a community college, in R. Benn and R. Fieldhouse (eds), *Training and Professional Development in Adult and Continuing Education*. Exeter: CRCE, University of Exeter.

Rogers, C. R. (1969) *Freedom to Learn*. Columbus, OH: Charles E. Merrill Publishing Company.

Schon, D. (1982) *The Reflective Practitioner: How Professionals Think in Practice*. New York : Basic Books.

Schon, D. (1987) *Educating the Reflective Practitioner*. London: Jossey-Bass.

Tough, A. (1971) *The Adults' Learning Project : A Fresh Approach to Theory and Practice in Adult Learning*. Toronto: OISE.

Chapter 12

Further Professional Development and Further Education Teachers: Setting a New Agenda for Work-based Learning

David Guile and Michael Young

The professional identities of further education teachers have been dramatically transformed because of the nature of organizational and curricula changes that are presently occurring in the further education (FE) sector. These changes are placing increased demands upon teachers; for instance, they are having to respond to:

- the pedagogic shift from an emphasis upon teaching to an emphasis upon learning and offering appropriate guidance to learners;
- the professional shifts from using fixed subject specialisms or bounded occupational skills as the basis for training to using the working environment as the natural site to acquire more broad-based or multi-skilled professional and managerial competences;
- the wider challenge of making contributions to developing the corporate identity of the college, company or training provider and assisting them to develop as learning organizations.

Three particular pressing issues are inhibiting FE teachers from undertaking further professional development to assist them to respond to these changes: status; accreditation and progression blockages, and the absence of a professional development strategy.

Status

FE has traditionally been the 'Cinderella' sector of the UK's education and training system. It has not been mandatory for FE teachers to hold a recognized teaching qualification. In fact, Department for Education (DFE) statistics indicate that in 1993 approximately 40 per cent of staff working in the FE sector did not hold teaching qualifications. Despite the significant number of staff still lacking initial qualifications, there has been some improvement since the mid-1980s when fewer than 50 per cent of staff employed full-time in FE had a recognized teaching qualification. This increase in the overall volume of trained staff in FE is probably attributable to the expansion of academic courses and the decision in colleges to employ qualified staff to teach on them, rather than any explicit strategy on behalf of colleges to professionalize the sector (Young *et al.*, 1995).

The professional development of teachers in-post has also been a marginal activity. Reliable statistics for FE teachers are not available, since it is only since colleges have become incorporated that they have begun to keep records of staff qualifications. However, the existence of long-standing and neglected progression blockages, which are discussed below, imply a general inattention to and lack of concern about this issue.

A further problem has been the under-resourcing and under-researching of the organizational, management and professional development needs of FE. There are no major university departments devoted to further education and there is no tradition of research or higher degree study in the field compared to that found in Germany (Young *et al.*, 1995). University departments of education have mainly concentrated upon the primary and secondary sector. The national interest in the 14–19 curriculum, which was followed by the introduction of the technical and vocational education initiative (TVEI) in the mid-1980s, did not lead to any corresponding interest in FE. The small amount of research from university education departments that was published was inclined to focus on post-16 progression, rather than on professional development needs.

The Staff College and the Further Education Unit (FEU), which in the past held, respectively, the remit for management and curriculum development within the FE sector, have, from time to time, commissioned small-scale research into professional development. However, the Staff College and FEU are being replaced by a new body, the Further Education Development Agency (FEDA). FEDA will aim to be the key commissioning agency for strategic research on behalf of FE; a director of research has been appointed, but it is too early to comment on the impact that the FEDA might make.

Accreditation and progression blockages for teachers

Historically, the accreditation options that have existed for FE teachers have been narrow and failed to provide opportunities for progression. Two options have existed. One option has been largely academic with an emphasis upon higher degrees which focus on book learning rather than on enhancement of professional practice. However, many universities set demanding standards as entry requirements, for example, the possession of at least a second class honours degree, and therefore FE teachers are often excluded from pursuing this route. The other option for FE teachers has been to attend the plethora of short courses on leadership, management development, etc., which have been offered by private providers of training or local education authorities. In the past most of these courses have been non-accredited, although some providers have now negotiated with universities to have their short course incorporated into local credit accumulation and transfer frameworks. They offer no clear route to higher level degrees.

The introduction of National Vocational Qualifications (NVQs) in the UK has provided an alternative structure of accreditation for professional development. A major aim behind the introduction of the NVQs was that they would provide forms of accreditation that were more relevant to workplace needs. FE teachers can, theoretically, pursue an award within the National Vocational Qualification framework; for instance, Training and Development Lead Body (TDLB), or Management Charter Initiative (MCI) accreditation. However, these awards were not designed for the FE sector and have been seen as lacking sufficient breadth (Chown and Last, 1993). This has led to some attempts to try and integrate certain NVQs with higher degrees.

The Institute of Training and Development (ITD), prior to its amalgamation to form the Institute of Personnel and Development (IPD), funded a national project to look at the fit between the TDLB standards and the Masters programmes offered by the business studies departments of several universities. This work has resulted in the development of Masters degrees in human resource development now offered by a number of universities. Although originally aimed at personnel who work as trainers and developers in the private sector, these degree courses are available to FE teachers. However, this provision of 'hybrid' higher degrees in some universities, i.e. modules combined with NVQ units, is only loosely related to the needs of FE teachers.

Absence of a professional development strategy

In the main, FE colleges lack an approach to strategic planning that relates further professional development not only to current but also to future work roles and the development of corporate capability. Colleges have made pragmatic decisions with regard to professional accreditation of their staff. Lecturers are being registered to become accredited NVQ assessors to enable them to assess students undertaking various NVQ awards. The gaining of NVQ awards is justified on the grounds of meeting the immediate college needs. However, considerable concern and criticism has been voiced by FE personnel about the validity of using TDLB standards as the basis of post-compulsory teacher training (Chown, 1992) and for further professional development. Some reservations have also been expressed by FE colleges about the atomized nature of MCI and TDLB awards, and in particular how far they enhance professional learning and the ability of staff to take on roles of wider responsibility (Ollin, 1994).

Prior to incorporation, some colleges used to offer support to staff to enrol for higher degrees and diplomas, since grants were available from both the Department for Education and local education authorities. However, the Further Education Funding Council (FEFC) does not explicitly allocate any funds for further professional development. This places the responsibility firmly with colleges. Financial support for staff who wish to enrol for Masters degrees is now strictly limited and dependant upon such courses being able to meet immediate training needs.

NATIONAL CONCERN ABOUT FURTHER PROFESSIONAL DEVELOPMENT

During the early 1980s a series of studies were published that focused upon the UK's poor economic performance compared with other leading industrial countries (MSC). One consistent feature of the studies was that attention was drawn to the poor quality of initial vocational education and training, and the further training and development of intermediate skilled employees and professional staff. A major government-sponsored review of vocational qualifications led to the establishment of the National Council for Vocational Qualifications (NCVQ). As Ashworth and Saxon (1990) have stated, the NCVQ's remit was to:

> bring together all vocational qualifications within a new
> national framework to be called the National Vocational
> Qualification (NVQ). This would embrace levels of award up to
> and including higher levels of professional qualifications and
> would describe standards in terms of 'competence'.

It was envisaged that the concept of competence would enable workplace skills, knowledge and the ability to perform relevant tasks to be assessed against explicit criteria at clearly different levels.

Strategic administration and responsibility for policy developments remained with the Employment Department. The NCVQ, in conjunction with industry lead bodies, was responsible for monitoring the actual development of occupational standards; and professional associations were invited to consider how their existing qualifications could be accommodated within the new NVQ framework. The intention was twofold. First, to create a framework that ultimately embraced all initial and further professional development qualifications. Second, to provide an alternative accreditation structure that enabled individuals who did not hold any formal qualifications to gain accreditation for their workplace skills.

Work-based learning

One aim of this new development was to promote the idea of work-based learning. The proposition was advanced that 'effective learning can take place at the work place, and not only in the formal academic setting of the lecture theatre and laboratory, and that we learn through the experience of work itself' (Employment Department, 1992, p.4). Two main avenues of activity were undertaken to advance and promote this new emphasis upon work-based learning. First, the Employment Department sponsored a variety of projects in universities that sought to identify ways of developing and accrediting students' generic skills; second, they funded the work-based learning in higher education programme. This programme concentrated on making specific links between how academic learning could be connected to, or seen to be part of the work role of an individual, and how some form of recognition could be given to such learning.

For some time, work-based learning had been an intrinsic part of the development for many professional groups, teachers, social workers and lawyers and accountants. It has also been a component of all sandwich degrees. However, the new focus which the Employment Department was advocating introduced a controversial idea. It argued that learning which does not take place in academic contexts was equally important as learning within higher education and was entitled to accreditation. The notion that 'all work-based learning is valid and creditworthy' (Employment Department, 1992) and its value could be assessed 'in terms which allowed it to be integrated – and possibly accredited – within academic programmes' is a clear departure from conventional higher education thinking and practice.

In the main, universities still retain the tradition of separating theory and practice, and rarely offer accreditation for the latter within the structure of degree programmes. Not only did most teacher training courses assess knowledge of educational theory separate from classroom practice, they rarely expected students to demonstrate the relationship between their theoretical and practical learning. Furthermore, although arrangements were usually made to assess the work placement within sandwich courses, all too often the assessments did not contribute to the final degree. As Young (1994) has indicated, the role of theory in such courses served at best as 'the intellectualisation of practice'.

Debates surrounding work-based learning

The debate about work-based learning in the UK has mainly centred around two themes. The first theme has been concerned with the potential and limitations of the concept of competence. Commentaries have highlighted its 'behaviourist' assumptions (Ashworth and Saxon, 1990) and the tendency of competency schemes towards 'reductionist' descriptions of work performance (Whitty, 1991). The second theme has focused upon operational issues, and in particular, the development of an appropriate method for establishing comparability and equivalence between academic and work-based learning.

More recent contributors to these debates have articulated the profound concern that in the process of developing comparability the traditional definition of 'academic competence', based upon knowledge of disciplines and notions of truth and objectivity, has been lost. It has been argued that in giving academic competence an operational twist, it comes to stand for 'know-how' and the ability to demonstrate skills (Barnett, 1994). Scepticism has also been expressed as to whether the capacity to perform various functions in the workplace can unambiguously be equated with an understanding of the ideas and concepts of relevant disciplines that might inform such actions (Eraut and Cole, 1994). In addition, criticism has been voiced about the assessment procedures associated with the new notions of competence, if they do not involve the explicit provision of evidence of an individual's understanding of the 'underpinning knowledge' of work roles (Black and Wolf, 1990).

Problems with current conceptions of work-based learning

One consequence of the domination of these two themes has been a tendency to lose sight of other equally important aspects of work-based learning. Work-based learning as defined within the Employment Department literature emphasizes the link between learning and the work role. It seeks to interrelate three essential components to support this process: first, structured learning in the workplace, second, on/off-the-job training opportunities, and third, identifying and providing relevant off-job learning opportunities. At the heart of the definition developed by the Employment Department lies a series of assumptions about the relationship between theory and practice. However, the main focus of the work-based learning debate, as outlined above, has led to diminished importance and consideration being accorded to the relationship between theory and practice.

All too often a rather narrow and 'technicist' perspective has prevailed. Many discussions about work-based learning in the UK have concentrated largely upon the methods and procedures that might guarantee employees' access to degree level study, i.e. accreditation of prior learning or experiential learning; and establishing comparability and equivalence between work-based learning and academic learning through the specification of learning outcomes. One result is that the relationship between the two different kinds of learning found in the workplace and in higher education (and therefore the relationship between theory and practice) has been marginalized (Young and Guile, 1995).

The traditional divide between theoretical and practical learning usually has the following three results. First, practitioners are left either with a knowledge of theory that appears to be disconnected from practice; second, they acquire the ability to systematically reflect upon their own practice; or third, they do not develop the concepts to help them to understand how forces external to the workplace may shape or influence professional practice. Many of the approaches to work-based learning in the UK, outlined above, are inclined to continue this divided tradition. They fail to pursue the connection between how adults actually learn at work and the contribution that theoretical concepts can make to assist individuals to understand what they are doing and why work practices are subject to change.

This devaluing of the theory–practice relationship has occurred for several reasons. First, as previously noted, competence-based approaches do not involve an explicit provision of evidence of an individual's understanding of the 'underpinning knowledge' of work roles. Up to now this has meant that the design of teaching/learning programmes for vocational awards has not specifically addressed the relationship between theory and practice. Second, there has been a failure to distinguish between the scholastic approach to the teaching of theory, a set of fixed definitions and disconnected from practical applications, and the idea of applied theoretical knowledge. In other words, the value of using theoretical concepts to establish a relationship with workplace reality enables individuals to comprehend what is happening, why it is happening and how it can be transformed (Engestrom, 1994). Another influence on the marginalization of the theory – practice relationship is the anti-intellectual tradition that lies at the heart of much of UK and USA 'enterprise culture'. This has been inimical to the idea of theory and intellectual leadership informing business strategy, let alone human resource development within organizations (Hamel and Praland, 1994).

Despite the limitations of many existing models of work-based learning the concept itself is innovative and extremely important, since it does place firm emphasis upon the importance of the workplace as a 'site' of learning (Streek, 1989) and extends the promise of forms of further professional development that relate more specifically to actual needs. However, the existing developments have failed to address how work-based learning can enable individuals to think in more theoretically informed ways about the nature of their work and the forms of further professional development they might need. These issues are explored in more detail in the next section.

EMERGING PROFESSIONAL DEVELOPMENT NEEDS OF FE TEACHERS

One of the implications of the skill audits being carried out by Training and Enterprise Councils (TECs) and other research about the future of work and associated skill requirements (British Telecom, 1993) is that the new jobs being created in the economy will require people with conceptual skills and knowledge. If occupational skill demands are going to require higher level conceptual understanding, then it follows that the demands on FE teachers will also be of a higher level. Such developments are likely to lead to a blurring of the traditional distinction between education and training, since the emphasis will increasingly be upon the combination of theoretical and applied learning. The implication of these developments is that FE colleges will confront a dual challenge. New human resource development (HRD) strategies will be required to enable staff to take up these new roles, and new curriculum delivery models will need to be devised to prepare students for future employment opportunities.

New work contexts in FE

Incorporation as autonomous organizations responsible for their own financial and strategic direction has led many colleges to introduce new organizational structures. Traditional bureaucratic and hierarchical structures have been replaced by different forms of matrix management, project teams and networks. One consequence is that FE teachers' new work contexts are now characterized by more open types of organizational and management systems (FEU, 1991). There have been two main manifestations of this change: a greater degree of responsibility has been devolved to teachers and trainers, and their professional identities have been transformed quite dramatically (Ollin, 1994).

The national trend towards modular courses and credit transfer between different courses has resulted in FE teachers having to accept a far greater degree of responsibility for redesigning course delivery and establishing a common means of measuring 'value added' across different programmes and qualifications. Substantial changes in the contributions to support the wider work of the organization have also had to be made. Teachers are required to adopt broader areas of managerial responsibility and are subject to greater degrees of professional accountability. This has meant that the traditional sense of security and guarantees of professional specialism associated with specific fields of the curriculum that arose from working within a fixed team, a specific location, homogeneous-aged client groups and at a specific level has been lost in many areas of further education and work-related training. Three main consequences of organizational change can be identified.

Three key needs

The effective use and integration of technological media to improve student learning and enhance teaching will be one of the most important challenges confronting FE teachers over the next few years. This requirement is a direct result of the development of modular curricula and the introduction of resource-based and open learning in many colleges. Such developments have sought to empower learners and remove the control of the learning process from teachers. In future, a key task for teachers will be to design appropriate learning activities and establish new learning contexts to support these more independent forms of learning. These new tasks will require specialist skill and pedagogic awareness; in fact, such expertise will be essential to the design of learning programmes which will have to strike a balance between the process of learning and the actual selection of the content to be learned (Heerman, 1984; Laurillard, 1993; Leclerq, 1991). A parallel but related development will be the need for teachers to work alongside, negotiate and liaise more directly with other professional and technical staff; for instance, personnel in libraries, information technology centres, freelance consultants, etc., in order to plan and coordinate the delivery of new educational and training programmes.

The introduction of core skills, an integral part of GNVQs, is also causing a re-evaluation of FE teachers' professional expertise. Core skills involve the delivery of general education within vocational courses. Two substantial problems exist. The diverse academic and occupational backgrounds of many teachers mean that they may require extensive professional support to enhance their capability to deliver core skills (Young et al., 1994). Another problem is that there are wide differences in research evidence about the feasibility and value of attempting to embed core skills within vocational courses, especially given the curricula and pedagogic challenges this task poses for teachers and trainers, and the lack of evidence to confirm the validity of this strategy (Green, 1995; Smithers, 1993; Wolf and Rapiau, 1993).

Finally, the Further Education Funding Council has accorded a far higher priority to the question of access and guidance in colleges and allocated an element of the overall funding to this function, thereby substantially increasing its importance. This issue has received further reinforcement from the recognition that, wherever possible, prior assessment of student/trainee learning must be taken into account (FEU, 1991). FE teachers are now involved with counselling students, assisting them to undertake self-assessment and producing action plans, and outlining strategies to further their progression. This helps students to exercise a greater degree of choice over the nature of their learning programmes and to identify the scope for credit accumulation and transfer between courses.

A new concept of teaching in FE

These new contexts and responsibilities have shifted the emphasis from the traditional model of learning, with its exclusive concern with the imparting of knowledge or demonstration of occupationally bound skills, to alternative approaches that focus upon the learner. FE teachers are now expected to apply their specialist knowledge and skill in ways that are not subject or occupationally specific, and to structure such knowledge and skills to respond to the needs of learners. The needs of the learner have been accorded a greater priority, and as a consequence teachers have to take up an extended range of roles. For instance, they need to be capable of acting as an instructor, facilitator, guide, broker, etc., depending upon the nature of the learning programme.

The shift to learner-led approaches has also involved teachers in making contributions within their respective organizations in ways that have not traditionally been associated with their roles (FEU, 1991; Shackleton, 1988). In particular, they are increasingly utilizing systems that ensure more comprehensive support and guidance for learners, displaying higher levels of self-management and working with a greater variety of teams and development of project team identities.

Recent research has demonstrated the specific nature of FE teachers' new roles and suggested how work-based learning could support those roles (Young and Guile, 1995). This research has argued that FE teachers possess two forms of specialist knowledge and skill which can be viewed as different varieties of theory: first, *curriculum theory* that is a part of academic and/or technically grounded disciplines, e.g. mathematics or media studies; and second, *pedagogic theory* that informs and underpins choices that teachers and trainers make about teaching, learning and assessment strategies. This has served the purpose of distinguishing between 'what it is' teachers are trying to get across and 'how it is done'.

This research has suggested that FE teachers will increasingly need to become 'connective specialists' (Young and Guile, 1995); in other words, to be able to utilize the two forms of specialist knowledge and skill which are required to operate in the new organizational contexts; and to develop inter-dependent relationships with colleagues who – as team members – have a joint responsibility to deliver particular curricula or training programmes. This new concept of the FE teacher role implies both a specialist and gener-alist dimension. The specialist dimension refers to both the curriculum and pedagogic expertise of teachers. It involves taking decisions about and making connections between:

- curriculum content, structure and patterns of delivery;
- the integration of resource-based learning and the more formal aspects of teaching/training;
- guidance and assessment of student learning;
- operating quality systems and establishing measures for added value;
- the balance between professional self-development and organiza-tional needs.

The generalist dimension refers to the professional competences that teach-ers require to operate within the wider organizational settings. It involves responding to:

- a more corporate, less autonomous concept of professionalism;
- thinking about work in system terms, including an emphasis on collaboration across team boundaries and effective networking, rather than from a perspective of the individual employee.

Limitations of current professional development

The current approaches to professional development, including the new developments of work-based learning, may prove to be inadequate to address the new challenges outlined above. Competence-based awards, as already noted, have been criticized for lacking a sufficient theoretical dimension. Yet the traditional academic approach, offering advanced quali-fications that fail to relate theory to practice, also limit their professional relevance for FE teachers. The demand of FE teachers' new work contexts is to 'connect' their knowledge and skill to broader organizational require-ments when compared with the past. This will involve them engaging in activities that require both their practical and theoretical learning and this implies that a reconceptualization of the relationship between theoretical and practical learning in further professional development is necessary.

RE-VISITING THE RELATIONSHIP BETWEEN THEORY AND PRACTICE

Two quite different concepts of theoretical activity are associated with continuing professional development; it is possible to distinguish between these concepts by employing the terms *theory* and *theorizing* (Young and Guile, 1995). The former is usually defined as learning associated with academic study. The *theory* that is learned involves the concepts and explanations developed through research and explored within disciplines (and in multi-disciplinary study). Theory in this sense is the product of the distinctive specialist activity of the academic staff of universities. It provides explanations and understandings of practical activity, but does not arise from the experience of that activity. Theory is created according to different rules and procedures and priorities to practical knowledge. It is theory in this sense and the rules and procedures for producing it that has formed the content of traditional academic masters degrees.

Theorizing, on the other hand, is the intellectual activity that distinguishes professions from other occupations. It refers to the process of systematically reflecting on one's own professional practice and discerning alternative or improved ways of resolving professional concerns. Practical learning involves this process of theorizing and learning and leads to the practical knowledge of professionals which is learned largely but not entirely in the course of work rather than by study, and is central to the process of intellectual apprenticeship that is involved in becoming a qualified professional.

The traditional divide between theoretical and practical learning leaves the practitioner with either 'theory' that is disconnected from practice, or the ability to 'theorize' practice but with no grasp of the forces shaping it. Some professional degrees have taken this idea of theorizing considerably further. By incorporating such strategies as action research which enhances the process of reflection, they have begun to give theorizing (and practical learning) a new status; they have shown how it can be made rigorous and systematic.

Approaches to work-based learning in the UK, as already noted, have, in the main, adopted one of two approaches to the question of theory and practice. The dominant tendency has been to down-play the question and to attempt to resolve issues about theory and practice through the assessment procedures. Certain projects, however, have been based on attempts to systematize the process of 'theorizing' as one basis for making theoretical and practical learning comparable and therefore suitable for the academic accreditation of practical or work-based learning (Anglia Polytechnic University, 1991).

Combining theoretical and practical learning

In order for FE teachers to develop the appropriate knowledge and skills they need to operate in their new work contexts they will need to engage in practical learning, i.e. reflection on their own practice or theorizing; they will also need to further their theoretical learning, i.e. understanding and using concepts which explain change in their practice but which do not arise from that work. It will not be possible to develop and keep in mind fixed solutions for every possible teaching dilemma. The problems that FE teachers will confront will be innumerable and cannot be foreseen. Therefore further professional training will need to support the development of 'theoretically thinking' teachers (Engestrom, 1994) who are capable of responding to pedagogic and managerial challenges.

The argument of this chapter, therefore, is that theoretical and practical learning need to be 'connected' in order to assist teachers to respond to their new professional challenges. This will help to overcome the problem of either equating theory and theorizing, or assuming that from the point of view of improving professional practice, it is only 'theorizing' that is relevant.

Outline of a connective model

The implications of a 'connective' model for further professional development have been explored in an Employment Department funded national development project, 'Work-based Learning for the Teacher/Trainers of the Future' (Young and Guile, 1995). The *connective* model developed by the project encourages the combination and interdependence of theoretical and practical learning. It has been proposed as the basis for both the accreditation of work-based learning and for an approach to staff development which responds to the new needs of FE teachers.

The 'connective model' would provide a role for:

- *theoretical learning*: theory would provide the concepts for analysing the problems that arise for professionals in their places of work;

- *practical learning*: workplace experience would be the key source of practical learning and of problems for analysis, for applying theory and for exploring the implications of different solutions to problems;

- *the relationship between theoretical and practical learning*: theoretical and practical learning are closely linked through partnerships in which universities and client organizations develop common long-term goals for further professional development.

Unlike the traditional view of universities as institutions committed to the preservation of traditional standards, the 'connective' model implies a different role for universities when supporting further professional development. The role of a university would be to act as a source of innovation and organizational change. The task therefore would be to identify for academic credit forms of learning in the workplace that enhance an individual's capacity to innovate; and to ensure that the concepts made available through university-based study also support innovatory processes in organizations. This implies that new criteria for partnership between universities and FE colleges would need to be set, since the goal of the 'connective' model would be to encourage students to develop critiques of and alternatives to existing practice and to apply the critiques and alternatives in the process of developing their professional capabilities. The daunting task of creating such new forms of partnership will ultimately be based upon negotiation, achieving a degree of trust and establishing an overall sense of common direction and purpose.

REFERENCES

Anglia Polytechnic University (1991) *ASSET, Vol. 1*. Cambridge: Anglia Polytechnic University.

Ashworth, P. and Saxon, J. (1990) On competence. *Journal of Further and Higher Education*, **14** (2), 5.

Barnett, R. (1994) *The Limits of Competence: Knowledge, Higher Education and Society*. Buckingham: SRHE and Open University Press.

Black, H. and Wolfe, A. (1990) *Knowledge and Competence*. Sheffield: Department of Employment.

British Telecom (1993) *Matching Skills: A Question of Demand and Supply*. London: BT Education Department.

Carroll, S. (1994) National standards for FE (an update). *Journal of the National Association for Staff Development*, January, 5–11.

Chown, A. (1992) TDLB standards and FE. *Journal of Further and Higher Education*, **16** (3), 52–9.

Chown, A. and Last, J. (1993) Can the NCVQ model be used for teacher training? *Journal of Further and Higher Education*, **17** (2), 15–36.

Elliott, J. (1993) *Reconstructing Teacher Education*. London: Falmer.

Employment Department (1992) *Higher Education Developments: Learning through Work*. Sheffield: Employment Department.

Engestrom, Y. (1994) *Training for Change*. London: International Labour Office.

Eraut, M. and Cole, G. (1993) *Assessing Competence in the Professions*. Sheffield: Employment Department.

Evans, K., Brown, A. and Oates, T. (1986) *Developing Work-Based Learning*. Sheffield: Manpower Services Commission.

Further Education Unit (FEU) (1991) *The Flexible College Part 2*. London: FEU.

Green, A. (1995) The European challenge to British vocational education and training, in P. Hodkinson and M. Issitt (eds), *The Challenge of Competence*. London: Cassell.

Hamel, G. and Praland, C. K. (1994) *Competing for the Future*. Cambridge, MA: Harvard University Press.

Heerman, B. (1984) *Teaching and Learning with Computers*. San Francisco: Jossey-Bass.

Hutton, W. (1995) *The State We're In*. London: Jonathan Cape.

Laurillard, D. (1993) *Rethinking University Teaching*. London: Routledge.

Leclerq, D. (1991) Multi-media training – trainers' skills, in *Vocational Training, Vol. 1*, pp. 28–32. Berlin: CEDEFOP.

Manpower Services Commission (MSC)/Department for Vocational Qualifications (1988) *A Review of Vocational Qualifications*. London: HMSO.

Ollin, R. (1994) TDLB standards and organizational development – are the standards old-fashioned? *Transition*, February, 12–13.

Shackleton, J. (1988) The professional role of the lecturer, in *Planning the Curriculum*. London: Further Education Unit.

Smithers, A. (1993) *All Our Futures – Britain's Education Revolution*, a *Dispatches* report on education. London: Channel 4 Television.

Streek, W. (1989) Skills and the limits of neo-liberalism. *Work, Employment and Society*, **3** (1), 89–104.

Young, M. (1994) New relationship between theoretical and practical learning (unpublished paper). Post-16 Education Centre, Institute of Education, London.

Young, M. and Guile, D. (1995) *Work-based Learning for the Teacher/Trainer of the Future*. London: Post-16 Education Centre, Institute of Education.

Young, M., Lucas, N., Sharp, G. and Cunningham, B. (1994) *Teacher Education for the Further Education Sector*. London: Post-16 Education Centre, Institute of Education.

Whitty, G. (1991) Competence-based teacher education: approaches and issues. *Cambridge Journal of Education*, **21** (3).

Wolfe, A. and Rapiau, M. (1993) The academic achievement of craft apprentices in France and England. *Comparative Education*, **29** (1), 29–44.

Chapter 13

Lifetime Learning and Professional Development

Malcolm Maguire and Alison Fuller

Issues related to the professional development of 'mid-career' managers are becoming increasingly important in the context of a burgeoning interest in, and adoption of, notions of lifetime learning. We examine the concept of lifetime learning and its relevance for the apparent disparities in participation in learning activities by different socio-economic and occupational groups through the example of Ford's Employee Development and Assistance Programme (EDAP). The Ford experience suggests that the relationship between social class and participation in learning is not as straightforward as some of the literature would lead us to believe. We then examine in greater depth the debates concerning the propensity for technical and managerial level workers to undergo programmes of training or education, before drawing attention to the relevance of a learning culture and change management to these issues.

LIFETIME LEARNING

The notions of *lifelong learning* and *lifetime learning* have become commonplace in recent years and have been assimilated into the rhetoric of politicians across the political spectrum. In the United Kingdom, the term 'lifelong learning' has come to be closely associated with the setting of the national targets for education and training (NETTs). Originally, the concepts grew out of a recognition that basic schooling cannot meet an individual's continuing educational needs, and that individuals should be able to participate in planned learning throughout life. Rogers (1992) argued that the way lifelong learning needs have been met has varied between countries. In America, for example, the notion of lifelong education was translated into the provision of *community education*, which aimed to integrate the educational provision of both children and adults. A more radical strategy, advocated by the OECD under the rubric of *recurrent education*, recommended a refocusing of the formal system of education, whereby adults would be able to opt in and out as they wished. Generally, considerable emphasis has been placed on adult education being used as a means to address inequalities of opportunities which exist in societies and to bring about political and social change. Under the all-embracing term of 'continuing education', it is regarded as the follow-on from initial education while being something quite separate. In reality, most of these terms have been intermingled and in some cases they have become confused and vague in meaning.

In Britain as elsewhere, studies have revealed significant disparities in the proportions of certain groupings of individuals who participate in learning. In particular, factors such as social class, gender and ethnicity have been found significantly to affect the learning process. The *Training in Britain* study (Training Agency, 1989) provided evidence of the relationship between previous education and participation in training, with those who receive higher levels of education being more likely to receive further training at work, and members of social class I being twice as likely as those in social class 3 to report receiving training in the previous three years. Edwards *et al.* (1993) attribute this situation to cultural factors, so that members of different social classes tend to adopt class norms which greatly influence behaviour. As far as the working class is concerned, 'a particular culture is engendered, a culture of non-participation, in which forms of provision are perceived to be part of a middle class culture'. Such notions may be called into question by the experience of employee development schemes (Maguire and Horrocks, 1995). What cannot be disputed, however, is that there currently exists in Britain an unevenness in the distribution of the proportions of different socio-economic groups who are engaged in learning activities. A recent review of the literature asserted that:

> The key message which emerges from the data ... is that those who have had the greatest exposure to learning and who may therefore be considered to have gained greatest benefit or reward from the system, are also those who continue to be exposed to, and derive reward and benefit from, the system.
>
> (Maguire *et al.*, 1993, p. 6)

In terms of motivations to learn, the literature suggests that individuals can have a variety of reasons for participating in learning, with a broad distinction often being made between job-related or career development reasons and non-work-related reasons, such as personal development. McGivney (1993) concludes that 'motivations vary according to age and gender: younger adults and men learn mostly for employment-related reasons, while older adults and women learn more for personal satisfaction, self-development, leisure purposes and family or role transitions.' The *Training in Britain* study categorized those who felt they had no need to participate as: (1) those who were happy to continue in their existing jobs and saw no need for training; (2) those who felt they had sufficient qualifications and could see no further benefit from vocational training, and (3) those in poorly paid jobs requiring no qualifications who saw training as only being useful in finding work. Such arguments lend weight to the contention that work-related reasons lie behind most decisions to participate in training, if not in learning activities more generally. The antipathy towards training on the part of workers in the lower levels of the occupational hierarchy is partly attributed by Rigg (1989) to the lack of opportunities afforded them by their employers. This may be compounded by a lack of reward for, or recognition of, learning on the part of employers.

Recently, the workplace has grown in prominence as an arena for learning. Traditionally, learning at work has been equated with training, which has been undertaken in order to impart specific job-related skills, or in order to inculcate a company ethos or culture. Research from different parts of the world has shifted this debate by suggesting that the way in which work is organized is of fundamental importance in understanding the process of skill formation, and overrides any concentration on individuals and the factors which affect their motivation. Research in the Far East attributed the higher productivity levels of Japanese firms to differences in organizational structure and the ways in which these differences influenced the process of skill formation. Japanese organizations enable employees to continue to move upwards in terms of income and status, but crucially they facilitate the acquisition of breadth and depth of skill (Koike and Inoki, 1990). In this context, motivation to train or acquire a skill is not a problem, as the individuals are embedded in an organizational structure which facilitates the acquisition of skill through time. Furthermore, research carried out in the USA and Poland suggests that the type of work undertaken and the degree of autonomy and responsibility enjoyed by those carrying out the work have a significant effect on the employee's intelligence and ability to learn (Kohn and Slomczynski, 1990).

It may be assumed from the above that those occupying managerial posts will exhibit a greater propensity to participate in learning activities, for both career and personal development reasons. However, the wide band of managers we have loosely grouped under the title 'mid-career managers', referring to those in their mid-thirties and forties who, having attained some experience in managerial jobs, are looking to progress, or at least consolidate their careers, may be said to be in a somewhat ambivalent position. On the one hand, they are seen as being of vital importance in any attempt to generate a significant enhancement of the skill levels of the national workforce as a whole, as exemplified by the proliferation of formal learning opportunities which would appear to be directed at them as a group (for example, MBAs, part-time degrees). At the same time, they are becoming increasingly vulnerable, due to a combination of labour market trends, technological change and ideas of strategic management which are leading to a process of 'delayering', 'downsizing' and generally reducing the size of the middle management group in many organizations. We therefore need to consider the available evidence about this group's propensity to participate in some form of learning activity.

There is relatively little research detailing the effect of age on managers' participation in training, with the exception of Warr (1993), who, on the basis of a combination of analysis of the Labour Force survey and a survey of managers, concluded that 'fewer older managers than younger ones take part in training' and that 'the amount of time spent in training is also lower at older ages'. While Warr does not discuss in any detail why older managers undertake less training than their younger colleagues, he suggests that managers, irrespective of age, believe that the need to acquire new skills and knowledge has become increasingly important in recent years, and this trend is likely to continue. Warr also found that older managers were apparently 'less confident in their ability to learn and less keen to take part in further training activities', and observed that a combination of older managers' reluctance to learn, their doubts about the outcomes of participation, and their superiors' scepticism about the cost-effectiveness of investing in their further training, conspire to ensure that this group is under-represented in many management learning activities. This mutually reinforcing dynamic would seem to contribute to a 'training-for-the-young' culture.

Warr's work points up three areas of interest for this discussion: (1) internal factors relating to notions of self-concept and image; (2) adult learning theory and lifetime learning and their implications for the target group, and (3) organizational change relating to the implications of flatter structures for management learning.

Burns (1982) contends that 'success in work/career appears to depend as much on how a person feels about the qualities and attributes he possesses as on the qualities themselves'. Thus the attitudes and behaviour of individuals cannot simply be inferred from variables such as socio-economic status, age and gender. However, it may be assumed that the self-image of individuals who have achieved managerial positions by the time they are in mid-career is likely to be shaped by the position and power they hold within hierarchical organizations. It could also be anticipated that the range of social interactions experienced by managers (e.g. with subordinates and peers) might help to reinforce a positive image. Burns argues that the self-concept consists of two fundamental components: *competence* and *belonging*. A positive self-concept requires individuals to feel that they are competent at their job or occupation and to feel that they are accepted by the groups that matter to them (e.g. family, work colleagues, etc.). The worth which individuals attach to themselves depends on their evaluation of themselves on these two counts. From a symbolic interactionist perspective, individuals' perceptions of self-worth will be affected by the types of inter-actions and social encounters they experience over time. This means that while we might superficially expect managers as a group to have positive self-concepts because of their socio-economic status, the range of individual experiences and interactions, coupled with personality differences, means that such inferences are likely to be grossly over-simplified.

Adult learning theory is of particular relevance for this debate. This has largely been concerned to understand how adults learn and how this knowl-edge could help practitioners and providers to design, structure and deliver learning opportunities. 'Andragogy' (Knowles, 1970; Jarvis, 1987; Brookfield, 1987) assumes that adults are ready to learn and are self-directed learners. Critics of this view have argued that the ability to be self-directed regarding learning may be true of some adults, but is unlikely to be a given condition of those with low socio-economic status (Huam, 1994). A variety of situational (e.g. time, cost) and dispositional (e.g. indi-vidual attributes and self-concept) factors interact either to inhibit or motivate the individual to participate in learning. Huam postulates that those with high socio-economic status are more likely to participate in train-ing. This observation is consistent with Warr's findings, in that the nature of the job affects managers' participation in and experience of training. However, participation in training activities because it is a requirement of the job is not the same as being 'ready to learn'. While theoretically it is logical to suggest that managers' readiness to learn will be more apparent than is the case for lower socio-economic groups, there is a need to critically examine this notion in order to further our understanding of decision-making processes among members of this heterogeneous group.

The literature on individuals' commitment to learning (Maguire *et al.*, 1993) suggests that variables such as age, income, gender, prior educational experience and factors such as time and cost, influence adult participation rates in learning activities. A major gap in the literature identified by Maguire *et al.* is the lack of 'studies of lifetime learning experiences of indi-viduals and even fewer studies of the role which training plays in these'. In addition, Fuller (1994) has stated that 'no matter what *use* and *exchange* value is attributed to training and qualifications in broad terms, individuals' own perceptions of self and career will affect how they experience such opportunities and will determine the meanings and values they attach to them'. It has also been established that lack of awareness of learning opportunities and of guidance provision are crucial factors in limiting participation.

Broad economic trends and changes in organizational structures, from the hierarchical to the flat, mean that previous assumptions about employment security for those reaching managerial positions are no longer valid. In consequence, organizational cultures and individual or collectively held values are susceptible to change (Handy, 1985). The key point to emerge from this is that change at the organizational level can relate to change at the individual level. It may be, therefore, that current trends in management careers and organizational staffing mean that mid-career or older managers are finding themselves in new situations which by their nature require learning.

One of the factors which may enable individuals to look positively on their demand for learning associated with a changed situation may be their view on whether individuals can change (Adler, 1991). It may be hypothesized that individuals who believe that people are able to change would be more likely to see learning as a way of bringing about self-improvement than those who take a more sceptical view of the individual's ability to change.

EMPLOYEE DEVELOPMENT

Partly as a result of a growing awareness of the differences in productivity and commitment to the organization achieved by the introduction of adaptations to organizational structures and espoused company cultures, there is a burgeoning literature and debate over the efficacy of the 'learning organisation' (Pedler *et al.*, 1991), with the learning requirements of managers emerging as a prime focus.

In the UK the notion of the learning organization has been one of a number of strands which, taken together, reflect a growing acceptance that it is not sufficient merely to provide training to a certain number of individuals in order to equip them with the skills required to fill identified skill shortage areas. Rather, there has to be a more fundamental reappraisal of, and attitudinal shift towards, the value attached to learning by society as a whole. The emergence of these ideas has spawned publications and initiatives, such as the National Institute for Adult and Continuing Education's (NIACE) *The Learning Imperative*, the RSA's *Learning Society* enquiry, led by Sir Christopher Ball, the RSA's *Learning for the Future* initiative and the Economic and Social Research Council's (ESRC) *Learning Society* initiative.

A significant trend which is highly relevant to this debate has been the spread of employee development schemes. While Ford's EDAP scheme is the best known, the list of companies operating similar schemes is growing rapidly. Payne's (1992) study of large firms which were either known to have set up employee development schemes or were regarded as leaders in the field of training showed that, unlike Ford's EDAP, which evolved from a trade union initiative, the vast majority of schemes were management initiatives. Crucially, such schemes are seen to encourage participation in learning. While, initially, this participation is often not work-related, it may subsequently lead to greater participation in, and commitment to, work-related training. The personal development of the individual is a key factor in these schemes. Bridge and Salt (1992) clearly differentiate between these types of schemes and work-based learning which tends to be vocational and job-specific.

Ford's EDAP was created in 1987 by a joint trade union and management agreement. Its main objective was 'to provide opportunities for personal development and training outside working hours for all employees of the Company' (Minutes of National Joint Negotiating Committee, Ford Motor Company Limited, 7 December 1987).

At that time, the improving of industrial relations within the company was an avowed aim of the agreement. On the basis of a similar programme which had been operating in the company in the United States, it was envisaged that up to 20 per cent of the company's employees would avail themselves of the opportunities available under the programme. Subsequently, the objectives were broadened to encompass career development and healthier lifestyles.

The programme itself was launched in 1989, with an initial allocation of £1,850,000 being apportioned to the EDAP Committees which had been set up within the various plants in the United Kingdom. Under the scheme, each Ford UK employee is eligible for an annual grant of up to £200 towards the cost of courses which have to be undertaken on a voluntary basis, out of working time, and to be distinct from all existing job-related training. From the outset, it was apparent that there would be no shortage of interest in, or enthusiasm for, the programme on the part of the employees. A survey of employees' opinions, carried out by the Trade Union Research Unit at Ruskin College, Oxford, in 1989, suggested that an overwhelming majority of employees would be interested (Hougham *et al.*, 1991). As it was, rather than the 5 per cent of employees who had been predicted to apply for grants, 15,000 employees, representing one-third of the workforce, applied for grants within the first six months of the programme's operation (Mortimer, 1990). Subsequent events have shown that this was no mere flash in the pan, for progress since then has been substantial.

Much of the publicity given to the success of the EDAP scheme has focused on the way in which large proportions of manual workers in the company have been attracted into participating in some form of learning activity. For example, '75% of all employees have taken part in EDAP programmes' (Mortimer, 1994). There has also been a tendency to show how that participation may have been initiated by the opportunity to engage in activities such as fitness training, or music tuition. What is less well known is the amount of activity which leads to the acquisition of professional level skills and qualifications. Professor Ken Mortimer, the Manager of Education Programmes for Ford of Europe, points out that in each of the three years from 1992 to 1994, 250 employees were studying for degrees under EDAP (Mortimer, 1994). At Ford's Halewood plant alone there is a B.Phil. programme, under the auspices of EDAP, which has enrolled 125 employees. Furthermore, Mortimer clearly sees EDAP as an essential plank in the process of continuous professional development, which is regarded as vital to the future success of the company. For the purposes of our discussion, two important points emerge from this consideration of employee development schemes. First, it would appear that the latent desire (and ability) to obtain high level qualifications is vast – it may also point to a disturbing under-utilization of talent throughout industry. Second, the ability of programmes such as employee development schemes to trigger a previously inert enthusiasm for learning applies as much to individuals occupying managerial positions as it does to those at the lower levels of the occupational hierarchy.

CULTURAL CHANGE AND LIFELONG LEARNING

An important implication of the evidence from the Ford EDAP scheme is that the demand for learning is linked to the availability of 'appropriate' learning opportunities. The appropriateness of these learning opportunities for technical or managerial staff is likely to be associated with access to professional qualifications, enabling experienced employees to upgrade their skills and certification in line with their on-the-job experience and to develop the skills and attributes required by changing organizational and technological work contexts. The Ford ASSET project provides one such example. In this scheme, the Anglia Polytechnic University and the Ford Motor Company are collaborating to enable engineers qualified to HNC/D level to gain a work-based honours engineering degree (Guise et al., 1995). Its aims are to:

- widen the opportunities for mature engineers to acquire a further professional and academic qualification based on their experience and learning at work;

- reinforce the concept of continuous professional learning.

While the first of these aims seems to be highlighting the benefits of the scheme to individuals – that is, the chance of gaining a higher level qualification by drawing on work-based experience and learning – the rationale underpinning the second aim is perhaps more ambiguous. However, a reading of some of the material accompanying the project reveals that a positive connection between continuous professional learning and organizational benefit is being fostered. The following quote illustrates this point: 'engineers and managers within Ford have stressed that a major expectation of professional engineers is the ability to take responsibility for one's own learning, a necessary skill in managing continuous technical and organisational change' (Guise *et al.*, 1995, p. 1). Such initiatives recognize the implications of changing patterns of production and work practice and their rationales strongly suggest that 'lifelong learning' or 'continuous professional development' for high level staff is necessary: for the individual in terms of protecting his or her position in a competitive labour market and for employers in terms of developing a workforce with the sorts of skills, attributes and attitudes likely to help the organization to survive and prosper.

However, the struggle to find working examples of learning organizations or companies (Taylor, 1994) indicates that while the rationales associated with lifelong learning sound attractive and plausible, the ability to deliver it to individuals and groups within organizational contexts is more difficult. One explanation for this may lie in the absence of a 'learning culture' being established in the workplace. Owen and Williamson (1995) identify three ways of facilitating the sort of changes necessary to develop a learning culture. These are termed 'culture management', 'empowered individualism' and 'labour processes'. The first refers to the way in which top management can determine an organizational or company vision and value set, which is then transmitted through a variety of mechanisms including management development programmes, training, internal and external corporate literature and publicity and so on. In this manner, certain 'cultures' have become associated with particular outcomes as in the connection that was established in the 1980s between 'quality' and 'excellent' business performance (see, for example, Peters and Waterman, 1982). Owen and Williamson (1995) argue that this approach to culture management is likely to be flawed as its focus is on changing the language of employee management and relations without changing relationships of power and control.

The 'empowered individualism' perspective is described as paradoxical because it attempts to facilitate individuals to become self-directed but fails to adapt existing organizational structures in such a way that they could enable employees to display qualities associated with self-direction (e.g. increased commitment, productivity and innovation). Alternatively, the 'labour processes' approach highlights the relationship between the way in which work is organized and learning culture. The suggestion is that conditions fostering learning, including two-way communication, collaborative problem-solving, integration of theory and practice, developmental (as opposed to judgmental) appraisals, can encourage the development of a learning culture. By implication, the existence of the converse conditions in terms of working relationships and task management may constrain the development of an educative environment.

The achievement of a learning culture at the organizational level may in reality depend on the implementation of all three perspectives. For example, a recent study of the training of air traffic engineers found that the way work was organized and tasks were managed contributed to the workplace being perceived by most respondents as a rich learning environment (Fuller *et al.*, 1995). In addition, messages emanating from the top were strongly advocating a 'quality' approach to the orientation of the business which many engineers felt was consistent with the 'professional' attitudes they brought to work. However, there had been very little attempt within this organization to 'empower' individuals through mechanisms such as continuous professional development programmes, even though the study revealed considerable enthusiasm among respondents for this type of initiative. As a result, the project indicated that the existence of appropriate 'labour processes' and 'culture management' without 'individual empowerment' was inhibiting the enhancement of individual skills and progress towards the goal of producing a highly adaptable and multi-skilled workforce: that is, the development of an established learning culture.

FINAL REMARKS

In this chapter we have outlined some of the key issues relating to the 'lifelong learning' of individuals. While some concerns particularly relevant to mid-career managers were highlighted, the overall conclusion drawn from the discussion is that the factors facilitating or inhibiting continuous employee development are likely to be similar in substance, if not in particular details, for groups at all levels. For example, the area of access to, and information about, learning opportunities is likely to be more problematic for those employees who have had little previous experience of training and qualifications, but will not be restricted to this group. It was pointed out that variables such as age can provide significant barriers to learning, even for those who have reached managerial positions. It was also contended that the availability of apparently appropriate learning opportunities such as those embodied in the two examples involving the Ford Motor Company, is a positive development. However, empirical evidence of the sort of learning organization and culture likely to facilitate individuals' ability to learn was sparse. The difficulty of achieving a learning culture provides, in our view, an important part of the explanation as to why the concept of lifelong learning is hard to translate into practice and why the talents and skills of individuals, including senior technical and managerial staff, may continue to be under-utilized in the future.

There would appear to be a pressing need to enhance understanding of the organizational structures and processes likely to facilitate or inhibit the development of learning cultures and to test practical ways of overcoming them: the role of change management is clearly crucial to this.

Viewing change from a different conceptual perspective, evaluators of the impact of educational innovations have utilized a model known as *stages of concern* to monitor individuals' responses to change (Hord, 1987). A seven-point journey has been charted which begins with a minimal reaction as participants are exposed to information concerning the proposed innovation and progresses to a final stage where those affected by the change are engaged in reviewing, and, if necessary, adapting the innovation to suit their needs. The strength of this approach is that it allows researchers to assess individuals' preparedness to change, and by inference their readiness to learn, through the way in which they are reacting to the organizational, cultural and wider labour market changes that surround them.

As we have pointed out, relatively little is known about mid-career managers' attitudes to, and experiences of, lifetime learning and continuous professional development. Adopting the above model could provide a fruitful framework from which to discover more about a group whose participation in a learning society may have tended to have been taken for granted.

REFERENCES

Adler, N. (1991) *International Dimensions of Organizational Behaviour* (2nd edn). Boston: PWS – Kent Publishing Company.

Bridge, H. and Salt, H. (1992) *Access and Delivery in Continuing Education and Training*. Nottingham: University of Nottingham and Employment Department.

Brookfield, S. D. (1987) *Developing Critical Thinkers: Challenging Adults to Explore Alternative Ways of Thinking and Acting*. Milton Keynes: Open University Press.

Burns, R. (1982) *Self Concept Development and Education*. London: Holt, Rinehart & Winston.

Edwards, R., Sieminski, S. and Zeldin, D. (eds) (1993) *Adult Learners, Education and Training: A Reader*. London: Routledge.

Fuller, A. (1994) New approaches to management, training and qualifications: perceptions of use and exchange. *Journal of Management Development*, **13** (1), 23–4.

Fuller, A., Davies, P. and Morgan, F. (1995) *Investigating OJT*, final project report to the Civil Aviation Authority. Leicester: Vocational Education and Training Research Associates.

Guise, S., Holman, M. and Winter, R. (1995) *The Ford ASSET Project: Professional Learning at Work*. Cambridge: Anglia Polytechnic University.

Handy, C. (1985) *Understanding Organisations*. Harmondsworth: Penguin.

Hord, S. (1987) *Evaluating Educational Innovation*. London: Croom Helm.

Hougham, J., Thomas, J. and Sisson, K. (1991) Ford's EDAP scheme: a roundtable discussion. *Human Resource Management Journal*, **1** (3), 77–91.

Huam, K. (1994) *Changing Mind-sets: A Case Study on Mid-career Workers' Training in Singapore*. Unpublished M.Sc. dissertation. Centre for Labour Market Studies, University of Leicester.

Jarvis, P. (1987) *Adult Learning in the Social Context*. London: Croom Helm.

Knowles, M. D. (1970) *The Modern Practice of Adult Education: Andragogy versus Pedagogy*. New York: Association Press.

Kohn, M. L. and Slomczynski, K. M. (1990) *Social Structure and Self-Direction. A Comparative Analysis of the United States and Poland*. Oxford: Blackwell.

Koike, K. and Inoki, T. (1990) *Skill Formation in Japan and South-east Asia*. Tokyo: University of Tokyo Press.

McGivney, V. (1992) *Motivating Unemployed Adults to Undertake Education and Training*. Leicester: NIACE.

McGivney, V. (1993) Participation and non-participation: a review of the literature, in R. Edwards, S. Sieminski and D. Zeldin (eds), *Adult Learners, Education and Training: A Reader*. London: Routledge.

Maguire, M. and Horrocks, B. (1995) *Employee Development Programmes and Lifetime Learning*. Working Paper No. 6, Centre for Labour Market Studies. Leicester: University of Leicester.

Maguire, M., Maguire, S. and Felstead, A. (1993) *Factors Influencing Individual Commitment to Lifetime Learning: A Literature Review*. Research Series No. 20. Sheffield: Employment Department.

Mortimer, K. W. (1990) EDAP at Ford. *Industrial Relations Journal*, **21** (4), 309–14.

Mortimer, K. W. (1994) *Continuous Professional Development*. Professorial Inaugural Lecture, University of East London, 10 November.

Owen, C. and Williamson, J. (1995) *The Development of 'Learning Cultures' in the Workplace: Some Phantoms, Paradoxes and Possibilities*. Hobart: University of Tasmania.

Payne, J. (1992) *Large Employers Survey Report*. Leeds: University of Leeds.

Pedler, M., Burgoyne, J. and Boydell, T. (1991) *The Learning Company*. London: McGraw Hill.

Peters, T. J. and Waterman, R. H. (1982) *In Search of Excellence: Lessons from America's Best-run Companies*. New York: Harper & Row.

Rigg, M. (1989) *Training in Britain: A Study of Funding, Activity and Attitudes. Individual Perspectives*. Sheffield: Training Agency.

Rogers, A. (1992) *Adults Learning for Development*. London: Cassell and Education for Development.

Taylor, C. (1994) *An Exploration of the Concept of the Learning Organisation and Its Applicability within a Local Authority Social Services Department*. Paper presented to 'Training and Development: Bringing Together Theory and Practice', University of Leicester, 3–4 September.

Training Agency (1989) *Training in Britain: A Study of Funding, Activity and Attitudes – The Main Report*. Sheffield: Training Agency.

Warr, P. (1993) Training for older managers. *Human Resource Management Journal*, **4** (2), 22–38.

Chapter 14

Management Development in Partnership: An Evaluation of a Qualification Programme for Junior and Middle Managers

Peter Simpson and Tony Lyddon

This chapter explores a number of issues arising from an evaluation of a qualification-based management development programme run in partnership between Bristol Business School (BBS) and Chep UK Ltd. While a number of Chep and BBS staff have been actively involved in this evaluation, the views expressed in this chapter are those of the authors and are not necessarily shared by others.

Over recent years, in response to national initiatives in management education and development, Bristol Business School has been developing a range of programmes to assist working in partnership with client organizations. The Certificate in Management and the Diploma in Management Studies have been designed to provide a comprehensive, yet responsive programme of education and development for junior and middle managers. When run in partnership these programmes comprise workshops on a range of topics covering all the major areas of management: finance, personnel, operations, marketing, information and strategic context. The participants are assessed in each of these areas through in-company projects and assignments. The Chep programme was one of the first of its type at Bristol Business School and is now entering its fifth year. It is designed for the education and development of lower and middle managers. At the time of this evaluation two streams of the Certificate in Management (CM) and two of Diploma in Management Studies (DMS) were underway, with the first CM programme completed. A third CM stream was about to commence.

One of the key benefits of a tailor-made programme run in partnership between the Business School and a single client organization is the ability to consider issues of organizational need in a focused and detailed manner. In a programme of this type which runs for several years, the scope for addressing these aspects of programme effectiveness is further enhanced. This chapter describes how the evaluation enabled us to identify a range of issues that were significant for the Chep programme.

BACKGROUND TO THE ORGANIZATION

Chep offers a wooden pallet and plastic container hire service to help manufacturing and distribution industries move products safely, swiftly and cost-effectively. The company has the largest pool of pallets in the world: over eight million are on hire and exchanged through its depot network, customers and delivery locations. Chep started trading in 1974 and grew rapidly in the 1980s to predominate in the food and drinks market and currently employs 1110 staff, about 170 of whom fall within the potential pool for this programme. However, Chep now faces the prospect of competition in a changing market and the challenge of growing new markets with existing and new products. In 1992 it launched its quality programme; it has gained ISO 9002 accreditation in Eire and plans to win this and the Investors in People award in the UK. Chep is using national standards of competence where these are available, and implementing the emerging National Vocational Qualifications system where benefits outweigh costs.

Chep has been committed to training and development for many years. Previous involvement in the management education schemes of GKN group (of which Chep was, at that time, a subsidiary) had been unsuccessful as participants saw them as too removed from work experience in Chep. In 1989 Chep recognized the benefits of adopting a more structured approach and linking in-company training to nationally recognized qualifications. Chep approached Bristol Business School through independent consultants, since when all developments have been undertaken in partnership. Chep's priorities for selection of an academic partner were the abilities to combine flexible and innovative delivery of programmes with the assurance of high standards of attainment, leading to nationally recognized awards.

Chep has traditionally operated in a dynamic but pragmatic manner, which allowed the company to meet customer needs and exploit the potential for new business. By the mid-1980s it was growing annually by 25 per cent to the point where there was a need to bring more formality and sophistication to the management of resources. At that time there was a continuing debate about the future direction, development and growth of the business which is only now coming into sharp focus. The need for smarter, more professional management was recognized – though there was less clarity about the numbers needed over the following five years. This became a major issue once growth tailed off in the early 1990s. Chep needed a change programme which allowed individuals to manage their own learning within a structured framework. The programme would have to train managers to apply learning to current business operations through practical assignments and to undertake projects to take the business forward in a more competitive operating environment. A formal qualification linked to the development programme was seen as a valuable incentive to the participants but was not the prime motivating force behind the decision to run the programme.

The first CM intake was requested in the autumn of 1990. Since then over forty participants have been involved, with others taking individual modules. Twenty-five participants have successfully completed the Certificate level and the majority of these have progressed to Diploma level. In 1992 a participant won an individual regional award in the UK's national training awards and the programme was commended by the Surrey Training and Enterprise Council in its annual business awards.

THE APPROACH TO EVALUATION

The aims of the partnership programmes at Bristol Business School are to provide both education of a nationally recognized quality and relevant, implementable outcomes for client organizations. In order to appraise the current performance of the various programmes run by the school, and to identify areas for improvement, six evaluation studies were undertaken (Simpson *et al.*, 1994). The evaluation of the Chep programme which forms the basis of this chapter was one such study.

The evaluation explored three main areas:

- individual and corporate objectives of the programme
- the perceived success of the programme against these objectives and in terms of quality of administration, inputs and outcomes
- the strategic and cultural context for a programme of this type

The longevity of the programme and the range of experiences of participants and managers provided considerable scope to perform an evaluation of this kind. Opportunities for gathering data included:

- module evaluation forms completed by participants
- semi-structured interviews
- group review workshops
- programme documentation

As a result of the commitment of Chep to performing this evaluation we were able to ensure that the main form of data collection in this evaluation was the second of these: semi-structured interviews. This provided a rich and extensive source of data. The interviewer made comprehensive notes at the time of each interview, attempting to capture the exact words and phrases of the interviewee. These notes were supplemented by reference to audio-tape recordings of the conversation where necessary. All current participants, human resources managers and a selection of line managers and board members were included in this process. This involved interviews with twenty-four participants, seven line managers, three members of human resources management and four board members. As some were wearing more than one hat, the total number of interviewees was thirty-two.

The outcomes of the research were of interest in a number of ways. First, they provided a greater understanding of the perceptions of the administration, design and success of the programme, facilitating ongoing improvements and modifications to the programme. Second, they high-lighted differing perspectives of the three groups of stakeholders interviewed: participants, line managers and senior managers. These find-ings have significant implications for the impact of programmes of this type. For example, line managers were found to be less committed and to demon-strate less ownership than senior managers who saw the programme as a strategic intervention. Addressing this issue has been of great importance in the facilitation of the transfer of learning from the programme to the work-place. Finally, they demonstrated the importance of locating management development initiatives within a clearly developed strategy for organiza-tional change and development. A need for sharper focus in this area was important for participants, strongly influencing their perceptions of the effectiveness of the programme.

The outcomes need to be viewed in the light of continuous improve-ments that were being made to the programme from 1991 onwards, not all of which were experienced by all participants.

STAKEHOLDERS' PERCEPTIONS AND PROGRAMME IMPROVEMENTS

The difficulties in evaluating the worth of a programme in a definitive manner are well documented (Easterby-Smith, 1986; Gibb, 1972; Hamblin, 1974; Hogarth, 1979; Rackham, 1973). As one line manager expressed it: 'There is a problem of attribution: you can't prove it. It's one of those things you have to take a leap of faith with.'

Consequently, the evaluation did not set out to prove the success of the programme, but rather to explore perceptions and possible improvements. We adopted a qualitative methodology that would give us access to a wide range of views. The interview data allowed us to gain a detailed picture of how the different stakeholders viewed the programme.

Overall, the ability to tailor the programme to the needs of Chep is seen as a key aspect of the programme's merit. Business School specialists collaborate with senior functional specialists from within Chep in the delivery of modules. A director argued: 'Learning materials from Chep, and Chep-based projects are important given the unique nature of the Chep business.'

The tailored nature of the programme received a range of positive comments from participants, for example:

'The programme has you working in your own environment: this makes it more realistic.'

'Working in partnership is a good thing. The Business School staff understand Chep, what we're talking about. Working with other providers is not so relevant.'

'I don't think any other courses I've been on have been as well conducted, open and work-related as these.'

'I prefer working with colleagues than with people from other organizations. It is more beneficial in terms of gaining broader perspective of Chep. This programme also helps to motivate because it is visible within the company. If I'm doing day-release at a local college, who cares? Here, the directors are watching.'

Another key factor in this partnership is the clear organizational commitment to the programme as an ongoing part of management development in Chep. It was noted earlier that the programme is now entering its fifth year. As one participant expressed his feelings on this: 'It is not just a case of "do the course and then bye bye". After CM there's the DMS. I like the way it is a progressive thing.'

Inevitably, alongside the general support and satisfaction with the programme, areas were identified which those interviewed wished to see changed. Within the context of an investigation of the organizational needs and the influence of the programme in meeting these needs, we were able to address apparent shortcomings and to implement improvements. The needs identified could be grouped under the following headings: succession planning, improving management competence, developing interpersonal skills, culture change, gaining a wider appreciation of the organizational context, developing a common management language, and tangible/intangible benefits. Some areas for improvement that were identified are discussed below.

Succession planning

The processes of nomination and selection for participation in the programme were identified as key aspects in meeting the needs for succession planning. This was a topic of particular importance to the line managers interviewed. In early cohorts the process was essentially one of self-selection, provided candidates could demonstrate the ability to cope with the academic demands. It later became evident that a number were placed on the programme who had already been identified by their managers as unlikely to progress into managerial positions. Consequently, a very strong argument was made by line managers that they should play a greater role in the process of nominating individuals to the programme. This was implemented, along with greater use of psychometrics in the selection process.

Interpersonal skills

It was argued by participants that interpersonal skills have not been sufficiently well catered for. Participants reported that there was little opportunity to continue developing skills once they have been covered on the programme. In part this is a consequence of undertaking a general management programme which attempts to cover a large number of areas: the programme gives an impetus, but the participants must assume responsibility for taking the learning further. This is difficult when their normal work roles do not provide opportunities. In support of this development Chep now offer training in relevant interpersonal skills alongside the provision on the partnership programme.

Tangible and intangible benefits

In general it was believed that most tangible organizational benefits would be obtained in the longer term. However, in addition to these, more immediate returns could be seen to have been achieved. It was widely argued that the projects and assignments were the major source of benefits for Chep arising from the programme so far. Participants cited numerous examples to illustrate both tangible and intangible benefits that they believed were obtained as a result of the programme. These examples demonstrated financial savings, improvements in quality, customer service and benefits in recruiting, retaining and rewarding staff. Given the importance of this there was considerable interest in addressing the processes of managing assignment design, including more extensive involvement of line managers in the identification of current needs.

The learning environment

Like many organizations, Chep has a well-equipped and functional training facility at their headquarters. Most workshops were run at this location.

However, proximity to support staff and telephones meant that the frequency of interruptions for participants, generally in the form of yellow 'post-its' requesting a return telephone call, led to a high proportion of the participants reporting difficulty in making the most of the learning opportunity. A venue that had a 'learning environment', remote from the workplace, was requested. Balanced against other needs, this has been addressed by scheduling a larger number of activities to be run away from Chep locations.

One of the difficulties of part-time study is to balance the demands of work with the demands of the programme. Participants requested clearer briefing at the beginning of the programme, and especially a better idea of the high workload to be communicated to allow improved management of an already long working week. These issues have been addressed effectively on recent programmes through extension of the induction programme, to provide more time to explore needs and expectations. Underlying this process is a greater appreciation of the need for participants to understand the culture of the programme, which is influenced not only by Chep but also by the Business School, an academic organization with very different values and norms of practice. Coming to an understanding and appreciation of these differing norms and their relevance for the learning process takes time.

Mentoring

Mentoring by line managers was almost unanimously viewed as ineffective. The fundamental problem was that there was little imperative for either the participant or the mentor to make contact. The role of the mentor was insufficiently defined in relation to the particular demands of the programme, which was compounded by the fact that these mentors could only have a limited understanding of the programme. The fact that the programme has been running for a number of years has made it possible to use previous course participants as mentors, as many are now middle managers. This has considerably improved the situation.

Programme structure

In the early stages of the programme there was an emphasis on participants taking responsibility for managing the learning process themselves. However, many lacked previous experience of tertiary education which led to problems with understanding some course requirements. A move towards greater structure on the programme has been well received by participants. The key factor is identifying those areas of the programme that are most baffling for the participant. For example, some disciplines were approached in an entirely new way and participants reported that they required more workshop time to cope with the testing demands of a new area of learning. Similarly, the completion of written assessments was a new and difficult discipline for some. A large number of participants requested that the administration of assessment be tightened up to provide a more helpful structure. A number have found difficulty understanding the specific requirements for projects and, without regular sessions with Business School staff, do not find it easy to get clarification. It is clear that participants' learning is enhanced by a teaching programme which balances traditional structures and organization with a more open, flexible approach.

Secretarial support

A final point believed by participants to be extremely important for the effective operation of the programme was that of secretarial support. The support provided was widely appreciated, but required more formal recognition by line managers. Secretaries were generally happy to type up work for students, but would not prioritize this if other tasks had to be done. Line managers were sometimes reluctant to sanction programme-related work and expressed unhappiness at the additional workload being placed on the support staff. This meant that participants felt unsupported and sometimes missed assignment submission deadlines.

In summary of this section, we would argue that the benefits of performing an evaluation of this kind were great, even though it does not 'prove' the success of the programme in a rigorous manner. What we gained was a greater understanding of the experience and expectations of all involved, either as participants or as line or senior managers. This has facilitated the improvement of the programme in a manner that has also allowed and encouraged the development of thinking throughout the organization concerning the purpose and benefits of management development of this kind. However, as well as enabling us to answer some questions, the evaluation has also raised questions of a different kind, some of which are less easy to resolve. In particular, we discovered some fundamental differences between stakeholders. These differences present a different form of challenge to those with the responsibility of managing this type of partnership.

DIFFERENCES BETWEEN STAKEHOLDERS

The programme was initiated at director level and the launch managed by the then management development manager on their behalf. Middle management was not involved in fundamental programme design. As such, the directors were the primary stakeholders in developing more professional middle management. In some respects, existing middle managers may have seen this as a threat, and increasingly so as growth tailed off in the early 1990s. From the beginning the roles and interests of the various stake-holders were quite different.

The three most important differences that were identified were: beliefs about succession planning; line manager involvement, and senior manage-ment commitment. Each of these was particularly significant in influencing participant attitudes and commitment to the programme. Given that partic-ipant effort and consequent performance on the programme is related to these factors, these are important issues to address if maximum value is to be gained from the investment in a development programme of this kind.

Succession planning

The programme has always had a role in developing individuals to prepare them to take up new or more significant management positions. Senior managers expressed confidence that the programme was catering effectively for succession planning. It was stated that some participants had indeed been promoted since taking part in the programme, and, although not the sole reason for their appointment, the programme was seen as having made a contribution.

In contrast, participants held a very different view of the relationship between the programme and promotion. Feelings were high and a number were disappointed and frustrated that there was a preference for recruiting from outside Chep. They felt let down. Seen from these very different perspectives, the correlation between the programme and promotion was given very different weight: participants' expectations were high, and not met; senior managers' expectations were moderate, and they were content with the results so far.

Since 1990 Chep has added psychometric profiling to the process of assessing long-term potential and career direction. This has improved the quality of selection decisions for the programme. In recruitment for the earlier streams the contribution to career progression was a major attrac-tion for many to make the effort to participate in the programme. In the briefing of more recent intakes the link between the programme and promo-tion has been played down, even though in practice the proportion gaining promotions is improving. It has been important to prevent expectations from reaching too high a level, while at the same time encouraging partici-pants to recognize the worth of the development process they are undertaking. However, it is likely that this issue is one that will persist on any programme of this type, as different stakeholders have fundamentally different criteria (Hogarth, 1979) for determining key programme outcomes.

Line management

The second area of difference was the extent of involvement of line managers in contrast to the participants. Inevitably participants will be the most fully committed of any stakeholders in a programme of development, but some participants found the almost total lack of involvement on the part of their line managers a significant problem, despite the fact that their involvement was actively encouraged. The line manager is crucial in the effectiveness of the programme for both a participant and the organization. This view was echoed by senior managers and participants as well as by a number of line managers themselves. A director argued: 'Line manager involvement is key. They will own it.'

The line manager is key in the sense that they possess considerable influence in the arena in which learning from the programme can be transferred to the workplace. If the line managers 'own' the programme, in the sense of recognizing the benefits for themselves, the individual and the organization, then they will work with the participants to find ways of putting the development of the individual to practical use. It is widely recognized that this notion of the transfer of learning (Casey, 1981) is fundamental when evaluating programme effectiveness. As one participant stated: 'Unless you can translate this learning back into the workplace then it's not really worthwhile.'

The effective use of real work issues for assessment projects is considerably simplified where the line manager is supportive and involved in identifying issues and prepared to address the implementation of recommendations. In a similar vein, some organizational projects will have their main benefit outside the department, and these require time away from the normal work of the participant. Without line manager involvement and support this is difficult. A number of participants reported line manager 'resistance' and 'disinterest'.

We were able to identify that the barriers to line managers' involvement included limited understanding of the programme, lack of organizational acknowledgement and support, wasted involvement in the past, changes to the programme, and resentment of the programme. An additional difficulty is the dispersal of line managers across eight locations throughout the UK in a number of functions. This hinders working with them as a group, either as managers or as a steering group. As a consequence of all these factors, working in different ways with the line manager on what mutual benefits can be derived from the programme is a difficult and time-consuming issue, but we have found it to be one that needs to be continually addressed.

Senior management commitment

The third area of difference we wish to discuss is that of the perceived commitment of senior managers. Senior managers expressed commitment to the programme, but there was less confidence among some of the participants that the senior managers were truly committed. The difference is demonstrated by contrasting the following quotes. A director argued: 'I started it. I would fight for it. But I can't get more involved.' A participant stated: 'Chep organization says the right words about commitment, but ... actions of senior management do not support the words.'

In a similar manner a number of other participants expressed frustration at the lack of involvement and understanding demonstrated by the senior managers. This form of frustration with senior managers is a common phenomenon in organizational life and is not limited to involvement in a management development programme. In some measure, receiving this form of criticism is part of the job for senior managers, and is clearly not always justified. However, we would identify a number of contributory factors from our evaluation. For example, one of the benefits of the course cited by the participants was the development of a common management language among all those who had participated. The level of debate and discussion on management issues was reported to have risen significantly as a result of the programme. Senior managers who had not undertaken this programme, or something similar, would not 'speak the same language', which creates a form of barrier. Indeed, there were a number of participants who argued explicitly that the senior managers needed something similar to the programme that they had undertaken, and Chep has now launched a one-week residential programme entitled 'Senior Management in the Service Sector'.

Another factor which contributed to the level of frustration among participants was a direct consequence of their learning: participants had become aware of the wider organizational context and had developed opinions on weaknesses in such areas as people management, information and control systems and strategic direction. The inability to influence these areas, or even to persuade senior management to discuss them, contributed to their sense of frustration.

Raised expectations

Again, as with the issue of succession planning discussed earlier, one of the results of a programme of this type is that awareness and expectations are raised. When these expectations cannot be fulfilled, the result can appear to be more negative than if the development had not taken place. It is however important and helpful for programme managers to be aware of these issues in order to manage expectations in as constructive a way as possible, and to temper the level of expectations of the scale and speed of change. Career development review processes are now in place to allow individuals to discuss their strengths, weaknesses and career direction to support existing line management appraisal. In hindsight, it is probable that the number of streams launched in the first two years aggravated the issue.

STRATEGIC DIRECTION AND MANAGEMENT DEVELOPMENT

The early 1990s were a period of considerable challenge for Chep. It has already been noted that the exceptional growth experienced in the 1980s had subsided and the threat of competition was increasing. Managers were exploring ways of addressing the new situation in which Chep found itself. Indeed, the management development programme itself was a part of the strategic rethinking that was occurring. The difficulties inherent in this strategic redirection must also be set in the context of the significant influence of the two major shareholders. Within this context, plans to expand into new product and market sectors came under greater scrutiny than before.

As we conducted this in-depth evaluation of one aspect of Chep's strategic activity, it was impossible to get away from the wider strategic context and the significance of a clear direction for the organization as a whole. This has been recognized elsewhere (Pate and Nielsen, 1987; Santhanaraj, 1990; Simpson et al., 1994; Vince, 1995) as an important element for programmes of this type. It was difficult to consider the key question of programme effectiveness in meeting organizational requirements when we were unclear about the organizational priorities for the programme. That is not to say that there was no strategy at all, but that the programme led to closer questioning in certain areas, exposing less clarity in direction than was required.

Some of the difficulties addressed in the previous sections can be seen to result from a lack of clarity in strategic direction. As has been argued, participation in the programme served to raise participants' awareness of managerial and organizational issues, and that awareness led to questions. Without a clear strategic direction the participants experienced considerable difficulty and frustration in attempting to resolve these issues. They could not find answers.

For example, what needs should the programme be meeting? The evaluation unearthed a list of seven areas of need. Are all these areas to be given equal weight or are some of greater significance for the organization? The differences in attitude to the role of the programme in succession planning is one that could gain some clarification if there were a clearly articulated strategy on preparing future management. What range of strategies are there to meet this need? What is the role of the management development programme in meeting this need?

The issue of line manager involvement would be more easily managed if the strategic significance of the programme were made explicit, and then linked to clearly identified aspects of the line managers' role. Similarly, the issue of senior management commitment and understanding could be considered more fruitfully if there were a clear strategy for senior management development. Additionally, some of the frustration with senior management over addressing identified problems could be alleviated if clear direction existed on the mechanisms for contributions from lower levels in the organization to the development of operational strategy. This is particularly pertinent when there is a structured process of investigating organizational issues, as occurs on a management development programme of this type. To have had a clearer strategic context for the programme would have facilitated the tailoring of the programme to meet organizational needs; for example, in identifying the type of projects to assign to participants. One line manager argued:

> 'We need the board to give top down strategy to get context ...
> we lack strategic guidance for managers tomorrow, to have
> training in thinking strategically. The best way is to involve
> participants in the strategic planning process. Give strategic
> projects to team members.'

These issues highlight the importance of a clear strategic direction not only to facilitate the evaluation of a management development programme, but also to enhance the ability of participants and other stakeholders to gain the most from the experience and investment. It is encouraging to report that since the completion of the evaluation, this strategic direction for Chep has been put in place and the business is being re-engineered to achieve it. It is equally encouraging to report that course members are heavily involved in this process.

IN CONCLUSION

It is important to set the evaluation of the Chep programme in context. Attention has been drawn to areas where problems were encountered. This has been done to stimulate discussion on issues that are difficult to manage and to move towards a greater understanding of the potential that exists for developing the notion of working in partnership. We have demonstrated how programmes of this type make it possible to address many detailed improvements in design, content and administration in relation to organizational as well as individual needs. It is inevitable that different stakeholders, each with their own sets of needs and expectations, will have differing views of what a programme of this kind should seek to achieve. We have explored some areas of difference which seemed particularly pertinent to us, and noted the importance of considering these issues when managing a programme of this type. The discussion in the final section demonstrates that working in partnership in this way is not only dependent upon but also makes a significant contribution to the wider strategic activity of an organization.

It is fitting to close by noting that the overwhelming message obtained from the evaluation was that the programme is viewed extremely positively by the majority of stakeholders. One of the most noticeable factors from the interviewing process was that while all respondents were open and at times very critical, there was a high degree of commitment to and valuing of the programme. A key factor contributing to this is the clear commitment to the programme on the part of participants and senior managers as an ongoing part of management development in Chep. Unlike some previous management education initiatives, this has survived the test of time.

REFERENCES

Casey, D. (1981) Transfer of learning – there are two separate problems, in J. Beck and C. Cox (eds), *Advances in Management Education*. Chichester: Wiley.

Easterby-Smith, M. P. V. (1986) *Evaluation of Management Education, Training and Development*. Aldershot: Gower.

Gibb, A. (1972) An investment appraisal of training. *Journal of European Training*, **1** (1), 19–33.

Hamblin, A. C. (1974) *Evaluation and Control of Training*. Maidenhead: McGraw-Hill.

Hogarth, R. M. (1979) *Evaluating Management Education*. Chichester: Wiley.

Pate, L. E. and Nielsen, W. R. (1987) Integrating management development into a large scale system wide change programme. *Journal of Management Development*, **6** (5), 16–30.

Rackham, N. (1973) Recent thoughts on evaluation. *Industrial and Commercial Training*, **5** (10), 454–61.

Santhanaraj, S. (1990) The Philips' approach to management and organization development. *Journal of Management Development*, **9** (5), 16–28.

Simpson, P., Grisoni, L. and Cox, R. (1994) Relative values: qualification programmes or non-assessed development? *Journal of Management Development*, **13** (5), 14–24.

Vince, R. (1995) Learning about management: an analytic large group in a management development programme. *Group Analysis*, **28**, 21–32.

Chapter 15

Stimulating Creative and Critical Energies in the Process of Organizational Change and Development

Boris Boulstridge and Neville Cooper

'Organisations learn only through individuals who learn. Individual learning does not guarantee organisational learning. But without it no organisational learning occurs' (Senge, 1990). If this premise is accepted, then individual learning is at the heart of organizational change and development. To test the premise we look at the extent to which experiential learning approaches have contributed to individual development, organizational learning and improved business performance at a factory site which is part of the advanced materials division of Courtaulds Aerospace. Two issues are given particular consideration:

- How effective is an experiential learning approach for individual and organizational development, and what is the relationship between individual and organizational learning?

- Can an analysis of this approach reveal general principles which could provide guidelines for the management of change and the creation and sustainment of a learning culture?

A clear view of the specific context on which the case study is based will help to clarify the reasons for the particular choice of development strategies. It will also provide a framework against which other organizations might wish to measure themselves.

THE PERFORMANCE FABRICS SITE

The business in question was the Courtaulds Aerospace performance fabrics site at Littleborough, Lancashire, which is involved in the manufacture of high-performance industrial fabrics. These find application in many fields including aerospace and defence industries. The business was formed in January 1992 by combining two former businesses located on the same site in

Littleborough. Although the original businesses had been free-standing, they were complementary in some areas (e.g. one weaving fabric and the other coating it to give heat resistance and non-stick properties). Notwithstanding their proximity, the businesses were vastly different in culture and ethos.

The two businesses had merged because of a need to concentrate on profitable core business, reduce costs and combine sales and technical activities. The business plan announced to the workforce and unions, which was accompanied by redundancy proposals, identified a number of key needs essential to future success. These were:

- A revised pay structure and harmonized employment terms and conditions. The existing pay structure was extremely complex and divisive with different schemes for shop-floor, supervisors, craft and managerial sectors. In the shop-floor area alone there were twenty-two different pay rates in a company of 300 employees. A new pay structure which encouraged flexibility between the former businesses was needed. Employment terms and conditions were similarly divisive and this and the pay structure were two of the main reasons why attempts at improving workforce flexibility had foundered in the past. These disparities had been seen as inhibiting flexibility and the development of the organization as a whole.

- Improved levels of quality and customer service. In a business based on a new and emerging technology, issues of product development and innovation were vital, and it was realized that innovation was a wide-ranging subject not related solely to product or technology but also involving approaches to people management and teamwork development.

- Improved health and safety performance. There was a strong imperative to reduce the unacceptable level of 'lost time' accidents.

Although the business objectives were clear, their fulfilment lay in addressing, in an innovative and effective way, four potential barriers to progress which were perceived to exist. First, it was believed that the existing functional structure of the business did not provide a basis for innovation, real teamwork and the changes in management style necessary for the achievement of step changes in quality and business efficiency. A change to a process and product-based organization was necessary for a real impact.

Second, there was a legacy of cynicism and suspicion following the redundancies consequent on the merger and it was recognized that if the new business were to succeed, the energies, abilities and commitment of individuals needed to be harnessed within a spirit of creative cooperation.

By such means, it was hoped, widespread ownership of the business needs would be encouraged and a basis for tackling them defined through increasing involvement and shared responsibility. This change in approach would severely challenge existing individual and organizational behaviour at all levels, not least among managers.

Third, similar business needs had previously been addressed in isolation by traditional methods such as productivity bargaining, quality circles and job evaluation. Benefits in the main had been limited or short term and the implementation of these approaches had been characterized by methods which were often confrontational and sometimes autocratic. These had tended to widen the gulf between management and shop-floor and had led to cynicism in many areas. Various well-intentioned initiatives addressing such issues as quality and productivity had been perceived as 'flavours of the month' and were often seen as distractions from the real task in hand by those charged with carrying them out.

Finally, training, where it existed at all, had mainly been the 'sitting with Nellie' type for the shop-floor, and off-the-job individual, external personal development courses for managers. It had never been really linked with business objectives and tended to perpetuate the shop-floor/management divide. Learning in the organization had not been a transformational experience either for the individual or the organization. An innovative approach to individual (and organizational) learning which engendered meaningful experiences would be central to any change process.

STIMULATING LEARNING IN THE ORGANIZATION

Given the relative ineffectiveness of previous development initiatives, it was realized that an approach which recognized that all the business needs were interlinked and could not be tackled in isolation was necessary. Key to this approach was a recognition that individual (and organizational) learning would be central to any change process. This was a significant challenge which demanded an appropriate management structure, a new direction in management thinking and a recognition that workforce and organizational attitudes and values were emerging as an important dimension of that challenge.

There also had to be a recognition that in matters of employee development and training, the managers had to be more directly involved. The development of people and the organization, and the training linked to it, had to become major elements of the managerial role. A strategy was needed which placed managers at the heart of the development process and challenged them to reflect on their management style.

Drawing upon previous, successful experiences of developing management teams within Courtaulds, the identification and development of a key learning team which would undertake a significant role in developing learning within the organization was seen as a crucial first step. The essential characteristics of this approach were that

- the team would be involved in a personal learning programme which developed teaching skills;

- as part of its own learning processes, the team would consider the question of how they, and adults in general, learn;

- an outcome of this project would be a programme which stimulated learning in the organization related to a key business need.

A pressing health and safety issue provided the initial focus for change and development and a radical approach to raising the threshold of safety awareness and performance was adopted. Managers were placed in a central role as designers and deliverers of a basic health and safety programme which all site employees would follow. The initiative had as its focus a one-and-a-half day programme based at the site training centre. This covered the safety issues relevant to the site but also had as its core the syllabus for the Institute of Environmental Health Officers Basic Health and Safety Certificate.

PRINCIPLES INFORMING THE LEARNING INITIATIVE

Adults learn throughout their lives, and experiential learning is vital in enhancing further learning, which in turn is best facilitated when adults perceive the interconnectedness and meaningful nature of what is to be learned (Brookfield, 1986). Consequently, both the learning programme for managers and the subsequent health and safety programme placed emphasis on active exploration of experience, participation and reflection, with a key focus on valuing both learning experiences and the learner. The idea of experiential learning has found its most articulate expression in the work of Kolb (1984). Kolb sees learning as a 'process whereby knowledge is created through the transformation of experience'. Emphasis is placed on the process of adaptation and learning as opposed to content or outcome. For Kolb, the cycle of learning involves four stages. An individual undergoes a 'concrete experience' as a result of which observations and reflections are made, which lead to 'abstract concepts and generalizations' constructing theories, and establishing principles which are then tested in new situations. This ongoing cycle shows that knowledge is 'being continuously created and recreated'. This thinking informed the approach to learning and teaching on site: the climate for learning was to be one which fostered team-work, sharing and openness, and encouraged the negotiation of learning activities. Additionally and crucially, the approach recognized that the content and context for learning had to be meaningful, the 'meaning' in this context being generated by the relevance and pertinence of workplace safety to individuals. This was extended by the active partnership of shop-floor employees in problem-solving and health and safety auditing and by partici-pation in health and safety management activities (cf. Illich, 1971, in whose view learning is the result of 'unhampered participation in a meaningful setting').

THE IMPACT OF THE INITIATIVES ON INDIVIDUALS

The development and implementation of these learning programmes had a profound impact on individuals and the organization. Those participating in the health and safety programmes as learners roundly endorsed its effec-tiveness. In the early stages of the initiative, a pilot course review was of particular significance in establishing the efficacy of the programme both in terms of its value in stimulating a positive attitude to learning and in its relevance to site safety. Comments from those who had agreed to participate in the pilot course tended to confirm the principles of adult learning and the experiential approach endorsed in the tutor development programme. Participants liked the learner-centred approach, they liked group work, they liked the way they were being encouraged to learn, they liked having their managers as tutors, they liked learning! A *meaningful* environment had been created. For many, the experience of learning itself had been fulfilling:

'This course has made me feel able to believe in myself being able to learn.'

'The tutors on my course made me feel at ease and able to speak out. As I am not normally able to do so this course has helped me greatly.'

For some, the experience of being on the programme showed that the company cared, and therefore began a reorientation of attitudes towards the business. The effect on the key management/tutor team was equally profound. They were also learners by virtue of engaging in a tutor develop-ment programme. Management development in the context of the design and delivery of learning programmes was stimulated by the following inter-linked experiences:

- *learning from experience*: the opportunity to immediately apply new learning through delivery and evaluation of the health and safety learning programmes was a significant factor in stimulating changes in perception, attitude and style.

- *receiving and responding to feedback*: seeking feedback from learners at all stages of the implementation process provided an essential framework of reference for assessing individual style, testing out principles and evaluating the impact of the programme. The feedback element had not featured in previous management style and the seeking of feedback, and action based upon it, was to be crucial to the success of the strategy.

- *perceiving a new role for managers*: the encouragement to critically reflect at all stages of both their learning and the stages of implementation of the health and safety programme was a vital dimension in the development of management learning. In the words of one manager, 'The reflection, evaluation and review process caused us to critically examine our function, role and performance from the people angle.' From an experiential learning perspective, this was a vital dimension in the development of effective learning. A number of key elements were built into the learning programme prepared for the tutor managers in order to stimulate the reflection process, including keeping a reflective diary and engaging in mutual support. These were supported by the regular review and evaluation sessions undertaken by both the tutor/manager group, and by the learners with whom they had been involved.

- *changed behaviours*: the mind shift which ensued led to new perceptions about personal interaction and communication in the fulfilment of a management role. This stemmed from the raised awareness of the needs of learning groups and how learning is brought about and led to 'a concern for the other' in any communicative context. One manager expressed this as a commitment to the principle (when communicating with people) of 'What are *they* going to get out of it, not what am *I* going to get out of it'. They also found a workforce more willing to listen.

- *risk-taking*: it is important to note here that for the tutor/managers launching into a teaching role this was a risk-taking exercise, given their previous lack of involvement in teaching, the somewhat cynical attitudes to training which existed and the uncertainty of outcome. No one had any real teaching experience and notwithstanding the managers' endorsement of the principles and practice of active learning approaches, this strategy was in essence an act of faith. A 'letting go of control', as one manager put it.

IMPACT ON THE ORGANIZATION

In terms of the extent to which this initiative began to influence other aspects of the business, the fact that learning took place in teams was significant. The development of managers' teaching skills and the design, delivery and evaluation of the health and safety programme took place in teams. An overarching factor was the existence of a challenging task which the management team faced (designing and implementing a learning programme). This was a task valued and owned by the team. Many participants in the various health and safety programmes commented, in their evaluations, on the value of the learning in a peer group setting and sought to carry on this spirit of team work in their places of work (in the context of both health and safety and other dimensions of work).

The sense of team work also extended to the tutor–learner relationship and the sense of developing partnership was palpable: people began to see one another as engaged in shared learning. The health and safety learning programmes established the beginnings of a notion of partnership between student and tutor (employee and manager), as well as creating the confidence for people to engage in more informed and active health and safety practice.

During and following the health and safety programmes, people talked and listened to each other more. Managers were seen as more approachable. The teaching and learning arena became a forum for the airing and sharing of other workplace problems which paid testimony to the communicative context that had been established. From a culture of cynicism and reluctance to be involved in training, a growing desire for learning emerged among employees. As one participant observed: 'People went away keen for the next course, even those who had initially refused to attend the pilot course.'

LINKED AND REINFORCING INITIATIVES

The extent to which the learning programme affected and linked up with other initiatives was a significant factor in the change process. Other areas of management activity beyond the realms of the teaching/learning situation began to respond to the style adopted during the teaching events and influenced approaches to other key business issues.

During the time that the health and safety programme was being introduced, management at Littleborough were preoccupied with delivering a promise to accommodate all employees with a pay structure which concerned fairness and relativity in pay rather than levels of pay. The relationship between the pay structure and the change process had four dimensions:

- Issues of training, quality, productivity and the reward and organizational structure were linked and any strategy which attempted change had to address and reinforce the links. It was thought that a skills-based pay approach could provide a way forward.

- Satisfying the workforce on pay issues was critical to harmonious industrial relations, establishing management credibility and rebuilding trust – without this nothing else worthwhile was likely to happen.

- The pay issue became the focus for developing greater coherence across a range of issues, and in the way management tackled problems generally – it was a key developmental experience for a young management team.

- An explicit relationship between skills and remuneration should further release workforce motivation to learn since it links learning to visible progression.

The pervasive impact of tutor training and the learning methodology linked up with the pay issue in a number of significant ways. Management approached the development of the skills-based pay structure on the basis of consultation with and participation from all sections of the workforce and treated the development as a new opportunity for engaging people in learning.

In addition to the pay issue, team briefings and union negotiation and consultation were directly affected by the new learning style. Team briefings become more two-way with managers taking time out to find out what people thought. This consultative approach also influenced dealing with trade unions, and whereas previously unions had dealt individually with management, 'single table' discussions became the norm with more emphasis on tackling issues as problems to be solved jointly. The experience of shop stewards in the health and safety learning process had led them to value this approach. The focus on communication generated by the health and safety programme stimulated a desire to focus on communication issues and a site-wide communication audit was conducted.

BENEFITS IN BUSINESS PERFORMANCE

What benefits have there been in business performance? In terms of health and safety, lost time accidents were reduced from twenty-five in the year prior to the full implementation of initiatives to three in the subsequent year.

The positive impact of learning, communication and team work, coupled with the changes in management style, played a significant part in improving commitment and morale, and contributed to improvements beyond those which might normally result from a training initiative. For example, absenteeism fell from 3.5 per cent to 1.7 per cent and disciplinary incidents from thirty-five to two per annum.

The desire for further learning led directly to the development of a business awareness programme which in turn has generated a better understanding of how the business operates. The teaching and learning approach has spread into standards identification, standards-based training and competence assessment which are at the heart of the skills-based pay structure, and have helped in the major steps made in improving quality. Skills definition, competence assessment and role clarification have prepared the ground for a change from a functionally based to a process- and product-based organization. The work on operating standards was key to the retention of BS5750 status in 1993 and the business was awarded Investors in People status in June 1994.

A LEARNING ORGANIZATION?

What then can be gleaned from the case study? Are there general principles which either echo the experiences of other organizations or might provide pointers for the development of the principles and practice of what has been called the learning organization?

The term learning organization, coined in the late 1980s, describes the characteristics of an organization or company which, in the face of continuing change and transformation, draws upon and develops the learning potential of the individual and the organization as a whole, to effectively direct, cope with and sustain meaningful change and development. Such an environment would be characterized by openness, collaboration and cooperation, flexibility and adaptability to change which would be congruent with 'the needs, aspirations and wishes of people inside and outside' (Pedler *et al.*, 1991). Pedler offers as a concise definition: 'A learning company is an organisation that facilitates the learning of all its members and continuously transforms itself.' In a similar vein, though with a slightly different emphasis, Hendry *et al.* (1994) offer: 'A learning organisation facilitates the learning of all its employees with a view to continuous improvement and innovation.'

The following summary points are, in our opinion, some of the characteristics of the case study which draw attention to the development of a learning organization at Littleborough.

Whole company involvement

The initiatives were company-wide and there was a sense of corporate involvement in the project from the site executive to the shop-floor. People believed in the project – in other words, there was a shared belief in and commitment to the principles and practice of the initiative. This company commitment, and in particular senior management commitment, was seen as crucial to the success of the project and was manifested in two ways:

- Nothing was seen as taking priority over attendance on the health and safety programme (therefore endorsing its importance in the minds of participants and the company at large).

- Managers, by teaching the course, were explicitly seen as committed to the project both in what they said and what they did. They had started to 'act the talk'.

Existence of a key learning team

The existence of a key team for planning, delivery and evaluation of the learning programmes was a significant factor in contributing to the success of the initiative. Indeed, the notion of team work both in terms of the actual team leading the course and as a principle informing the design and implementation of the programme was of great significance. From the perspective of development of the learning organization, the existence of learning teams is crucial. The notion of team work in its broadest sense becomes a principle informing both the spirit and practice of the learning organization. In the words of Senge (1990), 'Individual learning at some level is irrelevant for organisational learning. But if teams learn, they become a microcosm for learning throughout the organisation. Insights gained are put into action' (p. 236).

Creation of measured achievements

The creation of a process which promoted a feeling of achievement and gave the opportunity for accreditation for those in learning situations was of great importance. People following the health and safety programme had the opportunity to achieve the Institute of Environmental Health Officers' Basic Health and Safety Certificate. Managers, through their teaching role, could achieve the City and Guilds 7307 Further and Adult Education Teachers' Certificate. For many, accredited outcomes from a learning programme had a major impact on feelings of self-esteem and self-worth.

Cross-functional collaboration

Creating situations in which people could see and become involved in other parts of the business (and work together on these) was important. The management team which designed and implemented the learning programme was a good example of a self-managed, cross-functional, project team which succeeded despite previous experience of considerable functional demarcation. Without setting aside their functional perspectives, where these would have inhibited collaboration, no progress would have been made.

Creating supportive and meaningful climates for learning

The creation of forums for learning in which people were comfortable had particular significance. Contributory to this was the concern to set an appropriate tone for the learning programmes. A pre-programme brief and discussion was crucial here both in allaying fears about the programme and breaking down barriers between management and shop-floor. It was clear from successive course evaluations that the social experience of the course was vital in the minds of participants.

There was a crucial link between the learning programme and the shop-floor both in terms of the relevance of content and the ability to immediately apply new learning through relevant activities. 'In a learning organisation, you have to merge thinking and acting in every individual' (Senge, 1990, p. 238).

Valuing individuals and creating values

One of the characteristics of the learning organization is that it seeks to 'integrate the efforts of all involved into an effective working community, bound together by shared values and commitments' (Watson, 1994). The development of a value system to nourish the growth of and sustain a learning culture was created, and is being created, in three crucial ways: the adoption of a learner-centred approach; the development of a culture of openness, and a more constructive management–employee relationship.

The learner-centred approach was a distinctive and effective feature of the health and safety programme. This approach has had a pervasive impact on culture, values and behavioural style. The more people who participated in the programme, the more people wanted to go on it, and new attitudes and behaviours became pervasive once a certain percentage of people had been part of the process.

A general 'willingness to be open' was highlighted by one manager as the most significant outcome of the initiative. 'Openness' was a crucial issue not just towards discrete health and safety issues, but more broadly in terms of the extent to which the company (internally) adopted a set of attitudes and values of being open with itself.

Lastly, the health and safety programme provided a context in which managers performed different and more people-centred roles. These new roles in turn triggered a new and more constructive relationship with employees on a much broader basis.

A learning continuum

The implementation of the health and safety programme has motivated people both to go on the programme and to seek to further their learning beyond it. In the words of one manager: 'We have created a pull not a push!' People have, therefore, expressed a desire to become more involved in learning activities. The changed perception of the value of learning is an indicator of the 'push', and is highlighted well by the comment: 'It used to be a unique event to go to the training centre for a course, now it's the norm.'

The increased use of the training centre for a whole range of learning activities is a significant outcome of the programme. Further learning opportunities have been created by the development of a business awareness programme which, in conjunction with the health and safety programme, forms a foundation learning programme for all site employees.

External agents

The role of an external agent or agents in stimulating and nourishing developments was an important factor in the management of change on the site. Sources of ideas and vision came from the Advanced Materials Division, from links with the Man Made Fibres Industry Training Organisation, and from staff at Warwick University. The ability of external agents to work together with and give support to 'insiders' is important. The three key points emerging from the experience of the site management at Littleborough were:

- as an organization seeking external help, you have to know what you want from external sources;

- this external help should command trust, be independent of interest groups and share the values of the organization;

- part of the role of external support should be that of helping the company ask the right questions.

Process

One of the central lessons from the case study is about process. It is not just what you do but how you do it, when you do it, and how it fits together with all the other things you are doing, which is more likely to result in sustained, embedded change. The notion of process is crucial: 'becoming a learning organisation is a process ... a learning organisation is a direction not a prescription – a journey not a destination' (Hendry *et al.*, 1994).

The business now believes it has laid the foundation for major change in culture and structure which will transform the capability of individuals and teams to contribute to the achievement of business goals. This will benefit all concerned, be they customer, employee or manager. At the heart of this change is the basic belief in the need to value and develop every employee.

REFERENCES

Brookfield, S. D. (1986) *Understanding and Facilitating Adult Learning*. Milton Keynes: Open University Press.

Hendry, C., Jones, A. M. and Cooper, N. S. (1994) *Creating a Learning Organisation: Strategies for Change*. Sutton Coldfield: Man Made Fibres Industry Training Board.

Illich, I. (1971) *De-Schooling Society*. Harmondsworth: Penguin.

Kolb, D. A. (1984) *Experiential Learning: Experience as a Source of Learning and Development*. Englewood Cliffs, NJ: Prentice Hall.

Pedler, M., Burgoyne, J. and Boydell, T. (1991) *The Learning Company: A Strategy for Sustainable Development*. Maidenhead: McGraw-Hill.

Roose-Evans, J. (1994) *Passages of the Soul*. Shaftesbury: Element.

Senge, P. M. (1990) *The Fifth Discipline: The Art and Practice of the Learning Organisation*. London: Century Business.

Watson, T. (1994) Hype Versus Basic Instinct. *Observer*, 17 July.

Chapter 16

Best Practice for Continuing Professional Development: Professional Bodies Facing the Challenge

Clare Rapkins (*née* Madden)

In recent years there has been a proliferation of CPD policy-making by professional bodies in the United Kingdom. These policies are the means by which professional bodies have responded to the changes facing their members in: technology and knowledge; the demands for quality assurance and accountability from the public, and the need for improvement in economic competitiveness to respond to deregulation, the European Union's new market-place and, in some cases, demands for the rationalization of professions.

Most professionals have always kept up to date with developments and changes in their field of practice. Until recently however, such professional development has been largely *ad hoc* and a response to a specific and immediate need to be up to date. While it is recognized that such immediate requirements for professional development will always need to be met, the changing demands faced by the professions call for a more planned and structural approach to continuous learning for work. Professional bodies have, since the early 1980s, placed themselves at the forefront of the development of such approaches through continuing professional development.

CPD has been defined by the CPD in Construction Group as:

> The systematic maintenance, improvement and broadening of knowledge and skill and the development of personal qualities necessary for the execution of professional and technical duties throughout the practitioner's working life.

This definition highlights three crucial elements of CPD for the practitioner: it is systematic or planned; it is about broadening and deepening knowledge, skill and expertise, in addition to updating it; and it is a *lifelong* commitment to continuing professional competence (Clyne, 1995).

Drawing on the author's research (Madden and Mitchell, 1993) this chapter examines: contemporary policy and practice for continuing professional development (CPD) among a range of professional bodies; describes the two models of CPD policy and practice that result; and, from associated research into adult learning and analysis of the changing pressures on professionals in the 1990s, defines characteristics of *best* CPD policy and practice. The chapter closes with examination and analysis of CPD policy in the Chartered Institute of Public Finance and Accountancy.

A SURVEY OF CONTEMPORARY POLICY AND PRACTICE FOR CONTINUING PROFESSIONAL DEVELOPMENT

Twenty professional bodies representing a cross-section of contemporary professions in the UK were involved in a survey to identify contemporary CPD policy. They were categorized by occupational field, age and perceived status (i.e. 'old and established' versus 'new and/or developing'). Categorizing the professional bodies in this way helped in the identification of trends among those surveyed.

A survey framework was used to extract information from documentation supplied by the professional bodies. In-depth interviews were then carried out with sixteen of the twenty professional bodies in the sample. Five areas of CPD policy and practice were investigated using the survey framework:

- the profession and professional body (e.g. when it was established, whether it was regulatory);
- the organization of CPD policy (e.g. whether mandatory or voluntary, the reasons for instigating the policy);
- the form of the CPD provision (e.g. content, venues, form of learning, recommended number of hours per annum);
- promotion and marketing (e.g. how CPD was promoted and to whom);
- monitoring and evaluation (e.g. who does the monitoring and for what purpose).

MODELS OF CONTINUING PROFESSIONAL DEVELOPMENT

By examining the responses of professional bodies in our sample to the five categories of questions given above, we were able to identify trends in the type of CPD policy being adopted.

Professional bodies designated 'old and established', and which included regulatory bodies, tended to adopt mandatory CPD policies in order to demonstrate commitment to the professional standards and the continuing competence of members. The model of CPD provision developed on the basis of a mandatory policy is termed the 'sanctions model' of CPD.

In contrast, professional bodies designated 'new and/or developing', and which were largely non-regulatory, tended to adopt voluntary CPD policies in an attempt to raise the status and profile of the body through demonstrating the continuing competence of its professionals. The model of CPD provision developed on the basis of a voluntary CPD policy is termed the 'benefits model' of CPD.

The type of CPD policy adopted was seen to influence all facets of CPD practice and provision. A checklist of characteristics of the sanctions model and the benefits model are detailed in Table 16.1.

Table 16.1   Models of CPD policy and practice

	Sanctions model	**Benefits model**
Why have a policy	Means of demonstrating members are up to date	Means of raising status and profile of professional body
Type of policy	Mandatory; sanctions for non-compliance with requirements	Voluntary; incentives and rewards for participation
	Input-oriented (emphasis on number of hours undertaken, content amd process of learning)	Output-oriented (emphasis on learning resulting from participation)
Monitoring of CPD	Professional body monitors compliance with requirements	Self-monitoring of learning outcomes
CPD activities	Updating technical knowledge and skill	Updating, broadening and deepening knowledge, skill and expertise

CONTEMPORARY CPD POLICY AND PRACTICE

By examining the cases of individual professional bodies within the sample of twenty, it was possible to identify characteristics of good practice among those adopting the sanctions model and those adopting the benefits model of CPD policy and practice. Some of these characteristics are noted in Table 16.2.

RESEARCH IMPACTING UPON CPD POLICY AND PRACTICE

To further elaborate best practice, other areas of research that impact upon CPD were examined. The findings have been published and are here reproduced from *Continuing Professional Development: Perspectives on CPD in Practice* (Clyne, 1995).

Table 16.2   Characteristics of 'good' CPD practice

	Characteristics
Professional body	CPD coordinator/manager accessible and knowledgeable Continuum of education between pre- and post-qualification
Organization of CPD policy	Clear policy statement Clear aims for CPD Planned and systematic approach to CPD emphasized
Form of CPD provision	Recognition of range of CPD activities Work-based CPD recognized CPD provision available through professional body Provision accessible to all and inexpensive
Promotion and marketing	To employers as well as professionals To potential providers Emphasis on partnership between professionals, employers, providers and professional body
Monitoring and evaluation	Where necessary, then by quota Emphasis on individual professional identifying needs for CPD and evaluating the learning activities

Cognitive theories of adult learning

Continuing professional development aims to enhance professional competence so that professionals practise most effectively throughout their career.

By applying theoretical and practical analyses of adult learning literature we are able to deduce that if CPD is to be effective it must: meet the learning needs of professionals and their employers; be flexible enough to allow individual learning styles to be accommodated; and provide a number of learning opportunities (Madden and Mitchell, 1993).

Learning needs Practitioners will have different needs according to where they are employed, what their role is and what stage of their career they are at. In order to meet those needs the content of CPD must cover:

- updating and broadening of technical knowledge and skill;

- developing personal skills used by the professional, e.g. communication, interpersonal, information technology and negotiation skills;

- preparation for changing professional roles, e.g. developing or career enhancement, financial and staff management skills;

- development of professional specialist expertise.

Employers must also be taken into account. The role of the employer as an instigator, a facilitator and a funder of CPD cannot be underestimated and CPD must certainly reflect commercial and competitive realities. CPD must be a balanced partnership to include the players who stand to benefit from it: as well as the *professional* and *employer*, the *professional body*, which instigates the policy and places requirements on its professionals; and *society*, with its interest in high quality professional expertise.

All learning for CPD should be judged on the basis of its fitness for purpose. This is evaluated in terms of its effectiveness in updating and developing skills for practice. The value of CPD must therefore be evaluated on the basis of its outcomes for the partners involved. A training needs analysis and the assessment of the effectiveness in enhancing a practitioner's performance is appropriate for any model of CPD.

Learning style   Professionals are adult learners and as such they are voluntary learners (Knowles, 1980). Not only does this mean that they learn best when the content of learning is relevant and has direct and usually immediate application to practice, but also that the process of the learning must fit self-directed and self-motivated, autonomous individuals. Adults learn by building on existing experience and so the process of education or training should itself build on this experience and be practice- and problem-oriented and facilitatory rather than didactic (Madden and Mitchell, 1993). The process of learning to learn is vital if individual differences in learning style are to be fully exploited through self-directed learning processes. Many professionals rely on being supplied with facts by 'experts' as a means of updating and developing professionally. This approach is only useful when the professional is aware of what information he or she wishes to learn (i.e. objectives) and how best to learn this information.

Learning opportunities   CPD must then be appropriate in its content and process and in addition in the range of forms offered. Practical considerations such as availability, venue and cost must all be considered by the practitioner and employer when making decisions about CPD to be undertaken.

The changing professional environment

Research by Watkins *et al.* (1992) suggests that technological, social, economic, political and cultural developments are likely to affect work practice for professionals. If it is to be fully effective, CPD must take into account, and indeed drive and be driven by, the significant changes facing the professions in the next decade.

Increases in the use and integration of information technology into work remove some of the more humdrum but time-consuming work of professionals, leaving more time for higher level work; the delayering and downsizing of large organizations (the major employers of professionals) mean less opportunity for 'upward' career progression, and the likelihood that work will be project-based and multi-disciplinary; accountability to the consumers of professional services and the drive for quality, together with the removal of restrictive practices, require significant shifts in the work practices of professionals. All these factors imply the need for different types of knowledge and skill for tomorrow's professional with, for example, core personal skills of communication, interpersonal relations, negotiation, team work and selling coming to the fore.

Continuing professional development policy must not only reflect such changes, but should be pro-active in preparing existing, as well as new, professionals at all levels to practise effectively in this new environment and retain and develop competitive edge.

CHARACTERISTICS OF BEST CPD POLICY AND PRACTICE

By examining current CPD policy and practice in the context of theories of adult learning and the changing pressures facing professionals in their working lives, three groups of characteristics that have greatest impact on best CPD policy and practice emerge:

- policy and conditions for CPD

- the form and content of CPD provision

- quality assurance, monitoring and evaluation of CPD

Policy and conditions for CPD

A professional body must have a CPD policy that clearly defines the aims of CPD for that body and describes how these aims can be achieved. The policy itself may vary according to the nature and needs of the profession but it is best when it provides for structured, systematic CPD throughout a professional career.

To produce a CPD policy a professional body should have some awareness of the knowledge and skill required by members in their jobs. A good starting-point is the professional core of the education and training scheme. An analysis of professional competence would allow professional bodies to make further informed recommendations to professionals about what knowledge, skill or expertise needs to be developed or maintained at particular times in their career. It must be stressed however that a professional body would find it difficult to recommend anything other than 'typical' career stage needs as all professionals will differ in their own CPD needs given their different work roles and employers.

In establishing an environment favourable to CPD there should be acknowledgement and building of partnerships between all those who will benefit from and have responsibility for CPD: the individual professional, the professional body, the employer, providers and society. As the instigator of CPD policy the professional body must play a crucial role here. Professional bodies should inculcate the need for continuous learning into new practitioners during initial professional education to establish a synthesis of initial and continuing education. This reinforces the need for a continuing education from the initial professional qualification through CPD.

Practitioners must have support and guidance on CPD issues. This role may be undertaken by the professional body and the employer. Good practice can be shared by the increasing number of CPD professionals developing inter-professional networks.

The form and content of CPD provision

A range of CPD options must be recognized, both informal and formal activities, meeting the different learning needs, styles and opportunities of different practitioners. Where, when and how CPD is provided must suit the individual practitioner and the employer's needs. Emphasis should be on flexibility so that CPD can embrace on-the-job learning, short courses, conferences and modular or open learning, reading or secondments.

Attention needs to be given to updating professional or technical knowledge and skills but also to extending and deepening knowledge, skills and expertise. The professional body should collaborate both with a range of providers and other professional bodies to ensure that the widest range and depth of CPD provision is open to its members.

Although it is important to persuade practitioners to invest in their own CPD this will not be enough without the support of employers, who must be informed of the value and benefit of CPD to the organization in order that the best partnerships between employers, practitioners and the professional body can be forged. CPD should enhance, update or develop competence in practice, and cost can therefore vary considerably according to the form of

CPD chosen. Some of the most effective CPD takes place on the job, however, with little or no direct cost to the employer for fees or lost professional time and direct and immediate benefits where it matters.

Monitoring, quality assurance and evaluation

Resources should be concentrated on promoting the benefits and process of CPD and developing new CPD services. Where mandatory CPD policies exist or where members are rewarded for involvement in CPD, a quota monitoring system is advised, keeping monitoring cost to a minimum.

Most professional bodies already devolve responsibility for evaluation of CPD providers and provision to the professional. This is sensible and logical, given that CPD needs to fit the needs of the practitioner and the employer. A form of evaluation checklist from the professional body, however, may help individual practitioners in this process.

THE CIPFA STRATEGY FOR CPD

CIPFA is the Chartered Institute of Public Finance and Accountancy, the professional body representing some 12,000 qualified accountants working in public service. Although almost two-thirds of members are employed in the traditional sectors of local government and health, CIPFA's employment profile includes members in public service organizations now under private sector control (e.g. public utilities, gas, water, electricity). The public sector has experienced and continues to experience structural change. CIPFA is very conscious of the need to help its members to stay on top of this change and drive it. The maintenance and development of professional competence helps members to maintain and develop their competitive edge and operate more efficiently and effectively in the new climates they encounter. By planning and structuring career-long and career-wide professional development, members will not only be responding to change but shaping it, thus benefiting employers as well as themselves.

CIPFA defines CPD as 'a systematic and planned approach to the maintenance, enhancement and development of knowledge, skill and expertise that continues throughout a professional's career and is to the mutual benefit of the individual, the employer, the professional and society' (CIPFA, 1994, p. 1). This definition of CPD is in keeping with that of the 'CPD in Construction Group', emphasizing that it should be *planned*, *lifelong*, and a *partnership* between the professional, the employer and the professional body in the context of a wider society.

CIPFA has a voluntary approach to CPD centred on a flexible framework. Central to the approach is the building of a CPD portfolio throughout a member's entire career. The building of the portfolio is broken down into a cyclical process of identification of professional updating or development needs and the planning of activities to meet these needs, followed by the recording of activities undertaken (together with supporting evidence) and culminating in an appraisal of the outcomes of participation in these activities. This three-stage process is undertaken annually with each year feeding into the next.

Most crucially CIPFA asks its members to balance the type of activities undertaken for CPD in terms of their content (professional and management) and the method of learning (formal and informal). There is a belief that CPD should be met through a variety of activities from courses and conferences to research, presentations or running training courses, to informal learning methods such as secondments, informal discussion and reading professional journals.

Activities considered as appropriate are those that update, enhance and develop knowledge, skills and expertise for work. CPD can take place at any time in any place and cover any topic relevant to the member's professional development. It can also take place on the job or away from work, but as previously noted, should involve professional and management knowledge, skill or expertise.

Given that CIPFA has adopted a rewards-based model of CPD, to preserve consistency and fairness the Institute must ask participants to meet certain requirements and then monitor those requirements. The Institute has tried to keep its requirements to a minimum, the overriding principle being of individual continuous improvement; this is, of necessity, individualistic and subjective.

CIPFA has set minimum requirements in terms of the number of hours: at least 25 hours per annum, and over three consecutive years a total of 150 hours. The documentation to be returned to the Institute consists of a CPD proposal at the beginning of the year and a CPD record form at the end; the proportion of members who submit evidence of their activities each year is presently in the range 5 to 10 per cent. Finally, all members should identify professional (accountancy) and management (personal, staff or organization) needs and meet these through both informal and formal learning activities. This final requirement emphasizes the need for all CIPFA qualified accountants, whatever their present role, to remain in touch with issues affecting their own profession, and perhaps to widen knowledge and skill in areas yet to be encountered.

A CPD Certificate is awarded to members meeting the requirements detailed above over three consecutive years. This provides recognition of those who consistently, or continually, maintain and develop themselves for work and helps to encourage others to participate in the scheme. Members receiving the CPD Certificate after three years will be denoted by the letters 'Cert. CPD' in the *CIPFA Yearbook* for the following three years. After those three years the CPD Certificate lapses and members must continue to meet the requirements of the scheme in order to maintain their certificate.

This rewarding of participation in CPD combined with the flexible approach to what counts as CPD has created a lot of interest among the membership (45 per cent of the active membership having requested their CPD portfolio pack to date). This success must be built on in terms of the ongoing promotion of CPD to persuade both members and employers to adopt the strategy. The current strategy aims to involve as many members as possible, the creation of the CPD framework facilitating participation and the CPD Certificate recognizing that participation. This strategy must continue to be dynamic, with – in the future – increased emphasis being placed on evaluation of the outcomes of CPD.

REFERENCES

Chartered Institute of Public Finance and Accountancy (CIPFA) (1994) *CPD Framework*. London: CIPFA.

Clyne, S. (ed.) (1995) *Continuing Professional Development: Perspectives on CPD in Practice*. London: Kogan Page.

Knowles, M. (1980) Research and practice, in C. A. Madden and V. A. Mitchell (1993) *Professions, Standards and Competence: A Survey of Continuing Education for the Professions*. Bristol: Department for Continuing Education, University of Bristol.

Madden, C. A. and Mitchell, V. A. (1993) *Professions, Standards and Competence: A Survey of Continuing Education for the Professions*. Bristol: Department for Continuing Education, University of Bristol.

Rapkins, C. (1995) Professional bodies and continuing professional development, in S. Clyne (ed.), *Continuing Professional Development: Perspectives on CPD in Practice*. London: Kogan Page.

Watkins, J., Drury, L. and Preddy, D. (1992) *From Evolution to Revolution: The Pressures on Professional Life in the 1990s*. Bristol: Department for Continuing Education, University of Bristol.

Chapter 17

Evaluating the Impact of Professional Development for the Delivery of Community Pharmaceutical Services

Jennifer Tann and Alison Blenkinsopp

There are 18,000 community pharmacists working in the UK in a range of settings which encompass the smallest local pharmacy and the largest branch of Boots. Two major studies into the future of community pharmacy have been conducted and their findings published within the last ten years (Nuffield, 1986; RPSGB, 1992). Both documents describe what has come to be known as the 'future role' of the community pharmacist, centred around patient care and closer working with other health professionals such as the general medical practitioner. At the same time as these developments have been under discussion, the National Health Service has undergone dramatic changes. The separation of purchasers and providers, the move to a service based mainly in the primary care setting (NHS, 1990) and the shift towards a greater recognition of patients' rights via the Patient's Charter (Department of Health, 1991) are just some of the issues which have significant implications for community pharmacists' practice.

THE ORGANIZATION OF CPD IN COMMUNITY PHARMACY

The need not only for updating but for the acquisition of new knowledge and skills in preparation for a change in role, highlights the professional development challenges facing community pharmacy. The pharmacists' professional body, the Royal Pharmaceutical Society of Great Britain, expects pharmacists to engage in a minimum of 30 hours' continuing education each year, although this is not a mandatory requirement and the Society has produced a syllabus identifying the fields in which it expects pharmacists to keep up to date. Community pharmacists may participate in a range of CPD activities including in-house programmes (in the large multiples such as Boots, Lloyds and Safeway), reading professional journals or attending courses and seminars provided by organizations such as the

National Pharmaceutical Association and College of Pharmacy Practice. There have also been a few centrally funded local initiatives such as the clinical pharmacy project at Airedale Health Trust. The government sponsors some continuing education programmes for health professionals in primary care under Section 63 of the Health Act, but only one profession in health care has a national centre. The Centre for Pharmacy Postgraduate Education (CPPE) is a Department of Health funded unit which has been established to provide an infrastructure to design and deliver post-registration continuing education to community pharmacists in England (there is separate provision for Scotland, Wales and Northern Ireland). CPPE aims to bring together the service development needs which arise from government policies such as *Health of the Nation* (HMSO, 1992), with the profession's agenda for continuing education. A Steering Committee on Pharmacy Postgraduate Education (SCOPE) has been established by the Department of Health to inform the Minister of Health on matters concerning CPD in pharmacy. SCOPE has recently published a far-reaching strategy document in which it supports lifelong learning for all pharmacists.

Until the establishment of CPPE the responsibility for postgraduate pharmacy education was vested in the (then fourteen) regional health authorities, each of which appointed an organizing tutor, usually in conjunction with a local school of pharmacy. Practice varied across the country both in terms of the nature of the programmes and of their management. Programmes were funded under Section 63 of the Health Act, participants receiving travelling expenses and a contribution towards locum cover in their pharmacies. Some programmes were exclusively devoted to updating in aspects of pharmacy practice while others incorporated a multi-disciplinary element; for example, in aspects of management or information technology, the variance in curriculum being due to regional organizing tutors' interpretations of what it was appropriate to include under Section 63 (Tann, 1989). With few exceptions the approach was didactic, and depended on 'experts' who were invited to make presentations. The national provision of courses in 1990 and 1991 was 260, with a wide variation in supply between regions. Participation rates were estimated at between 10 per cent and 25 per cent of community pharmacists on the RPSGB Register in each region. Participant evaluation was limited to the completion of brief forms at the end of each course which served the dual purpose of providing evidence of attendance for the payment of travel expenses as well as a brief summary rating of the value of the course to the participant and his or her perception of the quality of the presentation. In a number of regions not even these most basic participant evaluation data were used in any systematic way to inform curriculum design (Tann, 1989).

The Centre for Pharmacy Postgraduate Education began to provide programmes in 1992. It is staffed by a full-time director and two assistant directors responsible, respectively, for distance and direct learning. Over seventy part-time pharmacist tutors have been recruited by the Centre. They have local responsibility for arranging workshop programmes in negotiation with the Centre and for facilitating local study groups. All tutors have undergone training in presentation skills and the facilitation of small groups and they also have regular updating. The Centre's programme comprises a mix of face-to-face provision (currently 600 interactive workshops each year) and distance learning (print-based, computer-assisted learning and video). In 1993 to 1994 over 43,000 print- and computer-based packages were requested by community pharmacists (CPPE, 1994a).

CPPE TRAINING MATERIAL

CPPE commissions training materials for its programme from specially recruited project teams. The programme contains activities which are largely in two categories: the updating of existing professional knowledge and skills; and the acquisition of new knowledge and skills to underpin the future role. A typical project team comprises a project leader (who may or may not also be the topic expert), a community pharmacist, a CPPE local tutor, one or more topic experts (who may be pharmacists) and, depending on the needs of the project, input from, for example, patients, GPs and other health professionals. Collaboration with external organizations is normal policy (e.g. QUIT for smoking cessation, the British Diabetic Association, the Health Education Authority). Each project begins with a diagnostic workshop facilitated by a CPPE Assistant Director to explore training needs. Members of the project team participate together with several community pharmacists. Materials for direct and distance learning are developed together so that they are complementary, although each is designed to stand alone. A series of 'CPPE standards' manuals have been developed and these are supplied to project teams to provide guidance, together with examples of materials and activities as well as instructions on CPPE house style. Manuals are available for workshops, print-based distance learning, computer-assisted learning and audio-visual materials (CPPE, 1993).

All workshop materials are piloted with at least one group of between twenty and twenty-five community pharmacists in different parts of the country. The workshop is facilitated by a CPPE tutor, who has not been involved in the development of the materials, to test the usability of the tutor pack. Pharmacists are invited to volunteer for pilot workshops through the normal CPPE workshop brochure and asked to stay for half an hour at the end of the event to provide written and oral feedback. In addition, an external evaluator is sometimes asked to attend the pilot workshop to comment on the training materials and their use by the tutor. The materials are subsequently amended by the project team.

Distance learning is piloted with twenty members of the CPPE's distance learning review panel. The panel currently consists of some 100 community pharmacists representing a range of ages, backgrounds and experience. Reviewers are asked to work through the package and complete questionnaires at key points, recording their views on the materials. Comments and suggestions for changes are encouraged and these are written directly on to the text for print-based packs. Topic experts, independent of the project team, provide reviews on points of accuracy and currency of information.

Evaluation of specific projects is commissioned by CPPE in order to follow up participants after they have returned to practice and to measure outcomes in terms of confidence, behaviour and attitude. Evaluation projects have been undertaken both in the areas of updating and the acquisition of new knowledge and skills. In both areas the focus has been on developments in the community pharmacist's role. An independent evaluation has been required in a number of projects funded by the Department of Health over the past six years.

EVALUATION: PURPOSES AND METHODOLOGY

One of the most problematic aspects of the evaluation of training interventions is whether any gains in knowledge and skill and/or changes in behaviour and work effectiveness can be attributed to a particular training event (Table 17.1). It is no doubt for this reason that particular emphasis is laid on output measures in the literature on evaluation (Connolly, 1988; Elkins, 1977; Bramley, 1991; Phillips, 1991). Knowledge updating and enhancement, such as the CPPE programme in asthma care, is an important aspect of community pharmacy CPD, for this profession is one in which

Table 17.1   Evaluation of training outcomes

- knowledge gain
- skill competency
  - hard
  - soft
- behaviour/attitude change
- change in work effectiveness

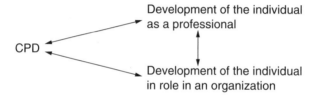

Figure 17.1   Complementary aspects of CPD

the rate of knowledge obsolescence is high, as is the potential risk to patients from dispensing errors. The fact that errors occur so rarely is clear evidence of the effectiveness of current knowledge-based learning in community pharmacy.

One of the less explicit features of CPD for the professions is the relationship between the development needs of the individual as a professional, with the requirements laid down by the relevant registration body, and the needs of the individual in role within an organization, however small. In community pharmacy this is demonstrated on the one hand by the RPSGB's syllabus for continuing education and on the other, by the wider business development needs met, in part, by the National Pharmaceutical Association, as well as by the different interpretations of what may legitimately be included under Section 63 of the Health Act (Figure 17.1).

Changes to skill levels may be considered along a hard–soft dimension. Hard skills consist of those necessary for the operation of particular pieces of equipment and might include the more mechanistic type of operating system to a particular protocol. In community pharmacy an example has been the training to enhance pharmacists' skills in the area of patient medication records (PMRs) and in particular to assist pharmacists to transfer from manual to computer-based systems. An example of softer skills is the training to encourage a more clinically based approach to community pharmacy. Changes in behaviour and attitudes are particularly difficult to measure, not least because, particularly in the case of attitude, much of it is self-reported. Examples of training interventions designed to achieve behaviour changes include interpersonal and facilitation skills for audit facilitators.

Changes in work effectiveness are a critical area in considering the outcomes of CPD (Cameron, 1980). They can be considered under five headings, as shown in Table 17.2. Some of these elements largely involve hard skills such as 'product goals' while others, such as 'resource acquiring', are broader and might include the management of professional boundaries between community pharmacy and other health carers. Similarly, the element described as 'constituencies' may involve some hard skills such as

Table 17.2   Measuring levels of work-based effectiveness

Focus	Explanation	Pharmacy example
Product goal	Measurement of work	Units dispensed; number of patients advised
System goal	Mode of functioning	Prescription dispensing procedure; response to symptoms process
Resource acquiring	Managing resource supplies	Purchasing; 'owings'
Constituencies	Meeting others' expectations	Professional/statutory obligations; GP relations; patient satisfaction
Internal processes; involvement	Staff integration; levels of conflict	Staff morale; job rewards

Source: 'Focus' adapted from Bramley (1991) and Cameron (1980)

meeting certain statutory and professional requirements but will also include potentially difficult soft skills such as pharmacist–GP work relations. And 'internal processes' are largely soft skills too, since they involve the management of the human resource in the pharmacy.

Above all, in seeking to achieve the application of new skills at work through learning, those responsible for curriculum design are seeking to effect a degree of learning 'embeddedness' through which the individual can apply new skills in new situations. A successful outcome of learning will be the level of effectiveness with which the skills are used, enabling the individual to cope with the new situation which, together with the sense of achievement in coping, leads to an increased likelihood of the individual applying the skills when necessary in the future.

A number of methodologies have been developed for the evaluation of training interventions, the most frequently used ones being shown in Table 17.3.

Table 17.3   Evaluation methodologies suitable for community pharmacy CPD

Methodology	When administered				
	Before	During	After	Follow-up	Use in pharmacy CPD
Questionnaire			•	•	•
Attitude scale	•		•	•	•
Observation/ behaviour scale		•		•	•
Tests	•		•	•	•
Interviews				•	•
Action plans		•		•	•
Peer performance contract		•	•	•	•
Action research		•		•	
Focus groups			•	•	•
Performance records				•	
Teaching/ learning style	•	•	•	•	•

As can be seen, the majority of these methodologies are used after a training or learning intervention, some immediately afterwards and others at a later follow-up date. One of the most commonly used and, to some extent maligned, forms of evaluation is the feedback questionnaire (Dickson, 1987). Some questionnaires are very simple, while others require some time for completion. The topics on which feedback is most generally sought include programme structure and format, teaching/learning materials, method of presentation, style of speaker, the learning environment and suggested improvements. From this it can be seen that this data collection method is of more relevance for the evaluation of inputs and process elements in a course rather than for an evaluation of what has been learned. There are, however, some obvious advantages as well as disadvantages to the feedback questionnaire. These are summarized in Table 17.4. Perhaps the most significant point here is that, on the whole, there appears to be little correlation between a good rating for a course and implementation of learning in practice, although some research (Elkins, 1977) does show a correlation between positive ratings and improved performance on the job. This is likely, however, to be the result of a self-fulfilling prophecy.

Immediate post-training questionnaires are completed by some 70 per cent of CPPE workshop participants and these provide a snapshot of participants' views on the relevance and value of the session. Data are optically mark-read on to a computer and analysed at tutor, regional and national level to give an overview and the opportunity to identify any local or regional differences in satisfaction levels. The form includes a section on the CPPE tutor's facilitation skills and this information forms part of the monitoring of tutor performance. Over 18,000 questionnaires have been evaluated to date, and besides informing curriculum design for future training interventions, they provide valuable data on pharmacists' perceptions of their future role. Forms were recently introduced into distance learning, but the response rate for these has been low (currently 12 per cent but gradually increasing).

The participant follow-up questionnaire is frequently used to attempt to measure the more lasting results of a programme, to compare responses with those provided immediately after the programme, to assess what opportunities participants have had for applying learning and to provide evidence of areas where participants have shown the most improvement.

Table 17.4 Advantages and disadvantages of feedback questionnaires

Positive	Negative
Immediate	Subjective
Valuable comments on training materials	Too polite
Easy to administer, tabulate, summarize	Good rating does not ensure implementation in practice

One of the difficulties, however, is to be sure that any change identified was due to the programme concerned. There is thus an issue of validity. Moreover, there is rarely a control group with which to compare the handling of problem-based situations in the workplace and, since there are few examples of pre-intervention testing of levels of skills and knowledge, there is no baseline from which to measure any change.

Changes in attitude can often be measured alongside other evaluation objectives in an informal way, such as the end-of-course discussion in which participants are invited to comment on what have been the most important learning points for them or what they will do more or less of when returning to work. A more structured form of measure is the semantic differential, where participants are asked to consider a particular concept and to mark where their opinion lies on a seven-point scale. Repertory grids are a more rigorous method of exploring people's attitudes towards a particular concept. Neither of these structured approaches to attitude change has been employed to any extent in the evaluation of pharmacy CPD. However, observation has been implemented both during particular training interventions to throw light on the teaching and learning process as well as in follow-up work-based situations, in the latter case using behaviour scales as a means of codifying different categories of behaviour. Where the major learning objective is an increase in knowledge, before and after tests are valuable. These can consist of open-ended questions, short answer items, multiple choice questions or the employment of a Likert scale for questions where individual responses are matched against the responses of a criterion reference group as, for example, in clinical pharmacy training.

A performance contract is cited in the literature as a way in which managers can agree with employees to monitor and support new learning at work. While this may be appropriate in the larger multiple pharmacies, some form of peer performance contract may be more appropriate for the independent contractor. This is emerging in the implementation of pharmaceutical audit where audit facilitators are contracting with their FHSA community pharmacy peers to undertake audit; and where groups of community pharmacists overcome initial concerns for the confidentiality of business information, they have formed peer support groups for audit. This may be quite close to action research as an approach for evaluating and continuing the learning process. However, so far as is known, there are currently no formal action research groups in community pharmacy, although in recent audit facilitator training the concept and practice has been introduced. Performance records may be used as an evaluative tool in the larger multiples but are not appropriate for the independent contractor. Focus groups, however, have a role to play both in the evaluation of training materials at the pilot stage of a new programme and in the follow-up on a learning intervention. Currently they are more regularly used in the former context in pharmacy.

There has been an increase of interest in the range of learning styles in different cohorts of learners and the implications for training interventions, both individually as well as in the groups. Inventories such as those of Kolb and Honey and Mumford have been used widely in training situations, the language of the latter appearing to be rather too management-oriented for most pharmacists. Other psychometric inventories can throw light on learning styles, notably the Myers-Briggs type indicator and KAI (Tann and Noyce, forthcoming). The Kolb Inventory can be matched with a McBer inventory on teaching style, based on the Kolb learning theory (Tann, 1993).

Interviews play an important part in evaluation. They have a role in the evaluation of approaches to course design and facilitation, as well as in following up participants after a training intervention. Specific techniques such as critical incident analysis can be employed in an attempt to determine changes in professional practice. While this is a time-consuming technique, the results appear to have a high validity (Spencer and Spencer, 1993) and can enable the skilled interviewer to test for a distinction between what people say they do and what they actually do. Interviews are also an appropriate way of undertaking an action plan audit. Action plans are frequently produced during a training event. They are less often followed up to ascertain what has been accomplished, what has not, and what has prevented the participants from achieving a specific task or aim. For the programme organizer, action plan audits are helpful in determining what has happened on the job as a result of a specific programme and whether the reported changes in effectiveness and behaviour were anticipated by the curriculum designers. An action plan audit has been carried out by CPPE on the Response to Symptoms training programme (CPPE, 1994b). In this case the follow-up interviews were conducted by telephone. From this it became clear that further attention needs to be given to considering ways in which pharmacists can set themselves realistic and attainable objectives.

RECENT INITIATIVES IN EVALUATING COMMUNITY PHARMACY CPD

Major initiatives have been taken in four areas identified as being important for the future role in community pharmacy. In 1989 a working part of the RPSGB deliberated on the question of distance learning as an appropriate form of postgraduate continuing education for pharmacists. One outcome was the commissioning of two distance learning packages on Services to Residential Homes (RH) and Patient Medication Records (PMRs) by the

Department of Health. For the first time the profession had been responsible for the selection of topics as well as the generating and editing of the learning materials. The two packages were competency-based rather than subject-based and were sent free of charge on request to all pharmacists. Each package contained a set of revision questions which were required to be completed and returned by pharmacists who sought certification of completion of the course, a requirement for those pharmacists seeking remuneration by family practitioner committees for the setting up and maintenance of a PMR or for registration to provide a service to specific residential homes. This was the first occasion on which answers to questions were required to be submitted prior to registration for provision of a new service as well as a financial incentive being involved. The submitted revision questions were analysed and a separate evaluation was commissioned to explore, in depth, the reaction of users of the pack to distance learning as a form of continuing education, comparing the self-reported competences of those who undertook to study the pack alone with those who studied the pack and also attended a workshop on the subject. In addition, evidence was sought on changes in professional practice, namely the extent to which respondents had sought registration for providing services to RHs or had established PMRs. The methodology adopted was a long, mailed questionnaire.

The study, completed in November 1990 (Tann, 1990), showed that pharmacists were increasingly accepting distance learning as an appropriate medium for continuing education, 48 per cent of respondents acknowledging that they had undertaken distance learning before, in marked contrast to surveys carried out between 1978 and 1988 (Tann, 1989). Seventy per cent of respondents to the survey were male and over 70 per cent were contractors, suggesting that distance learning appealed to male managers and owners of pharmacies who were unable or unwilling to attend the courses which were then run in the regions. The workshops introduced participants, many probably for the first time, to role-plays as well as case studies and presentations. Since both the setting up of a PMR system and the negotiation involved in seeking to provide services to residential homes require interpersonal skills of a high order, role-play is a particularly relevant medium for training. It does, however, require sensitive and expert handling and while there is no evidence that role-play was not well handled by facilitators, there was a mixed reception from participants. Nevertheless, almost two-thirds of the attendees at the PMR workshop believed that attendance had provided help additional to that available in the distance learning pack, a view endorsed by 90 per cent of respondents to the Services to Residential Homes workshops.

While outcomes are difficult to measure from post-training surveys – and the fact that respondents self-report on their own behaviour must be taken into account – there was a reported noticeable increase in levels of confidence and 24 per cent of respondents to the mail survey of participants in the residential homes distance learning pack reported an increase in the number of residential homes for which they provided a service, while 93 per cent of respondents to the PMR mail survey had begun to use a PMR system. In a number of cases respondents were changing from a manual to a computerized system. There was also an increase in the number of PMR systems covering all prescription patients.

Approximately 49 per cent of respondents believed that their behaviour towards prescription patients had changed. Moreover, and most importantly, 37 per cent of respondents to the PMR survey reported a change in their relationships with GPs. And overall 81 per cent of respondents to the RH distance learning pack believed that they felt more confident about providing a service to residential homes. The significance of this major training intervention should not be underestimated. Not only did the distance learning packs reach a large number of practitioners, but they were studied by a group of pharmacists which had been until then notable in its absence from face-to-face continuing education.

An important experiment was conducted over a three-year period from 1991/92 to 1993/94 in the North Western Regional Health Authority when, under an inter-university scheme (known as CONTACT), participants in a programme of continuing education could receive a CPD certificate on the successful completion, including assessment, of six out of twelve modules. The programme was evaluated by a follow-up participant questionnaire, observation, interviews with tutors, administrators and participants and learning and teaching style inventories over a three-year period. Particular emphasis was given to the stated or implied learning objectives devised by tutors, participants' satisfaction in terms of individual learning objectives, the adequacy of instruction for the assignments, the adequacy of feedback on completion of assignments, the relationship between teaching and learning styles and the format of workshops and style of pedagogy. The three-year study resulted in two reports (Tann, 1992, 1993) and a number of recommendations which informed the emerging national continuing education programme for community pharmacists. CPPE has now negotiated a relationship with the newly established CONTACT, with a view to exploring future options for accreditation.

In 1993 a major national initiative to introduce the pharmacy profession to audit was introduced. The Department of Health funded the appointment of an audit fellow to the staff of the RPSGB with a remit to increase national awareness of audit. A consortium, of which CPPE was a partner, was formed to produce a distance learning package entitled *Moving to Audit*. This was distributed in the Autumn of 1993 to all contractors and was available on demand to others. The Department of Health commissioned a study to evaluate the effectiveness of the year-long awareness programme. The methodologies employed included a before and after survey, interviews with individuals conducting local projects, interviews with key personnel in the field of audit in Scotland and, at intervals during the period, with the RPSGB's audit fellow. While the emphasis was on measuring changes in awareness, the project also sought to identify changes in practice. In terms of awareness raising, the evaluation showed that almost 90 per cent of pharmacists were aware of the RPSGB's policy on audit. Awareness was raised through the *Moving to Audit* package, public lectures and local meetings addressed by the audit fellow, articles in the *Pharmaceutical Journal*, and through networks. By the end of the year, implementation of audit had increased in the hospital sector while remaining fairly low in community pharmacy (Hanson and Tann, 1994). One of the innovative features of *Moving to Audit* was the inclusion of a series of challenges. Pharmacists were invited to complete the first challenge on which they received feedback from the audit fellow and a second challenge was sent to them together with a pre-printed response card. The response cards contained space for comments on the distance learning pack and CPPE commissioned an evaluation of these comments. These showed that the style of the pack elicited extremes of reaction from those respondents who found it challenging, well designed and helpful, to those who considered it to be juvenile, patronizing and stating the obvious. Respondents were on the whole consistent in their perceptions of the package. Those who had initially thought that both the materials and the programme for audit training good, on the whole stayed with that view and conversely those who were opposed to audit and reacted negatively to the learning material did not, on the whole, change their view (Tann and Platts, 1995).

The audit fellow has now been reappointed for a further three years and the Department of Health has funded two pilot projects on audit facilitation in the West Midlands and North Thames regional health authorities. These pilot projects are also being evaluated, the training of audit facilitators comprising an element of the evaluation. Observation of the training event for the West Midlands facilitators informed the design of the curriculum for the training intervention for the North Thames facilitators, the latter event being longer and more focused on the process skills required by facilitators in role. The evaluation methodology has also involved the shadowing of facilitators, employing an observation schedule developed for the purpose, as well as interviews with FHSA pharmaceutical advisers and each audit facilitator to explore their different interpretations of the role.

In comparing reactions to different training methodologies over the period 1988 to 1995, it becomes clear that approaches to the continuing education of pharmacists have been informed by evaluation, that the uptake of continuing education has greatly increased, that participants have been exposed to a range of intervention techniques and find them acceptable and less threatening than formerly, and that distance learning is far more widely accepted. With the launch of a strategy for pharmacy continuing education by SCOPE and its enthusiastic endorsement by the RPSGB, continuing education will make an ever more important contribution to the development of pharmacists in their future role.

REFERENCES

Bramley, P. (1991) *Evaluating Training Effectiveness*. Maidenhead: McGraw-Hill.

Cameron, K. (1980) Critical questions in assessing organisational effectiveness. *Organisational Dynamics*, Autumn, 66–80.

Centre for Pharmacy Postgraduate Education (CPPE) (1993) *Standards for Print-Based Distance Learning Materials; Audio Visual Materials; Computer-Based Distance Learning Materials; Standards for Workshop Materials*. Manchester: CPPE.

CPPE (1994a) *Annual Report*. Manchester: CPPE.

CPPE (1994b) *Evaluation Report: Response to Symptoms*. Manchester: CPPE.

Connolly, S. M. (1988) Integrating evaluation, design and implementation. *Training and Development Journal*, February, 20–1.

Department of Health (1991) *Patient's Charter*. London: HMSO.

Dixon, N. M. (1987) Meeting training's goals without reaction forms. *Personnel Journal*, August, 108–12.

Elkins, A. (1977) Some views on management training. *Personnel Journal*, June, 305–11.

Hanson, S. and Tann, J. (1994) Evaluation of the introduction of pharmaceutical audit. *Report to the Department of Health*. London: HMSO.

Health of the Nation (1992) London: HMSO.

National Health Service (NHS) (1990) *National Health Service and Community Care Act*. London: HMSO.

Nuffield Foundation (1986) *The Report of a Committee of Enquiry Appointed by the Nuffield Foundation*. London: Nuffield Foundation.

Phillips, J. J. (1991) *Handbook of Evaluation and Measurement Methods*. London: Kogan Page.

Royal Pharmaceutical Society of Great Britain (RPSGB) (1992) *Pharmaceutical Care: The Future of Community Pharmacy. Report of the Joint Working Party on the Future of the Community Pharmaceutical Services*. London: RPSGB.

RPSGB (1995) *Guide to Medicines, Ethics and Practice*. London: RPSGB.

Spencer, L. M. and Spencer, S. M. (1993) *Competence at Work: Models for Superior Performance*. London: Wiley.

Tann, J. (1989) Evaluation of continuing education for community pharmacy in eight RHAs. *Final Report* to the Department of Health.

Tann J. (1990) Comparative evaluation of the effectiveness of distance learning for community pharmacists in four modes. *Report* to Department of Health.

Tann, J. (1992) Effective community pharmacy. *Report* to CPPE.

Tann, J. (1993) Effective community pharmacy. *Year Three Report* to CPPE.

Tann, J. and Noyce, P. (forthcoming) *Pharmacists' Learning Styles and the Implications for Training Interventions*.

Tann, J. and Platts, A. (1995) Moving to audit – an analysis of comments from respondents to challenges. *Report* to CPPE.

Index